Untimely Beggar

For Courtney,
with my
best wishes,
Patrick

Untimely Beggar

POVERTY AND POWER FROM
BAUDELAIRE TO BENJAMIN

Patrick Greaney

University of Minnesota Press

Minneapolis

London

Material from chapter 4 was previously published in "The Richest Poverty: The Encounter between Zarathustra and Truth in the Dionysos-Dithyramben," in *Nietzsche-Studien* 30 (Berlin: Walter de Gruyter, 2001); copyright 2001; reprinted with permission of Walter de Gruyter. Material from chapter 7 previously appeared in "Montage and Identity in Brecht and Fassbinder," in Gail Finney, ed., *Visual Culture in Twentieth-Century Germany: Text as Spectacle* (Bloomington and Indianapolis: Indiana University Press, 2006), 154–63; reprinted with permission of Indiana University Press.

Published by the University of Minnesota Press
111 Third Avenue South, Suite 290
Minneapolis, MN 55401-2520
http://www.upress.umn.edu

Library of Congress Cataloging-in-Publication Data

Greaney, Patrick.
Untimely beggar : poverty and power from Baudelaire to Benjamin / Patrick Greaney.
p. cm.
Includes bibliographical references and index.
ISBN: 978-0-8166-4950-1 (hc : alk. paper)
ISBN-10: 0-8166-4950-2 (hc : alk. paper)
ISBN: 978-0-8166-4951-8 (pb : alk. paper)
ISBN-10: 0-8166-4951-0 (pb : alk. paper)
1. Poverty in literature. 2. Power (Social sciences) in literature.
3. European literature—19th century—History and criticism.
4. European literature—20th century—History and criticism.
I. Title.
PN56.P56G73 2008
809.933556   dc22   2007033545

Printed in the United States of America on acid-free paper

The University of Minnesota is an equal-opportunity educator and employer.

12 11 10 09 08   10 9 8 7 6 5 4 3 2 1

For my parents

Contents

The Beggar and the
Promised Land of Cannibalism

Poverty and Power

At a lively street fair, the narrator of Charles Baudelaire's 1855 prose poem "An Old Acrobat" spots a "poor acrobat, stooped, obsolete, decrepit, a human ruin" whose "absolute misery" so disturbs him that he is momentarily blinded by tears and stops breathing. When he recovers, he only has time to ask himself "What to do?" before he is pushed along by the crowd.[1]

About eighty years later, in notes found among his papers, Walter Benjamin imagines a ship resolutely pushing off from Europe's shores, manned by Paul Klee, Bertolt Brecht, Adolf Loos, and others. These artists, architects, and writers turn their backs on millennia of culture, leaving behind "temples full of images of man, solemnly bedecked with sacrificial offerings." They are headed for "the promised land of cannibalism," where man will consume himself and become something else. Benjamin christens the vessel *Poverty*.[2]

These scenes confront us with two quintessentially modern topoi: urban *misère* and the dream of a posthumanist future. Poverty names socioeconomic destitution as well as the abandonment of cultural traditions, and in both texts, the experience of poverty opens up onto something else: the remedy sought in the question "What to do?" and the flight into the promised land. A cursory glance at other key modern texts in French and German reveals that poverty's range is even wider: forms of voluntary poverty are the exemplary virtues in Friedrich Nietzsche's *Thus Spoke Zarathustra* and in Brecht's early poetry; for Stéphane Mallarmé, "the true state of the literary man is poverty";[3]

Robert Musil describes the utopian telos of *The Man without Qualities* as "an impoverishing ecstasy";[4] and Martin Heidegger closes his "Letter on Humanism" with the dictum, "Thinking is descending into the poverty of its provisional essence."[5] Such a broad semantic scope leads, at first, to a doubt—that we are dealing here with a watered-down, metaphorical understanding of poverty—and to a number of questions: What is it about poverty that allows it to assume such a broad range of meanings in authors from Mallarmé to Brecht, from Marx to Nietzsche, from Baudelaire to Heidegger? How can it unite such ideologically and historically disparate figures? How can it denote both the pitiable state of a street performer and the messianic goal of Benjamin's crew? And what does urban poverty have to do with Mallarmé's *Un coup de dés* and Zarathustra?

This doubt can be allayed and the questions answered by a simple, well-known fact: in the nineteenth century, the poor were associated with power. They were destitute, but they also embodied productive and destructive forces. Their labor power and revolutionary potential situated them in the center of any wider consideration of Europe's political and economic reality as well as any reflection upon its future. The link between the poor and power also made them a focal point for the modernist aesthetic concern with the representation of potential and virtuality. If the treatment of the poor in literary and philosophical texts was to be faithful to their "powerful" constitution, they had to be represented not only in their actual state but also in relation to their potential. This challenge aligned the theorization and representation of poverty with the more general modern project of orienting literary language and philosophical thought according to forces and possibilities, a task that is evident in a wide range of figures and concepts, from Nietzsche's overman to Mallarmé's absent flower.

Untimely Beggar investigates the coincidence of these two modern literary and philosophical interests: representing the poor and representing potential. In readings of texts from the period between the publication of Baudelaire's poems in the 1850s and the composition of Benjamin's texts of the 1930s, this book pursues several lines of inquiry: it analyzes theories and representations of poverty and power; it reexamines relations to the poor by submitting to critique notions such as identification and community; it explores the concurrent emergence of modern modes of writing, a fascination with ascetic traditions, and an intense philosophical and literary interest in socioeconomic poverty; and it argues for the importance of the encounter with poverty for philosophical and aesthetic notions such as Mallarmé's virtuality, Nietzsche's overman, and Benjamin's aura.

Although the authors will be treated here in the context of a general, modern interest in poverty, *Untimely Beggar* does not offer a survey of the treatment of poverty in nineteenth- and twentieth-century literature and philosophy. Instead, the seven chapters that follow this introduction focus on the effects of the encounter with poverty on a number of major French and German authors, who were selected because of their prominence in literary history, the importance of poverty to their writing, and the close relation of poverty to their other, better-known notions or figures. Based on the readings of these authors, I will argue that poverty, far from being one modern theme among others, occupies a central position in the development, in France and German-speaking Europe, of key concepts and modes of writing in the nineteenth and twentieth centuries.

Untimely Beggar identifies and analyzes what might be called a minor tradition of writing about poverty within the larger traditions of modernism and the history of the representation of poverty in Europe. The tradition begins with the theoretical and literary confrontation with urban poverty and industrial capitalism in Marx, Baudelaire, and Mallarmé; it continues in Rainer Maria Rilke's development of nineteenth-century conceptions of poverty, power, and community, which draws on Nietzsche's thinking about asceticism; and it closes with a consideration of poverty in Brecht and Benjamin, who refer to all of these writers and work on the threshold of an era characterized by new forms of impoverishment, production, and destruction. This study ends before the genocide of European Jewry during the Nazi era, which radically changed the way that European writers and thinkers understood power and weakness. After 1945, artists, writers, and thinkers once again explicitly claimed the rubric of poverty for themselves; the best-known examples are Jerzy Grotowski's poor theater and the Italian artists grouped under the term *arte povera*.[6] A continuation of this study might

show how, in different contexts and with other intentions, they reacti-
vated parts of the tradition of representing and conceptualizing poverty
that will be investigated here.

I will return in the first and last chapters to the scenes of poverty in
Baudelaire and Benjamin sketched out above, but, for now, they can
serve as a double emblem for the book's object of study: the specifically
modern concurrence of misery and promise in texts about poverty.

Hannah Arendt and the Language of Compassion

Poverty was not a novum for literature in the nineteenth and twentieth centuries, and authors from the period self-consciously draw on a
millennial corpus of writing about poverty that includes the Franciscans, Meister Eckhart, and Rhenish mysticism, as well as carnivalesque
and picaresque writing. Baudelaire and Mallarmé's poems on beggars
depend on and depart from their predecessors in French poetry, from
François Villon to Victor Hugo; Nietzsche's critique of the ascetic ideal
emerges from a confrontation with the history of Christian thought and
morality; Rilke's *Book of Hours* reinterprets Franciscan poverty; and
Benjamin and Brecht come at the end of this new, modern canon of
writing on poverty in which they participate while also referring back
to figures such as St. Francis and John Gay.[7]

Against the backdrop of these traditions of thinking about and representing poverty, nineteenth- and twentieth-century writers respond
in historically specific ways to the new forms of poverty that emerge in
the wake of the economic and political changes brought about by
industrialization and the accumulation of capital. In the nineteenth
century, the poor appear to be inherently powerful, and this intimate
tie to power means that poverty resists being isolated as an object or
phenomenon, and not only in literature and literary criticism. The historian Louis Chevalier shows in his *Laboring Classes and Dangerous
Classes in Paris during the First Half of the Nineteenth Century* how the
term "poverty" *(misère)* does not designate the condition of distinct
"unfortunate classes, but the far more complex relationship between
those classes and other classes."[8] For Chevalier and for many scholars
of the nineteenth century, poverty is not a condition "but the passage

from one [condition] to the other . . . , an intermediary and fluctuating situation rather than a status."⁹ Even in this brief citation, we can see how poverty is always more than a theme or topic, because, as a "passage" and an "intermediary and fluctuating situation," it cannot be isolated as a thing or topos and thereby forces a reflection on the limits and possibilities of literary language.

The representational challenge posed by the poor is at the center of Hannah Arendt's *On Revolution,* in which the analysis of the poor focuses on the "discovery," during the French Revolution, of the political power of the poor—the new belief that the poor were "la puissance de la terre." The chapter "The Social Question" begins with this definition of poverty:

> Poverty is more than deprivation; it is a state of constant want and acute misery whose ignominy consists in its dehumanizing force; poverty is abject because it puts men under the absolute dictates of their bodies, that is, under the absolute dictate of necessity as men know it from their most intimate experience and outside all speculations. It was under the rule of this necessity that the multitude rushed to the assistance of the French Revolution.¹⁰

The poor have been stripped of their humanity and subjected to the "dictate of necessity," which they eventually come to represent politically. Arendt credits Marx with the elaboration of this Revolutionary insight "that poverty can be a political force of the first order."¹¹

The new understanding of the poor brings about a new relation to them: compassion, which previously operated "outside the political realm" but then became "the one force which could and must unite the different classes of society into one nation."¹² The language of compassion aims "to lend its voice to suffering itself," whose demand is simple: "bread!" Arendt describes a figural operation whereby others speak for the poor—or, more precisely, whereby others speak for the suffering of the poor. This operation cannot be described as "giving voice to the voiceless" but, instead, as giving voice to a dehumanizing force that could never speak and for which the term "voiceless" would therefore be improper, because such a designation would presuppose the possibility that this force actually could have a voice.

Compassion for Arendt brings about a transformation of political life whose effects can best be seen in the change in political language: "Passion and compassion are not speechless, but their language consists in gestures and expressions of countenance rather than in words."[13] The language of compassion reveals an

> incapacity (or unwillingness) for all kinds of predicative or argumentative speech, in which someone talks to somebody about something. . . . [I]t will shun the drawn-out wearisome processes of persuasion, negotiation, and compromise, which are the processes of law and politics, and lend its voice to the suffering itself, which must claim for swift and direct action, that is, for actions with the means of violence.[14]

For Arendt, the invasion of politics by the "social question" is a catastrophe, because it marks the end of a political culture of debate and discussion. The poor, submitted to the dictates of necessity, become necessity's dictators. But it is possible to understand this change in political discourse differently.

Impoverished Language

The appropriate rhetorical term for the kind of speech described by Arendt is prosopopeia, the figure that bestows the ability to speak upon absent persons or inanimate objects. The poor often appear in literary and political discourses as the object of this figural operation that presents them as silent, addresses them, and postulates their ability to respond. In this way, language orients itself according to silence, the absence of the beggar's voice, and becomes impoverished, stripped of an actual interlocutor and centered on a lacuna. But this absence cannot be understood merely negatively, as we can see in Paul de Man's description of prosopopeia as "the fiction of an apostrophe to an absent, deceased, or voiceless entity, which posits the *possibility* of the latter's reply and confers upon it the *power* of speech."[15] Reading Arendt's discussion of the language of compassion together with de Man's definition, it is possible to conclude that the suffering of the poor is endowed with a power that, however, remains abeyant. Suffering appears as a possible, inhuman speaker.

Arendt's "language of compassion" thematizes poverty, but it also belongs to a process in which language itself is reduced. Its "predicative and argumentative" aspects are stripped away, and in this fashion language becomes poor. The poor embody labor power, and the language that speaks for their suffering reduces itself to a mere potential so as to approximate their power. The similarity of socioeconomic poverty and linguistic poverty lies not just in the phenomenon of reduction but also in their shared relation to power. Language becomes poor in a way that is not metaphorical, because it reduces itself to potential when faced with the poor, and, in this way, it attempts to become similar to the very power that it represents. The phrase "impoverished language" could not be replaced by phrases such as "reduced language" and "minimalist language," because they would miss the essential relation to power in texts about poverty.

When considering this approximation of thematic and linguistic potential, it is tempting to go one step beyond the establishment of a mere similarity based on a relation to power and to claim that language does what it says, but this would ignore impoverished language's highlighting of what Arendt calls a linguistic "incapacity." When language is truly impoverished, it suspends communication and the kinds of discursive speech that would allow for language to present themes, including the theme of poverty. In the example of prosopopeia, the power of language appears in the positing of an unrealized ability to speak. Since an impoverished, potential language cannot thematize socioeconomic poverty or anything else, there can be, strictly speaking, no simultaneity or identity of thematic and linguistic poverty. Adequation cannot be the measure for an operation that is centered on forces. In the place of communicative speech that would relate the concerns of an already existing group of poor people, something else emerges that is powerful without conveying the voices of the poor or any other constituted group.

This is why the representation of the actual conditions of poverty as a theme does not do justice to the reality of poverty in capitalist societies, in which the poor exist not only as their misery but also as a power. In the texts I read in the following chapters, the appearance of poverty is doubled. The thematic representation of the poor as an actual individual or group characterized by socioeconomic misery alternates with nonrepresentative moments in which literary language interrupts its presentation of what is and reduces itself to the potential for representation.

Literary language acknowledges in moments when it becomes poor that poverty creates not an identity but a capacity, even if it appears in privative form as an incapacity.

The Poor and the Worker

The linkage here of the term "poverty" with the labor power that is usually associated with a specific group of the productive working class anticipates chapter 1's analysis of Marx's understanding of the relations among different groups of the poor. Marx argues that capitalist societies reach a stage at which they require a "reserve army" and "relative overpopulation" of potential workers just as much as they need an active population of actual workers. Those who do not work and even those who cannot work are essential to the process of production in the stage of the accumulation of capital that coincides with the period in which some of this study's texts by Baudelaire, Mallarmé, and Nietzsche were written. To belong to the working class does not require employment or active, direct participation in production, but, instead, a relation, no matter how estranged or latent, to the process of production.

In my discussion of Marx, I focus on recent readers of Marx who have emphasized how, in his texts, the proletariat is not a fixed group joined by the activity of work or by an identity or set of characteristics. They are united only in their usability, which Marx famously calls their "freedom" to sell their labor power.[16] Marx attempts to establish a rigorous categorization of the diverse population of the relative overpopulation into groups that are more or less removed from the process of production: the urban unemployed who are searching for work; the rural population on the verge of moving to the city; and the old and infirm who can no longer work. I argue that Marx's characterization of these groups fails to distinguish "pauperism," the unproductive, obstinate, and disabled poor, from the groups of the working class that are actually or potentially productive. For this reason it is possible to say not only that, in *Capital,* every worker is poor but also that the poor are all workers. A similar line of reasoning leads Michael Hardt and Antonio Negri to insist, in *Multitude,* "There is no qualitative difference that divides the poor from the classes of employed workers."[17]

The terminological overlap between the poor and the working class is a result of the nature of the fluctuating reserve population that Marx tries to classify. There appear to be idle, unproductive social groups, but the process of production is able to accommodate them and even needs them for its proper functioning. The following passage from *Capital* formulates this in the form of a "law" that relates the working poor to the unemployed reserve army and the most destitute groups of the poor:

> The greater the social wealth, the functioning capital, the extent and energy of its growth, and therefore also the greater the absolute mass of the proletariat and the productive power of its labor *[die Produktivkraft seiner Arbeit]*, the greater is the industrial reserve army. The same causes which develop the expansive power of capital *[Expansivkraft des Kapitals]*, also develop the labour power *[Arbeitskraft]* at its disposal. The relative mass of the industrial reserve army thus increases with the potential of its wealth *[Potenzen des Reichtums]*. But the greater this reserve army in proportion to the active labour-army, the greater is the mass of a consolidated surplus population, whose misery is in inverse ratio to the amount of torture it has to undergo in the form of labour. The more extensive, finally, the pauperized sections of the working class and the industrial reserve army, the greater is official pauperism. *This is the absolute general law of capitalist accumulation.*[18]

The general law of capitalist accumulation posits the interdependence of capitalism's power of expansion, the intensification of the proletariat's power, and the growth of a part of the working class that no longer can or no longer wants to sell its labor power: those who are grouped under the rubric of pauperism. A few sentences later, Marx reformulates this law: "Accumulation of wealth at one pole is, therefore, at the same time accumulation of misery."[19] The poor and even the most destitute appear here in a complex network of forms of power—productive power, labor power, the expansive power of capital, power in reserve—that determines their presentation in Marx and the other authors in this study. Instead of an identity or an attribute, poverty names a changing position constituted by relations among forms of power.[20]

Relating to the Poor

Conceiving of poverty's appearance in nineteenth- and twentieth-century literary texts in terms of power means that relations with the poor can no longer be thought of primarily as relations between subjects (author/beggar or almsgiver/beggar) or as a purely economic relation between bearers of already established attributes (the rich/the poor). These relations are still at play in encounters with the poor, but they are secondary with respect to the relations determined by power. The conceptual shortcomings of such intersubjective conceptions of relations are apparent in the ease with which they can be reversed in interpretations that show that, actually, the poor are rich and the author, too, is a kind of beggar. Such reversals empty the terms of all specificity: the poor are truly rich only if one thinks of their incapacity as a kind of plentitude that they own, and the authors to be studied here are poor only if one understands poverty in a metaphorical way that strips it of its incapacity and socioeconomic destitution.

Such intersubjective conceptions of the relation to the poor also betray their vacuity by the facility with which they can be conceived of in terms of identification: the rich authors or narrators, in this view, identify with the poor souls they see on the street. None of the texts under discussion in this study can be summarized in this way, because the relation to the poor is far too disturbing to be conceived of solely in terms of identity. The poor seduce, threaten, stupefy, paralyze, beat, blind, and persecute the narrators who present them, and to think of these relations solely in terms of identification would be to simplify and pacify relations that are best conceived of as an intimate antagonism or even violence that threatens every form of identity and that forces the writers in question to develop new understandings of relation and community. Our encounters with the urban poor in the twenty-first century continue to bear signs of this disturbance that found its first modern articulation in the texts of the mid-nineteenth century.

The Untimely Beggar

In many of the texts to be analyzed in this book, it is the beggar who marks the place of this nonidentitarian aspect of poverty. But the appearance of the beggar as the figure par excellence of poverty is surprising, because historical analyses of poverty in the nineteenth century show how the figure of the beggar surrenders its exemplary status to more modern, timely figures of poverty such as the worker.[21] Beggars are un-timely figures, left over from political, religious, and literary discourses that saw them as representatives of poverty. But this unhistorical aspect of literary beggars bears witness to something more essential than a mere clinging to tradition. They appear both as a remnant of the past and as an omen for a possible future, and their untimeliness aligns them with the disruptive temporality of revolt and revolution.[22]

The figure of the beggar undergoes far-reaching transformations in the nineteenth century. For the modern poet, beggars are no longer what they once were. The beggar invited in to tell his story in Victor Hugo's "The Beggar" ("Le mendiant") and the poor street musician followed home to his garret and paid to relate his biography in Franz Grill-parzer's "The Poor Musician" ("Der arme Spielmann") evolve, in the mid-nineteenth century, into Baudelaire's speechless, uncanny *pauvres* viewed either from a distance or in a violent, barely linguistic proxim-ity in the section of *The Flowers of Evil* titled "Parisian Scenes" and in his collection of prose poems, *Le spleen de Paris*.[23] From Baudelaire on, the beggar appears as an emblem of the power of the poor and only sec-ondarily, if at all, as the bearer of an identity or history. This under-standing of the poor belongs to a more general shift in the nineteenth century described by Michel Foucault in *The Order of Things* as the invention of "a depth in which what matters is no longer identities, distinctive characters, permanent tables with all their possible paths and routes, but great hidden forces."[24] The poor were essentially related to these forces, and so, according to Foucault, was literature, which appeared in the nineteenth century to lead "language back from gram-mar to the naked power of speech" that had been banned in the consti-tution of language as the object of new forms of scientific knowledge.[25]

A New Kind of Power

Literature and poverty thus meet not only as representation and its object but also as two forms of power, and the elaboration of this rela-tion of forces is the task of this book. By emphasizing the place of power in its investigation of the relation of socioeconomic poverty and forms of linguistic poverty, this book sets itself apart from recent studies of poverty in nineteenth-century poetry and impoverished subjectivity and writing.[26]

Although removed historically and thematically from *Untimely Beggar,* Leo Bersani and Ulysse Dutoit's *Arts of Impoverishment: Beckett, Rothko, Resnais* is close to the present study's interpretation of the relation of poverty and power. These authors show how Samuel Beckett, Mark Rothko, and Alain Resnais share an interest in actualizing, within their respective art forms, those forms' origins, and, in this way, I would argue, they continue the investigation of the power of literature and art whose origins can be found in texts about the poor by Baudelaire and Mallarmé. Beckett's writing imagines the "originating of a speech it cannot remember ever not having"; Rothko's art "renders concrete a coming-to-appear" and the advent of differentiation; and Resnais's films "[lead] us to reenact what might be called our extensive identity," which distances us from our claim to mastery of the world and ourselves by assigning us to "shifting positions within an untraceable network of forms in communication."[27] Bersani and Dutoit identify in these artists the attempt to confront us with forms of origination and becoming that threaten and "impoverish" our notion of subjectivity and community. Their works offer us very little or nothing except this reduction, and, as Bersani and Dutoit write, "If there is nothing to appropriate within the work, we can no longer be, in our relation to the work, appreciatively appropriating subjects."[28] This nonappropriating relation to the work of art "trains us in new modes of mobility" that *Arts of Impoverishment* tentatively proposes as a model for a form of "political and cultural resistance" for an "unlocatable" self that would be "impoverished and dispersed."[29]

Bersani and Dutoit leave unexplored the relation of socioeconomic poverty to the forms of impoverishment that they find in the three artists named in the title. I argue in my final chapter that the forms of linguistic impoverishment that first emerge in the encounter with the poor eventually strain to separate themselves from this thematic link to the point of becoming indicative of modern writing in general, and *Arts of Impoverishment* serves as evidence that there are definite historical boundaries to the validity of my claim for the linkage of socioeconomic and linguistic poverty.

Bersani and Dutoit are closest to the present book's interests in the final sentences of their introduction, when they suggest that the impoverished self may give birth to "a new kind of power."[30] Their notion of a text "training" us to cultivate a power makes explicit the relation of their reflections to ascetic traditions (*askēsis,* "training").[31] Asceticism is to be understood in the sense Nietzsche gives to it in his undoing of the ascetic ideal and in Foucault's understanding of ascetic methods as "the arts of existence . . . by which men not only set themselves rules of conduct, but also seek to transform themselves."[32] For Bersani and Dutoit, literature becomes a training ground for the development of impoverished selves, selves who discover and cultivate a new kind of power that is not mastery.

This impoverished relation to power has significant consequences. In the final pages of the first volume of *The History of Sexuality,* Foucault offers an abbreviated formulation of the objective of political struggles that can no longer be understood in terms of sovereignty. In emerging biopolitical societies, no longer did one await or demand "the coming of the emperor of the poor, or the kingdom of the latter days, or even the restoration of our imagined ancestral rights."[33] In these regimes, "what was demanded and what served as an objective was life, understood as basic needs, man's concrete essence, the realization of his potential *[accomplissement de ses virtualités],* a plenitude of the possible."[34] Foucault restates this objective as the newly articulated "'right' to discover *[retrouver],* beyond all the forms of oppression and alienation, what one is and all that one can be."[35] Biopolitics constitutes its subjects as the bearers of potential, their "own" potential that they have a right and duty to explore and realize. The concept of impoverished writing claims a similar goal, but with a slight difference. It calls into question the biopolitical hold on potential by depriving the subject of the relation of mastery and authority: yes, there is potential, but no, it is not mine. Impoverished writing simultaneously focuses attention on power and releases it from its dependence on an appropriating subject.

For the modern writers I read here, it is poverty that brings them to an experience of virtuality and potential and that leads them to develop forms of impoverished writing. The beggar's silent gaze and incoherent cry interpellate nineteenth- and twentieth-century writers and thinkers,

forcing them to attempt to formulate notions of language and subjectivity that respond to the scenes of poverty that they witness and the
modern forms of impersonal power in which they are implicated.

A Modern Tradition

I begin my reading of poverty and impoverished writing by offering, in
chapters 1 and 2, a theoretical and literary framework for understanding modern concepts of poverty and power. Chapter 1 examines Heidegger's reading of power in Aristotle's *Metaphysics* and shows how Marx
and Foucault develop this notion of power in their discussion of the
poor. Chapter 2 then explores, in readings of Foucault and Baudelaire,
forms of power in literary texts about the poor. Drawing on chapter 2's
conclusions about language and power in Foucault and Baudelaire, chapter 3 analyzes the privative concepts that determine Mallarmé's formulation of a virtual and impoverished literary language.

Chapter 4 broadens the scope of investigation by discussing Nietzsche's engagement with the ascetic tradition of voluntary poverty.
Although Nietzsche does not explicitly link voluntary poverty with socioeconomic conditions, his texts play a key role in twentieth-century
representations of poverty in German literature and philosophy. The
reading of Nietzsche begins with a presentation of his critique of Christian understandings of language, difference, and asceticism and then
considers the two capital forms of poverty in Nietzsche's works: "the
gift-giving virtue" in *Thus Spoke Zarathustra* and the "poverty of the
richest" in his cycle of poems titled *Dionysus Dithyrambs.*

Chapters 5 and 6 constitute an in-depth study of Rilke's treatment
of the poor in texts written between 1903 and 1910. The two chapters
synthesize the results of the previous chapters, which offer interpretations
of ascetic and socioeconomic poverty in nineteenth-century writers who
remain central to literary and philosophical developments in the twentieth century. Chapters 5 and 6 show how Rilke, an avid reader of French
poetry and Nietzsche, explicitly reworks nineteenth-century understandings of poverty and poetics to offer new concepts of identity and
community. Chapter 5's reading of his cycle of poems titled "The Book
of Poverty and Death" offers a critique of the notion of aestheticization

that has been crucial to the reception of texts about poverty and to many readings of Rilke and other authors of the fin de siècle. Chapter 6 demonstrates how Rilke's continued confrontation with urban poverty led him to rethink his relation to the poor by presenting a community without identity in his only novel, *The Notebooks of Malte Laurids Brigge*. Drawing on Heidegger's notion of "being-with," and its elaboration in texts about community by Maurice Blanchot, Jean-Luc Nancy, and Giorgio Agamben, chapter 6 shows how Brigge's loss of every form of identity (his home, his name, his family, his class standing, his self-understanding as a writer) coincides with his awareness of a new kind of community with the urban poor whom he encounters on the streets of Paris.

Chapter 7 presents Benjamin's notion of the "poverty of experience" as the conclusion to a modern tradition of writing about the poor that begins with Baudelaire. It reveals this concept's importance for Benjamin's writing in the 1930s, in which it emerges along with other, better-known Benjaminian notions such as reproducibility, quotability, and the aura. In the book's final instance of impoverished writing, the impersonal, citing "I" of Brecht's early poetry presents as exemplary its abjuration of every possession and every relation that might bind it to its language or identity. For Brecht and Benjamin, the linguistic and conceptual traits that once were associated with the themes of poverty and the beggar become part of a modern, urban "attitude." In his essay "Experience and Poverty," Benjamin explicitly distances his articulation of the poverty of experience from the tradition that bestowed poverty with the beggar's face and voice, thereby presenting the poverty of experience as the end of one epoch in the understanding of poverty and the beginning of another.

In the notes that describe the ship named *Poverty*, Benjamin eventually strikes the sentence that christens the ship. The ship's name bears witness to the hope invested in poverty, and its erasure corresponds to the impoverishment of the figure of poverty in Brecht and Benjamin. Poverty is reduced to its potential aspect, stripped of its traditional attributes, its explicit relation to socioeconomic conditions, and even its own name. Chapter 7 concludes the book by arguing that this move is made in accordance with a logic inherent to figures of the poor, whose silenced voices and hidden faces betray the approach of their future disappearance.

Impoverished Power

The Marginality of the Poor

In the introduction to the first edition of the first volume of *Capital,* Marx presents as the object of his work "the capitalist mode of production and the relations of production and forms of intercourse that correspond to it."[1] The first volume opens with an analysis of the commodity, the "elementary form"[2] of the "wealth of societies" (the book's first words), and proceeds to unveil the "secret" that lies behind it, the "expropriation of workers" (the last phrase of the first volume).[3] At the heart of this secret lies a relation between two powers: labor power and the expansive power of capital. This chapter will focus on a specific aspect of this tense relation, one that is most visible in Marx's brief discussion of pauperism. For Marx, pauperism—a term used to group together the lumpenproletariat, criminals, the disabled, the unemployed, and others—seems at first to constitute a merely marginal phenomenon, but I will argue that the treatment of pauperism is essential to the concepts of the proletariat and labor power in *Capital.* Pauperism is "dead weight" and yet also a "necessary condition" for capitalist production, Marx tells us, and my reading examines the repercussions of this seemingly paradoxical coincidence of nonproductivity and production.

To develop further the analysis of pauperism in *Capital,* I turn to Foucault's notions of disciplinary power and biopower, which focus expressly on those groups of the poor that are not economically fruitful. The relation of Marx and Foucault has already been the focus of a great deal of scholarly attention. In 1991, Étienne Balibar felt compelled to preface a long article on Foucault and Marx with something like an excuse: "one assumes that the question of the relation of Foucault and Marx . . . already lost its interest and use at the end of the 1970s."[4] But Balibar goes on to say that "a real struggle with Marx accompanies Foucault's entire oeuvre" and concludes by insisting on the advantages of the continued, comparative investigation of these two independent theoretical models that "inevitably" confront each other.[5] A reconsideration of this confrontation is particularly advantageous for thinking about poverty, because their texts offer different—and, I will argue, complementary—notions of the relation of productive and unproductive groups of the poor. Both thinkers insist, in different ways, on the importance of even the most destitute and disabled workers within the process of production.

In Marx and Foucault, the treatment of poverty and pauperism goes hand in hand with the invention of new concepts of power, and their texts belong to a tradition of thinking about power and potential that stretches back to the Greeks. To introduce this tradition and to define the concept of power that will be central to this book, I will begin this chapter with a discussion of Heidegger's treatment of the philosophical notion of power in his 1931 lecture course on Aristotle's *Metaphysics, Book Θ 1–3*, Aristotle's treatise on power *(Kraft* or *dunamis).*[6] I will then look to the texts of Marx and Foucault to elaborate the forms of power specific to the poor. Chapter 2 will broaden the discussion of Foucault to include his theorization of literature's relation to power and production. Foucault's concepts will then guide my first detailed reading of literature, chapter 2's interpretation of the language and "crazy energy" of the poor in Baudelaire's *Le spleen de Paris.*

Heidegger Defines Power

The importance of Heidegger's lecture course for my study lies in its investigation of three relations in Aristotle's text: the relational essence of power; the relation of power and impotence; and the relation of power and *logos*. In the first sentences of his treatise, Aristotle reduces the many senses of power to one basic definition that is already relational. This is Walter Brogan and Peter Warnek's translation of Heidegger's translation from the Greek:

[A]ll the meanings of "power" . . . have the character of something like an origin which rules over and reaches out, and are (therefore) addressed by referring back to the first way of being a power (or an origin). This first way means: being an origin of change (a ruling over and reaching out for change) in another or to the extent that it is another.[7]

A power is the *archē*, the origin that contains within it the relation to "another" in which it effects a change or transposition. This will be the central, guiding definition for Aristotle and Heidegger, and it shows how power is always relational. At first glance, this seems to match up with our commonsensical notions of activity and passivity, according to which an active power affects a passive object. But Heidegger argues that, for Aristotle, another relation is more essential: the relation between a power that suffers change and a power that resists change.[8]

Heidegger explains that the order of presentation in Aristotle's text avoids an understanding of power as active or passive in a way that is faithful to his guiding definition, which "does not imply [an active] *dunamis* isolated unto itself *(poiein),* in addition to which then other further meanings are listed."[9] Thinking about power in terms of activity and passivity would inevitably make activity the center of attention and make it seem as if there were an independent agent that acts against a secondary, merely reactive passivity. In Heidegger's interpretation, Aristotle's emphasis on suffering and resisting power directs our attention differently and orients it according to the experience of power, in which "*that which resists* is the first and most familiar form in which we experience a power."[10]

One of the most extensive modern accounts of the encounter with power as resistance is offered by Marcel Proust at the beginning of *In Search of Lost Time,* as he describes how the madeleine evokes a sensation that resists repetition and understanding. It emerges, at first, only negatively and as resistance: "I cannot distinguish its form, cannot invite it, . . . cannot ask it to inform me."[11] The withdrawal of the sensation's origin initiates the narrator's quest to encounter something that exists only potentially. And it is only when the narrator stops actively "wanting" to "compel" the origin to reappear that this indeterminate something begins to emerge:

> I clear an empty space in front of it; I place in position before my mind's eye
> the still recent taste of that first mouthful, and I feel something start within
> me, something that leaves its resting-place and attempts to rise, something
> that has been embedded like an anchor at a great depth; I do not yet know
> what it is, but I can feel it mounting slowly; *I can measure the resistance,* I can
> hear the echo of great spaces traversed.[12]

The narrator's attempts to grasp the sensation give way to a kind of
expectation. The encounter of the narrator and the sensation's origin
takes place not between an active and passive force but between a force
that makes itself ready to receive the arrival of a force that is at first re-
sistant. The sensation of the madeleine is accompanied by a resistance
to "grasping" and to creation, and it is only after this experience of a
resistance to the narrator's every exerted force that there can be a revelation: "suddenly the memory revealed itself."[13] The account of how
Combray "sprang into being, town and gardens alike, from my cup of
tea" reveals how the enactment of a force—here, the ability to understand the origin of a sensation and, ultimately, the ability to write Proust's
novel—begins with an experience of resistance.[14]

Power appears first as resistance to change, and Heidegger shows
how only in the encounter with resistance "do we experience a wanting to be able, a tending to be able, and an ought to be able."[15] Suffering and resisting powers are inseparable in a way that bears witness
to how power is primarily a relation among powers. Heidegger insists
that "the outwardly directed implication belongs to the being-power of
power."[16] There is no such thing as a single, isolated power; instead,
there are always two powers that face each other as different and distinct. This is "the divisive, simple essence of power-being."[17] It would
be a misreading to conclude from this that the two powers are identical, because the ontological unity of the relational being of power
"demands precisely the ontic discreteness and difference of beings."[18]
Such an essential, joining split is central to Marx's analysis, already
cited in my Introduction, of the interdependence of the powers of capital and the proletariat: "The same causes which develop the expansive
power of capital *[Expansivkraft des Kapitals],* also develop the labor
power *[Arbeitskraft]* at its disposal."[19] Capital's expansive power emerges
together with labor power. But the two powers of capital's expansion

and the worker's productivity are ontically different even though they ontologically require each other to exist.

Heidegger develops the reading of the essential relationality of power when he discusses how a power is enacted. He uses the example of a human capability: a sprinter before the start. Heidegger writes, "What exhibits itself to us [in this sprinter] is not a human standing still, but rather a human poised for the start; the runner is poised in this way and is this utterly and totally. . . . The only thing needed is the call 'go.'"[20] In this moment, the runner is fully capable and ready for the gun, but the runner's capability is no less actual if the gun does not go off. To think about what it means for a capability to be actual—for a capability to be qua capability and not just in its enactment—requires that one also think of the runner's ability in its potential not to pass into enactment. A power possesses a realm in which it can be enacted, but a power can just as well be deprived of that realm. To be capable means always to be in a relation to nonenactment, to holding back, and to impotence.[21]

For Heidegger, the definition of power must reserve a place for non-enactment, which can take three forms: interrupting one's work; finishing a project; or abandoning a project.[22] In all three instances, the capability does not disappear but is withdrawn, and Aristotle insists on this as part of his argument against the hypothesis of the Megarians, who saw the actuality of a capability solely in its enactment and thus understood its nonenactment as its nonexistence.[23] For Aristotle, a power that is not enacted is nonetheless actual, and this claim is crucial for understanding the power of those among the poor who are not productive.

Amputated Power

In Heidegger's discussion of actuality of a latent power, the example of a potter's capability figures prominently. When we see the potter in a tavern, Heidegger writes, he has the capability to make mugs even though he is not at his wheel enacting this capability.[24] It is "in him" at the end of the day just as much as it is when he is making a mug, and Heidegger argues that the capability remains even when the potter stops working in a more definitive way:

> Such a loss can come about if, for example, the potter through some misfortune
> . . . loses both hands. Then we say: for him pottery is finished. But this being
> finished is a totally different occurrence from, say, when the potter takes his
> leave from the wheel and the workplace. Indeed, even with such a loss of hands,
> the capacity has not utterly disappeared, in the sense that the Megarians
> wanted to be able to assert, namely that it is simply gone. It is merely in a
> certain way no longer at hand [vorhanden].[25]

Even after the loss of his hands, Heidegger argues, the potter's capability is still actual and merely cannot pass over into enactment, a privation that we have seen to be essential to the actuality of every power. His ability is only "in a certain way" no longer at hand, which would be a grotesque understatement only if his capability were to be understood to be actual only in its enactment.

Only if we think of power in terms of nonenactment can we understand why we think that the potter's capability is still there, in some way, when he has no hands. In the final pages of the lecture course, Heidegger returns to the example of the disabled potter:

> Now it becomes clearer how the actuality of dunasthai [capability] is to
> be comprehended through echein, having and holding, namely as holding
> oneself in readiness, holding the capability itself in readiness. This being held
> is its actual presence. In the example mentioned earlier, the potter who had
> lost both hands, the moment of passing beyond, of going over, is in a certain
> manner no longer at hand; the being held is no longer complete; the readiness
> is interrupted.[26]

The disabled potter's readiness is "interrupted," and his capability cannot pass into enactment but is no less actual. In fact, the loss of his hands calls more attention to the specific actuality of a capability in its independence from enactment. The potter's dismemberment is exemplary for potential's not being at hand and yet still being actual, because the stumps emphasize the impotence that is not extraneous but essential to all forms of power.

What Heidegger says of the specific privation of the blind applies equally to the example of the potter: "To not find the transition to . . . : this is not nothing, but instead can have the pressing power and actuality of the greatest plight and so be what is properly urgent."[27] Just as we first encounter a power in resistance, we might also be drawn to

think about the specific actuality of a power only when we are confronted with the impossibility of its enactment. The "non-" of a capability's nonenactment is not a negation of its actuality but a specific
mode of privation that belongs to the capability, and the "urgent" demand of this privation and the consequences for understanding power
may be what make the appearance of the poor in the nineteenth century so compelling. Only in our coming to terms with the incapacity
of beggars and the most destitute does the full understanding of the
power of the poor become possible, because in these figures the implication of power and impotence becomes apparent and allows us to
understand the kind of actuality specific to power.

Logos and the Work

The poor embody an awesome capability that is deprived of its enactment and that in its very suspension calls out "urgently" for literary
representation. The relation of power and language occupies a central
position in Heidegger's lecture course. In Aristotle, the relation of logos
and power is intimate and relies on the wider Greek sense of the term
logos. The Greeks had "no word for language in our sense," and Heidegger argues that the acceptation of *logos* as language is secondary.[28]
Speaking, the making present of things in language, repeats the more
original way in which *logos* first makes things present to us. The Hei-
deggerian account of *logos* makes clear how language is never simply
added to a phenomenon and, by extension, how the literary presentation of poverty is intimately related to the act of presentation that allows
for us to see poverty at all.

Logos, for Heidegger, must perform a selection as it reveals the world;
it separates what is to be revealed from what is to remain hidden. It is
"the site of the manifestness of the contraries" of appearance and withdrawal.[29] *Logos* understood in this way also governs all human skills
and capabilities, because it directs their enactment according to contraries, determining what is to be produced and what is to be left unrealized. All production is "interspersed with alternatives: this, not that;
in this way and not in another way," Heidegger writes, and, for this
reason, "Production, in the way of proceeding that is appropriate to it,

is in itself a doing and leaving undone—a doing something and leaving its contrary alone."[30] Not only when in the middle of making the mug, but even when setting out to make it, the potter has in mind the *telos* of his work, an image *(eidos)* that is given to him by *logos* in its selecting and selecting out. Heidegger calls this the *Gesammeltheit* of production, its "being gathered" or "collectedness" to which limitation and exclusion also belong: I will make this mug and not that one, I will proceed in this way and not in that way.[31] Just as a power necessarily maintains a relation to its own impotence, production always includes a relation to what is not produced and to nonproduction:

> Only because being gathered into one belongs to every work *[Werk]*, no matter how unimportant and trivial, can the production of a work be disseminated [or distracted, *zerstreut*] and careless and the work be disorderly, that is, a non-work *[ein Unwerk]*.[32]

Privation accompanies every act of production as the possibility of an unordered work and, more important, as the necessity of leaving undone in every act of doing. To collectedness belongs the possibility of distraction; to the careful activity of production belongs a kind of carelessness. Every work emerges in relation to a nonwork, because the *logos,* in every act of production, includes and excludes, does and leaves undone. As Charlotte Witt writes, "[T]he presence of the form in the artist's mind and the steps to its realization are shadowed by its contrary, the privation."[33] For every human capability, "*logos* is named the unitary, singular *archē*" that joins within itself these contraries.[34] Like the ontological concept of power, *logos* is essentially divided and divisive.

The poor often appear in literary texts as the privative aspect of these two "logical" divisions, as the nonwork and impotence that seem to be outside of the process of production. The disabled worker first poses the question of how to consider the power of the poor in a way that does not reduce it to its enactment. Heidegger presents impotence not as power's negation but as a privative mode of its appearance, in which it is held back from enactment and thus implicitly held open for other, possible enactments. The power of the poor is similarly open, and it appears at first as forms of resistance—obscurity, absence, and distance—that, in the nineteenth century, became the object of an attempt to illuminate, make present, and integrate.[35] But the poor resist the forms of identity that would dispel their obscurity and obfuscate their relation to power and impotence.

Marx and the Accumulation of Misery

As I mentioned earlier in this chapter and in the Introduction, the labor power of the working class emerges in relation to the expansive power of capital. The working class appears as both the object and the future agent of expropriation, and the first aspect appears nowhere more clearly than in the pages of *Capital* dedicated to the accumulation of capital. The twenty-third chapter of *Capital*, titled "The General Law of Capitalist Accumulation," links the accumulation of capital to the "accumulation of poverty":

> Accumulation of wealth at one pole is, therefore, at the same time accumulation of misery, the torment of labour, slavery, ignorance, brutalization and moral degradation at the opposite pole, i.e. on the side of the class that produces its own product as capital.[36]

To explain this link, Marx traces capitalist accumulation and its effects on the composition of the working class through three historical stages. He begins by relating how, during the initial phase of the accumulation of capital, the ratio of constant capital (the value of the means of production) to variable capital (the value of labor power) remains stable: the demand for new workers increases at the same rate as the development of the means of production.[37] Then, in the second subchapter, he describes how the continued reinvestment of surplus value in the means of production eventually allows for such an intensification of productivity that the composition of capital changes.[38] Fewer workers are needed to produce a greater amount of surplus value. With the accelerated accumulation of capital, the number of required workers continues to grow, but this occurs in an ever reducing proportion to the growth of constant capital.[39] This change in the makeup of capital creates a new kind of worker population, which Marx presents in the third section of chapter 23:

> Capitalist accumulation produces, and produces indeed in direct relation with its own energy and extent, a relatively redundant working population,

i.e. a population which is superfluous to capital's average requirements for its own valorization, and is therefore a surplus population.[40]

The sudden expansion of capital "produces" a surplus worker population, which, far from being excluded from production, then becomes a necessary component of the continued expansion of capital. The "available industrial reserve army" of workers can be moved from one branch of industry to another, "released" (*freigesetzt*, a term usually reserved for the release of energy) and used somewhere else or not at all: "Modern industry's whole form of motion therefore depends on the constant transformation of a part of the working population into unemployed or semi-employed 'hands.'"[41] The acceleration of the accumulation of capital takes place only as long as there is the constant demobilization, dispersal, and redeployment of its variable component, which is forced in this way to respond to the transforming needs of the process of production.

Pauperism

The fourth section of chapter 23 of volume 1 of *Capital* specifies the three groups that make up the relative overpopulation: they are "floating," "latent," and "stagnant." The floating population exists at the "center of modern industry" and is constantly repelled and absorbed by industry's fluctuating needs; "latency" characterizes the rural population that is "constantly on the point of passing over into an urban or manufacturing proletariat"; the "stagnant [*stockend*] form" is employed, but only erratically, and its wages are lowest, its conditions the worst.[42] It is important to note that for Marx, stagnancy does not at all denote a lack of productivity, and, in fact, he insists expressly on the necessity of this final group as "an inexhaustible reservoir of disposable labor-power" and "a broad foundation for special branches of capitalist exploitation."[43] All three groups of the reserve army of the proletariat are included in their very distance from production in the accumulation of capital, because this distance is what allows them to be dismissed and redeployed elsewhere.

The tripartite classification of the forms of overpopulation is supplemented by a distinct set of categories that belong to what Marx calls "the sphere of pauperism." Pauperism and poverty were two clearly differentiated terms in the nineteenth century. In the texts of Marx's contemporaries, the term "poverty" designates a natural state from which one could free oneself by means of work and savings; it is a remediable state of lack. The term "pauperism" designates the set of behaviors and beliefs of those poor people who claim poverty as a permanent condition or culture with its own morality and codes of conduct; it is a state of alterity that is not reducible to a condition of having less.[44] The mid-nineteenth century saw a number of attempts to understand and include the poor in a new society that valued, above all else, useful work and production, because poverty's alterity represented a menace. Since pauperism claimed another set of values, it seems to present the possibility of another society, and it thus appeared to many nineteenth-century reformers to be "virtually revolutionary."[45] Marx's presentation of pauperism reveals, at first glance, at least a terminological proximity to this tradition:

> Pauperism is the hospital of the active labour-army and the dead weight of the industrial reserve army. Its production is included in that of the relative surplus population, its necessity is implied by their necessity; along with the surplus population, pauperism forms a necessary condition [Existenzbedingung] of capitalist production, and of the capitalist development of wealth.[46]

The first sentence here seems to exclude pauperism from the process of production: it is the "hospital" and "dead weight" of the working class. But the next sentence places pauperism at the very center of production: it is a necessary condition of capitalist production. With this move, Marx departs from the traditional understanding of pauperism. In *Capital,* pauperism denotes a specific group within the relative overpopulation that is excluded as "dead weight" from the active working class but that is nonetheless essential to the process of production.

This split position is not unique to pauperism, because the entire relative overpopulation can be said to be both marginal and central. Both as workers and when unemployed, the members of the reserve army are always caught in a double movement of inclusion and exclusion. Even as unemployed, they are always included, putting pressure by the very fact of their existence on the employed to work harder and for less and functioning as a necessary reserve for future expansion. Even when they are employed, they are always potentially excluded, threatened with replacement by the unemployed or with obsolescence due to increased productivity, and the members of the reserve army are always eventually excluded when the extreme demands of work use them up.

Simultaneous inclusion and exclusion characterize the relative overpopulation as a whole and not only pauperism, but there must be something specific to the sphere of pauperism that necessitates its special treatment in *Capital.* The next sections will attempt to identify what sets pauperism apart from the rest of the working class. This is an important question for the current study, because most of the figures to be treated in the following chapters (street musicians, beggars, vagabonds) would fall under the category of pauperism.

The Disabled Worker

Pauperism occupies a prominent position in Marx's text even though it is excluded from his initial classification of the three forms of relative overpopulation. After describing the three categories of relative overpopulation, Marx presents pauperism as its final, deepest "sediment" and begins a new paragraph whose structure mirrors the classification of the relative overpopulation by including three categories and an excluded group:

> Finally, the lowest sediment of the relative surplus population dwells in the sphere of pauperism. Apart from vagabonds, criminals, prostitutes, in short the actual lumpenproletariat, this social stratum consists of three categories. First, those able to work. One need only glance superficially at the statistics of English pauperism to find that the quantity of paupers increases with every crisis of trade, and diminishes with every revival. Second, orphans and pauper children. These are candidates for the industrial reserve army and . . . are enrolled in the army of active workers. . . . Third, the demoralized, the ragged, and those unable to work, chiefly people who succumb to their incapacity for adaptation, an incapacity which results from the division of labour; people who have lived beyond the worker's average life-span; and the victims of industry, whose number increases with the growth of dangerous machinery, of mines, chemical works, etc., the mutilated, the sickly, the widows, etc.[47]

Pauperism includes the able, the disabled, and the lumpenproletariat, which is not identified with either attribute. But this heterogeneity is not unique to this "sphere." Something similar can be seen in the general understanding of the working class in *Capital*. To understand the relation of pauperism to the working class, it is worth recalling how Marx formulates the worker's sale of his or her labor power as the necessary condition of capitalism:

> For the transformation of money into capital, therefore, the owner of money must find the free worker available on the commodity-market; and this worker must be free in the double sense that as a free individual he can dispose of his labour-power as his own commodity, and that, on the other hand, he has no other commodity for sale, i.e. he is rid of them, he is free of all the objects needed for the realization of his labour-power.[48]

Under the conditions of capitalist production, labor power is a potential that must be sold to be actualized. In a later section of *Capital*, Marx will thus describe the worker as a "personal source of wealth, but deprived of any means of actualizing *[verwirklichen]* that wealth for himself."[49] The worker is "deprived" of the means of realizing his labor power, and he or she appears as a "bare corporeality" that is separated from the means of production. This "confiscation"[50] of the worker's activity in large-scale industry only continues a process begun in the preceding age of manufacturing:

> [Manufacture] cripples the worker, making him a monstrosity by furthering his particular skill as in a forcing-house, through the suppression of a whole world of productive drives and inclinations, just as in the states of La Plata they butcher a whole beast for the sake of his hide or his tallow. . . . If, in the first place, the worker sold his labour-power to capital because he lacked the material means of producing a commodity, now his own individual labour-power withholds its services unless it has been sold to capital. It will continue to function only in an environment which first comes into existence after its sale, namely the capitalist's workshop. Disabled by nature *[Seiner natürlichen Beschaffenheit nach verunfähigt]* from making anything independently, the manufacturing worker develops his productive activity only as an appendage of that workshop.[51]

Only when the worker is an "appendage" can his or her labor power be enacted most fully. This potentializing disabling is not merely an unfortunate result or side effect of production; it is what allows the worker to become part of the capitalist process of production and what allows this process to function.[52] In this way, Marx reveals the bond that joins the worker's disabling and the intensification of his or her productivity.

The grouping together in the sphere of pauperism of those "able to work" and "the demoralized, the ragged, and those unable to work" thus only redistributes attributes among workers that are usually concentrated in *Capital* in a single worker. In Marx's analysis, the worker is disabled even when she or he is able to work and even when he or she is most productive, because the capitalist process of production always alienates ability from the worker and allows for its realization only after its sale and separation from the worker. "Pauperism is the hospital of the active labour-army and the dead weight of the industrial reserve army," but the factory is itself a hospital, and the worker is dead weight even as she works, as an "appendage," to produce wealth.

In *Capital,* the borders defining pauperism are porous. It may be impossible to isolate pauperism because of the way in which the working population in general is disabled and potentialized, included in and excluded from the process of production. The ranks of pauperism swell and shrink with every boom and crisis, and its place in Marx's categorization of the relative overpopulation is itself unstable, distinct from and yet dovetailed with the relative overpopulation.[53] Why, then, does pauperism merit its own supplemental place in Marx's chapter on the relative overpopulation?

The Unnameable Proletariat

Pauperism's resistance to classification reveals something essential about the constitution of the proletariat. Nicholas Thoburn has shown how the proletariat "exists in Marx's texts as a non-identitarian mode of practice" appropriate to capitalism, which, in general, "assembles not distinct entities—say, workers, machines, and natural objects—but *relations* and *forces* across and within apparent entities."[54] Thoburn argues against Jeffrey Mehlman, Peter Stallybrass, and others, who insist on the lumpenproletariat's heterogeneity and difference in what they understand as

Marx's overall characterization of a homogeneous proletariat. Thoburn's analyses reveal how, in Marx's texts, the proletariat and the lumpenproletariat are not groups but "modes of political composition" and how Marx criticizes the lumpenproletariat not as an already constituted group but as a "tendency toward the maintenance of identity":

> The lumpenproletariat is a mode of practice that seeks not to engage with the manifold relations of the social toward its own overcoming, but to turn inwards towards an affirmation of its own autonomous and present identity.[55]

Unlike the proletariat, the lumpenproletariat is not engaged in the "expansive 'fluid' state of material life in [the] specific sociohistorical relations" of capitalism.[56] The lumpenproletariat attempts to create an identity that would be sheltered from the forces that constitute capitalism, which, "unlike all previous modes of production," aims not to "conserve a set of relations and identities" but, instead, to create a state of "constant change—'constant revolutionizing of production, uninterrupted disturbance of all social conditions'—as it seeks to continuously maximize surplus value in a process of production for production's sake."[57] Thoburn shows how Marx repeatedly criticizes the lumpenproletariat's attempt to claim an identity, and he argues that Marx does this to "sever" the lumpenproletariat from the anti-identitarian mode of composition that is the proletariat.[58]

Thoburn's critique of the lumpenproletariat would seem to clash with my earlier insistence on its inclusion in the reserve army, because its tendency toward the maintenance of an identity would seem to be incompatible with the reserve army's necessary fluidity. But Thoburn's reading of Marx's "continual excision" of the lumpenproletariat implies that it, too, is engaged in a constant process of transformation. Marx has to keep returning to the lumpenproletariat because its attempt to claim an identity keeps changing. The tendency to maintain an identity fails in the face of the "constant revolutionizing" that it cannot escape. The previous reading of *Capital* showed how the lumpenproletariat and the sphere of pauperism are not islands of nonproductivity, sheltered from work and power, and for this reason, they too are caught up, despite themselves, in the process of production.

Just as the lumpenproletariat should not be romanticized as the site of difference outside of a homogeneous proletariat, pauperism should not be understood as a privileged site of disability and impotence. If there is something specific about pauperism in *Capital*, it is its resistance to being classified as a discrete group.[59] It emblematizes the imbrication of power and impotence in *Capital* that is essential to the makeup of the proletariat as a whole. The "excessive and thus superfluous" relative overpopulation and even its "lowest sediment," pauperism, are products of capitalism that remain productive even when they seem to be most unproductive and even when they are "stagnant." Superfluity and stagnation are essential elements in the emergence of labor power, just as pauperism is an essential element of the proletariat. The groups within the relative overpopulation represent not discrete identity categories but, instead, moments in the processes of inclusion/exclusion and disabling/potentialization that constitute the proletariat. The supplemental role played in *Capital* by pauperism and its motley crew of constituents, including the lumpenproletariat, indicates that pauperism is not heterogeneous to the proletariat, but a symptom of the essentially heterogeneous constitution of the proletariat.

Thinking of the proletariat not as an identity category but as a "mode of political composition" poses a challenge to traditional models of politics. Thoburn develops a theory of the "minor politics" appropriate to this understanding of the proletariat by drawing on the collaborative works of Gilles Deleuze and Félix Guattari, but a more schematic version that emphasizes the role of literature in a minor politics can be found in Deleuze's short text "Un manifeste de moins," on the Italian playwright and director Carmelo Bene. Deleuze explicitly distances his presentation of a minor politics from one that would understand Bene's theater as the representation of a conflict between the poor Italian South and the rich North: "there is no cult of poverty" in Bene.[60] A minor politics stages a conflict not among already existing groups but between a minority as "the power *[puissance]* of a becoming" and a majority, which "designates the power *[pouvoir]* or the impotence of a condition, of a situation."[61] More than a conflict, a minority engages in what Deleuze calls "variation," which may occur, in the theater, because of an actor or director who exercises "the authority of a perpetual variation, as opposed to the power or despotism of the invariable"; it would be "the authority, the autonomy of the stammerer, of he who has won the right to stammer, as opposed to the 'proper speech' of the majority."[62]

A text or production whose practice of variation would allow for this stuttering to be heard would not give a voice to the proletariat or any other already existing minority, because such a process would be a kind of ventriloquism in which only already constituted voices could be heard. Instead, literature's variations allow for something to appear that is not yet a voice but, instead, the potential for a voice. For Deleuze, the "antirepresentative" function of an art of the proletariat would "make present and actual a potentiality" and "constitute in some way a figure of minority consciousness."[63] A key aspect of such a potentiality would be its distance from enactment. For many authors of the nineteenth century, such an antirepresentative, potential figure emerges in the encounter with the poor and especially in relations with beggars.

Thoburn argues that the proletariat exercises a disaggregating force by overcoming work and its identities from within, drawing on capitalism's forces and not relying on a position of already established exteriority. Instead of constituting an identity, the proletariat constantly changes according to political conditions and events, and, as Thoburn writes, "Marx leaves the proletariat as something which must constantly find its own forms, and invent its own techniques from the specific configuration of work . . . that the proletariat finds itself within at any one time."[64] For this reason, the proletariat is "unnameable" for Thoburn, and I would argue that the impossibility of distinguishing pauperism in *Capital* is a sign of this general unnameability, because it shows how the poor can be, in the words of Hardt and Negri, both "unlocalizable" and "the foundation of the multitude."[65] For Hardt and Negri, the poor are "the figure of a transversal, omnipresent, different, mobile subject" because of their "indispensable presence in the production of a common wealth."[66] This is clear in *Capital*, which shows us how their indispensable presence is never the presence of an identity.

The sphere of pauperism emerges in *Capital* to bring together a heterogeneous group joined only by movements of inclusion/exclusion and potentialization/depotentialization. Thoburn's insistence on the unnameability of the proletariat and the impossibility of celebrating the lumpenproletariat as the location of difference in Marx highlights the importance of understanding that pauperism is not an identity or a group external to the working class. Pauperism is contiguous to and interwoven with the proletariat, and it forces us to consider the non-identity of the proletariat as a whole, the specific form of nonidentity characterized by power in its relation to impotence and in its specific form of actuality that is not only enactment.[67]

Disciplinary Power

Marx shows how capitalism's development "produces" a relative over-population and pauperism, and he reveals how the continued accumulation of capital requires disabled and able members of these groups. This notion of capital as productive and not merely as repressive served as a model for Michel Foucault's articulation of his notion of power. In an interview following the publication of the first volume of *The History of Sexuality*, he makes what he calls a "presumptuous comparison" of his notion of power to Marx's, and he presents as exemplary in this respect Marx's examination of poverty:

> What did Marx do, in his analysis of capital, when he encountered the problem of the poverty of the workers? He rejected its usual explanation as the effect of natural scarcity or planned theft. He said in essence that, given what capitalist production is, in its basic laws, it cannot not produce poverty. Capitalism does not have as its raison d'être the starvation of workers, but it cannot develop without starving them. Marx substituted the analysis of production for the denunciation of theft. Mutatis mutandis, that's a bit like what I wanted to do.[68]

Foucault is speaking specifically here of his own inquiry into the relations of power and sexuality, but the notion of power as productive is not unique, in his works, to the *History of Sexuality*. Foucault's relation to Marx's notion of the productivity of power and the problem of poverty extends far beyond this cursory comparison.

For Foucault, poverty was "le grand problème . . . du XIXe siècle," and, although he never dedicated an entire work to it, a concern with poverty and Marx's texts appears in *Madness and Civilization, The Order of Things, The Archaeology of Knowledge, Discipline and Punish, The History of Sexuality*, and a number of essays and interviews.[69] One of

Foucault's closest points of contact with Marx is the analysis of disciplinary power in *Discipline and Punish,* in which he demonstrates how, in the course of the seventeenth and eighteenth centuries, a reform of the French justice system established a "punishment without torture" and regularized a penal system that had until then been characterized by "innumerable authorities" and by "innumerable loopholes."[70] Foucault couples the power to punish with new disciplinary techniques that were used in schools, hospitals, and, eventually, the military.[71] He describes how military regulations, factory construction, and school dormitory regulations aimed to create "the obedient subject" and a "docile body":[72]

> Discipline increases the forces of the body (in economic terms of utility) and diminishes these same forces (in political terms of obedience). In short, it dissociates power from the body; on the one hand, it turns it into an "aptitude," a "capacity," which it seeks to increase; on the other hand, it reverses the course of the energy, the power that might result from it, and turns it into a relation of strict subjection. If economic exploitation separates the force and the product of labour, let us say that disciplinary coercion establishes in the body the constricting link between an increased aptitude and an increased domination.[73]

This passage is close to Marx's description of the separation of labor power from the worker. Disciplinary power "increases" an "aptitude" or "capacity" and closely links this increased ability with a form of "domination" and not, as in Marx, with disability. The disabled, enabled worker in Marx takes on a different form in disciplinary power's establishment of a subjected, capable individual. The relation of the disciplinary individual to the new forms of work in the capitalist process of production occupies Foucault throughout *Discipline and Punish.*[74] One sentence in the key paragraph on this question makes clear the interdependence of the rise of disciplinary power and the accumulation of capital: "Each makes the other possible and necessary; each provides a model for the other."[75]

This link of capital and disciplinary power should not distract from the fact that, despite the affinities that link Foucault and Marx, disciplinary power is not exhausted by its uses in capitalist production. Foucault explicitly presents his work as a departure from Marx.[76] Disciplinary power, for Foucault, "may be identified neither with an institution nor with an apparatus" and thus is not identical to or controlled by economic interests.[77] He writes about how the kind of work performed by "the insane, the sick, prisoners . . . has a value that is, above all else, disciplinary" and that "the productive function is clearly 'zero' for the categories that concern me."[78] In the eighteenth century, Foucault argues, the function of work exceeded the merely economic benefits and created disciplined individuals whose productivity was not the primary concern.

The close link that joins production and nonproductive individuals is central to Foucault's work, and this is where Foucault's relation to Marx overlaps with his sustained interest, from *Madness and Civilization* on, in poverty. In *Madness and Civilization,* Foucault describes the discovery of the power of the poor:

> The eighteenth century discovered that "the Poor" did not exist as a concrete and final reality; that in them, two realities of different natures had too long been confused. On the one hand, there was *Poverty:* scarcity of commodities and money, an economic situation linked to the state of commerce, of agriculture, of industry. On the other, there was *Population:* not a passive element subject to the fluctuations of wealth, but a force which directly contributed to the economic situation, to the production of wealth, since it is man's labor which creates—or at least transmits, shifts, and multiplies—wealth.[79]

The perception of the poor is split, as the condition of poverty and the force of a population become visible separately.[80] The poor, as population, are productive and, as in Marx's analysis of the relative overpopulation, essential to the expansion of the economy. But, unlike Marx, who insists on the inclusion of the sick and disabled poor in the processes of production, Foucault summarily excludes them from production:

> The sick man is dead weight and represents a "passive, apathetic, negative" element, and he takes part in society only as a consumer. . . . He is the negative element par excellence, poverty with no way out and no options, no virtual wealth. He alone demands total care. But how to justify it? There is no economic utility in the care of the sick and no practical necessity.[81]

In this passage from *Madness and Civilization,* Foucault seems to limit the role of the poor to that of "dead weight" and "consumer," while

Marx emphasizes the necessity of this "dead weight" in the accumulation of capital. But the sick poor, being "without virtual wealth," are excluded here only to be included elsewhere, in the new apparatus of assistance developed in the eighteenth century: "All human life, from the most immediate sensations to the most elaborated social forms, is taken up into the network of the obligations of care."[82]

Foucault intends with the phrase "all human life" the sentiments of those who help the poor just as much as the lives of the sick poor who are the beneficiaries of these new forms of public assistance. His analysis takes account of the epoch's "economic and social thinking on poverty, sickness, and care."[83] Having been excluded from the processes of production, the sick poor become the locus for the elaboration of a new "social space of sickness" whose investment with power becomes an object for other studies by Foucault.[84]

Biopower

Foucault's analysis of the poor in *Madness and Civilization* ends with the discussion of the discovery of the power of the population, because it is at this point that the poor are perceived as distinct from the mad. But Foucault later returns to the figure of "population" when, in the 1970s, he begins to work on another concept of power. It is almost as if *The History of Sexuality* picked up where the analysis of poverty left off in *Madness and Civilization*. Disciplinary power focuses on the individual and the individual's body, and, in the second half of the eighteenth century, Foucault argues, a new form of power, "biopower," emerges, which accompanies the already existing disciplinary techniques and disciplined bodies by creating a wider support and point of application in humanity as a mass phenomenon and as "life" or "species."[85] This new "biopolitics of the population" takes account of and manages birth and death rates, illness, and public hygiene.[86] Of course, just as there was discipline in less structured forms before the rise of disciplinary power, so too there were institutions that engaged with humanity as a mass and as life, but, with the emergence of biopower, "there are mechanisms that are more subtle, more rational, of insurance, individual and collective savings, [and] security."[87]

The biopolitics of the population deals with reproduction and the "very important problem, dating from the beginning of the nineteenth century (at the moment of industrialization) of aging, the individual who falls outside the field of capacity or activity—and also accidents, infirmities, [and] various anomalies."[88] Disciplinary power joined with biopolitics "in the form of concrete arrangements [agencements concrets] that would go to make up the great technology of power in the nineteenth century."[89] Biopower thus has a double object and support: the disciplinary, trained, anatomo-political body and the mass phenomena of life that cannot or can no longer be trained. The rapid development of new institutions and fields of research and policy (on birthrate, death rate, longevity, public health) allowed this new power to take hold in these areas in new ways.[90] Biopower's "grande technologie à double face" aimed to "invest life through and through," and its testing ground and privileged point of application always included the poor.[91] The formulation of power investing "life through and through" rephrases and completes the task implied in *Madness and Civilization* in the claim that "all human life, from the most immediate sensations to the most elaborated social forms, is taken up into the network of the obligations of care."[92]

Although Foucault's notion of power departs from Marx's in its emphasis on power's relative independence from economic interests, Foucault continues and complements Marx's analysis of the accumulation of capital and the emergence of a relative overpopulation. *Discipline and Punish* investigates the disciplinary techniques that Marx identified as essential to the development of capitalist production, and the notion of biopower expands the interpretation in *Capital* of the sphere of pauperism and the worker's body by offering a further explanation for the inclusion of both capable and disabled life within capitalist production. In the first volume of *The History of Sexuality,* Foucault explicitly invokes Marx when he describes biopower as an "indispensable element in the development of capitalism," making possible (without being subordinate to) "the adjustment of the accumulation of men to that of capital, the joining of the growth of human groups to the expansion of productive forces and the differential allocation of profit."[93] Foucault also explicitly anchors his periodization of power in two moments in the history of capitalism: the initial stages of capitalist production in which it was necessary to "form a 'labor force'" by means of disciplinary power and the "epoch of *Spätkapitalismus*" in which the demands of production became more complex and required the development of biopower.[94] "The development of capitalism . . . would not have been possible without the controlled insertion of bodies into the machinery of production and the adjustment of the phenomena of population to economic processes," Foucault writes.[95] The analysis of sexuality and biopower remains linked to Foucault's earlier texts on disciplinary power and their concern with the accumulation of capital and modern processes of production.[96]

For Foucault, biopower, with its double emphasis on discipline and population, is indispensable for the accumulation of capital. My readings of Marx showed how the porosity of the sphere of pauperism bears witness to the linkage of ability and disability in the capitalist process of production. In this process, labor power emerges simultaneously with a produced and productive incapacity, which Marx insists is a "necessary condition" of capital. Foucault continues this examination of incapacity in industrial societies by elucidating the central place of nonproductive trained labor in the development of disciplinary power and the crucial role played by biopower's investment of nonproductive life. There is something about the power of the poor that, even when reduced to impotence, remains central to "capitalist production and the development of wealth" (in Marx) and power (in Foucault). In their texts, the understanding of incapacity and nonenactment is just as essential as the analysis of productivity, and the importance of this unactualized power can be seen in the prominence given by Marx to pauperism and by Foucault to the sick poor, unproductive yet disciplined bodies, and biological life. Biopower and pauperism emerge in the texts of Foucault and Marx as markers of the central place of impotence and nonenactment identified by Heidegger in the structure of power, and the following chapters will explore how these and other privative aspects of power appear in literary texts about the poor. My literary readings will pay special attention to the way in which the poor emerge in tandem with "modes of composition" that resist the attribution of identities and communities based on identification. The next chapter will build on this chapter's analyses by looking at the relation of power and language in texts by Foucault and Baudelaire.

Let's Get Beat Up
by the Poor!

Infamy

In an essay titled "Lives of Infamous Men" that dates from the same period as the first volume of the *History of Sexuality*, Foucault presents some of the implications of his notion of biopower for literary representation. The essay formulates the conditions under which a form of life that is "infamous" and "insignificant" (*infâme* and *infime*) comes to light in historical and literary texts.[1] Since the time of his work on *Histoire de la folie* in the late 1950s, Foucault planned to present archival material from the Hôpital général and the Bastille, short notices and narratives of episodes about the lives of criminals and the poor and their relations with these institutions.[2] The documents present obscure lives in their "encounter with power," which "snatched them from the darkness in which they could, perhaps should, have remained."[3] These lives appear only insofar as they are illuminated by power, and Foucault insists, "it is doubtless impossible to ever grasp them again in themselves, as they might have been 'in a free state.'"[4] But this restriction, far from limiting their interest or importance, reduces each of these infamous lives to "the most intense point," "the point where its energy is concentrated" and "where it comes up against power, struggles with it, attempts to use its forces and to evade its traps."[5]

Although Foucault insists on the nonliterary quality of the texts he would have assembled in his proposed collection, he closes his essay with a discussion of how the new form of power that illuminates these existences also brings about "a whole new regime of literature."[6] He argues that until the seventeenth century, daily life becomes "capable of being said *[dicible]*" only if "traversed and transfigured by the legendary," but, in the seventeenth century, Foucault writes, literature takes on the new task of illuminating "the most nocturnal and most quotidian elements of existence" and becomes

> determined to seek out the quotidian beneath the quotidian itself, to cross boundaries, to ruthlessly or insidiously bring our secrets out in the open, to displace rules and codes, to compel the unmentionable to be told[;] it will thus tend to place itself outside the law, or at least to take on the burden of scandal, transgression, or revolt.[7]

Power "incites, provokes, produces" these texts, and "it makes people act and speak."[8] Produced in this way, the voices of the infamous are always contained and excessive; they respond to a demand to speak while simultaneously "displacing rules and codes" and calling into question the very imperative that compels speech. Transgression must be understood here in the specific context established by the discussion in chapter 1 of power in Marx and Foucault: poverty's singular combination of capacity and incapacity is threatening and potentially transgressive because it marks the place of something within the process of production that could transform or destroy it.

The Crowd's Uncanny Presence

Literature must tell a certain kind of secret that is the "most insufferable" and "the most common." Foucault's focus remains on the apparatus that provokes the revelation of this secret and not on the secret's content. His interest lies not so much in what the secret reveals as in the fact that it is told and how it is provoked to appear. This interest in the secret should be carefully circumscribed so as not to reduce Foucault's conception of literature to a thematic presentation of secrets, and a similar caution is necessary when approaching an often cited remark by Walter Benjamin that will frame the following discussion of Baudelaire: the claim that the crowd is a "secret presence" in Baudelaire's poetry.[9] This phrase has been taken to indicate a "hidden theme" that is there like any other theme, just not in the foreground of Baudelaire's texts. It would then suffice to reveal that it is a theme for the secret to be disclosed and its force exhausted. The claims made in "The Lives of Infamous Men" about the production of secrets have to do with an earlier epoch, but at the very least the essay's lexical resonance with Benjamin alerts us to the necessity of carefully considering the secret as having more than just a thematic interest. The German phrase *heimliche Gegenwart,* which is translated as "secret presence," evokes a wide range of associations implicit in the German term for "secret," *heimlich*—if they can still be called implicit almost a century after Freud's essay "Das Unheimliche" ("The Uncanny"). This term indicates that the crowd is "at home" in his texts, and because of an intimacy with its putative opposite, *unheimlich,* it is also disturbingly uncanny, as the readings that follow will show.

The crowd is not a theme or motif that, although it is lurking beneath the surface of Baudelaire's poems, could be illuminated and made to appear by the reader and critic. The crowd is present in a way that is *heimlich.* Its multiplicity is uncanny, which is why Benjamin cites Hugo's description of its absence as the "silence of a throng" *(Schweigen eines Gewimmels)* immediately after presenting its "secret presence."[10] In his translation, Benjamin uses the term *Gewimmel,* which is used in German to denote a mass of living beings or fantastic creatures, including swarms of locusts, frogs, and worms.[11] He also compares the crowd to *le troupeau mortel* of Baudelaire's poem "Danse macabre" and goes on to describe its "presence" in "A une passante," in which it appears only as a "roaring" in the background, as what makes the poem possible without appearing as a theme. Its secret presence is also uncannily doubled in a number of *Doppelgänger* that appear in poems such as "Les sept vieillards" and "Les petites vieilles," and its secret is reflected in the eyes of such uncanny figures as the dandy.

The crowd is a specific kind of uncanny presence, like the supplemental presence of pauperism that unsettles Marx's classification of the reserve army and the "secret" *(Geheimnis),* in the last sentence of the first volume of *Capital,* that is "loudly proclaimed" by political economy: "the expropriation of the worker."[12] Benjamin's discussion of the secret presence of the crowd focuses on "A une passante," in which, as Benjamin writes, "the very crowd brings to the city dweller the figure that fascinates" but that appears, only implicitly, in the incipit: "The street roared around me, deafening!"[13] Baudelaire offers a formulation of this implied relation to the crowd in his essay "The Painter of Modern Life":

> The crowd is his element, as the air is that of birds and water of fishes. His passion and his profession are to become one flesh with the crowd. . . . He is an "I" with an insatiable appetite for the "non-I."[14]

Serving as a necessary background, the crowd provides the modern artist with an opportunity for communion and consumption: his union with the crowd and his nourishment by means of contact with it. Benjamin emphasizes the tension of this consuming communion by presenting Baudelaire's place in relation to the crowd as a threshold. Baudelaire "guarded this threshold" and maintained the tension, which differentiates him from Hugo, who attempts to hide it and overcome it:

> [Hugo] wanted to be flesh of their flesh *[Stoff sein von ihrem Stoff]*. Secularism, Progress, and Democracy were inscribed on the banner which he waved over their heads. This banner transfigured mass existence. It was the canopy over the threshold which separated the individual from the crowd.[15]

Hugo's identificatory banner serves two functions: it glorifies the crowd and obscures the differences that constitute it and separate it from the writer and, as Benjamin makes clear, from every individual. "Hugo placed himself in the crowd as a *citoyen*," Benjamin writes, whereas "Baudelaire divorced himself from the crowd as a hero," and much of Benjamin's reading of Baudelaire concentrates on this heroic conception of the poet.[16]

Bored Community in *The Flowers of Evil*

For Benjamin, the modern hero is not a role but the ability to change roles: "Flâneur, apache, dandy, ragpicker were so many roles to him. For the modern hero *[Hero]* is no hero *[Held]*; he is a portrayer of heroes. Heroic modernity turns out to be a *Trauerspiel* in which the hero's part is available."[17] The hero role can be occupied by any one of these other modern types. Benjamin then cites two stanzas from "The Seven Old Men," including the line "I roamed, stiffening my nerves like a hero"

(Je suivais, roidissant mes nerfs comme un héros).[18] Later in that poem, we read, "Indignant as a drunk who sees the world / Double, I staggered home" (Exaspéré comme un ivrogne qui voit double / Je rentrai . . .).[19] Baudelairean heroism is not the vehicle—the *héros* in the first simile—but the openness of the "I" that allows it to be both *comme un héros* and *comme un ivrogne*. Benjamin claims that heroism is a term that Baudelaire uses to present a shifting state that otherwise would have no name; behind the masks is not an identity but an "incognito."[20]

The role of hero is only one of the many that can be occupied by Baudelaire's heroic, transformable, and productive incognito. Another role is the dandy, who contains "the last spark of heroism amid decadence," Baudelaire writes in "The Painter of Modern Life."[21] The dandy is "rich in native energy" and is an example for Baudelaire of "an energy" that one finds "in all excess."[22] This energy, however, is latent, which is why Baudelaire imagines a passerby who thinks of the dandy: "A rich man perhaps, but more likely an out-of-work Hercules."[23] In the mid-nineteenth century, even mythological figures join the ranks of the reserve army.

Benjamin cites all of these remarks on the dandy and claims that his traits bear "a very definite historical stamp";[24] his Herculean strength and nonchalance reflect the English merchant class's control of an international commercial network to whose "tremors" they had to react with the greatest discretion. The dandy's "tic" is "a clumsy, inferior manifestation of the problem," a crack in the surface that reveals a powerful, hard-to-control interior similar to the productive incognito of the poet.[25] According to Benjamin, this simultaneity also explains Baudelaire's interest in ships, because "the ships combine airy casualness with readiness for the utmost exertion *[Krafteinsatz]*."[26] The Baudelairean ship remains in the harbor, idle, just as modernity has no need for the hero, who, like Hercules, is unemployed. The ship's immobility sets Baudelaire apart from the artists, writers, and thinkers in Benjamin's fragment that I cited in the introduction. Their ship, initially christened *Poverty*, breaks with a Baudelairean tradition as it sets sail.

In his prose poems about crowds and the poor, Baudelaire repeatedly emphasizes their "energy," and the dandy's relation to the crowd can be understood as a link between "energetic" figures. Based on a shared energy and incognito (and not on identity), this community, too, is a secret presence in Baudelaire. In Benjamin's account, Baudelaire understands the lumpenproletariat as racially different; he claims that the poet subscribes to contemporaneous accounts of the poor as "a class of subhumans which sprang from the crossing of robbers with prostitutes."[27] Such an account is close to the conventional understanding of pauperism mentioned in chapter 1. Benjamin cites as evidence of this view the poem "Abel and Cain" and compares it to Marx's juxtaposition of a "race" of commodity owners and a "race of those who possess no commodity other than their labor power."[28] Benjamin's insistence on Baudelaire's presentation of the poor as different comes after he cites a poem by Charles-Augustin Sainte-Beuve in which a different kind of relation with the poor appears. Sainte-Beuve laments the fallen condition of a coachman ("Comment l'homme peut-il ainsi tomber?") and "asks himself whether his own soul is not almost as neglected as the soul of the coachman."[29] "Abel and Cain" could not conclude more differently: "Rise up, Race of Cain / and cast God down upon the Earth."[30] Instead of insisting on the identity or link of the souls, Baudelaire invokes the destructive difference that the poor embody, and he posits other forms of community based on forms of energy that undo identity by revealing, in the face convulsed by the tic, a transformability that makes identity possible.

My analysis of the poor in Baudelaire will adopt Benjamin's term of "secret presence" to understand the mode of appearance of the poor, especially those figures on the edge of the crowd that Baudelaire thematizes, such as the beggar and the street performer. The secret of the poor in *Les fleurs du mal* is, in some ways, an open one and in no way limited to the *Tableaux parisiens,* because they are already invoked in "To the Reader," the provocative opening poem of the collection. In the first stanza, we read: "we feed our amiable remorse / the way mendicants nourish their vermin"; and the fifth stanza offers this extended comparison:

> Like the debauched poor man who kisses and bites
> the martyred breast of an ancient whore,
> we steal a clandestine pleasure,
> squeezed with effort, as if from an old orange.

[Ainsi qu'un débauché pauvre qui baise et mange
Le sein martyrisé d'une antique catin,
Nous volons au passage un plaisir clandestin
Que nous pressons bien fort comme une vieille orange.][31]

The poor appear here as the vehicle in two very different similes: they are life-sustaining in the first stanza, and in the fifth stanza they are able to extract pleasure from even the most exhausted object of desire. There is something about the poor that allows them to be both a source of nourishment and to draw from what seems to be able to offer no more pleasure. They are able to sustain others, and they find sustenance where it is least likely. This double function points to their privileged relation to potential, which permits them, in these lines, to serve as a vehicle for the opening of *Les fleurs du mal* and to offer a common ground for the speaker and the reader, this "we" that emerges in both similes on the threshold of the collection in a relation that one reader calls "the intimacy of an obdurate collective."[32] The poem's final stanzas postulate as the ultimate ground for "our" relation the ugliest and foulest of vices, "Boredom which with ready tears / dreams of hangings as it puffs its pipe."[33] Ennui here is a kind of inaction that dreams of murderous action; the impotence of boredom nourishes fantasies of the extreme exercise of power.[34] (And the comparison of the poor and "clandestine joys" shows how Baudelaire associates the poor with secrets.)

The poem then concludes with these famous lines that bind the reader and writer in the shared knowledge of boredom, in an insult, and in a claim of fraternity: "Reader, you know this squeamish monster well /— hypocrite reader,—my alias,—my twin!"[35] This is the first indication of the uncanniness of the presence of the poor: their role in the formation of an antagonistic community based not on identity but on hypocrisy and the shared potential or openness of boredom.

"This Crazy Energy"

In *Le spleen de Paris,* the relation to the poor becomes an explicit object of investigation in prose poems such as "The Bad Glazier," "Widows," "The Old Acrobat," "The Pauper's Toy," "The Eyes of the Poor," "The Counterfeit Coin," "Windows," and "Let's Beat Up the Poor!" The poor and "the mute eloquence of [their] beseeching eyes" are an essential part of the experience of the city in these texts.[36] Their destitution is described in detail, and their exposure to the passerby's gaze appears positively as an exposure to "life"[37] and to being "refashioned,"[38] which attracts the poet "irresistibly."[39] In an extended reading of "The Counterfeit Coin," Derrida writes, "[B]eggars can signify the absolute demand of the other, the inextinguishable appeal, the unquenchable thirst for the gift," and their force and the pull of their withdrawal are inescapable for the narrator of *Le spleen de Paris.*[40] The poet would like to be able to awaken poverty's latent "energy," which can best be done by exposing them to danger and violence. When this energy is hidden, the poet performs a series of more or less outrageous provocations full of risk for the poor and for the poet himself, such as giving a counterfeit coin as alms and beating a beggar to a pulp. As Anne-Emmanuelle Berger writes, it is important to remember while reading *Le spleen de Paris* that the narrator's "philosophy of the *promeneur*-moralist-logician . . . is almost always an experimental philosophy," and I would argue that the narrator's "experimental disposition" is guided by an interest in the power of the poor, the power of the poet, and an understanding of the relation that joins them.[41] This incitement of the poor awakens their force as well as some force in the poem's narrator, as when he drops a flowerpot on a poor glazier's wares so as to awaken his own energy in a way that recalls the bored hangman and reader in "To the Reader." The narrator makes the link explicit: "It's the type of energy that springs from ennui and daydreaming."[42] The poem opens with a description of "characters" who are "purely contemplative and completely unsuited for action" but who

> sometimes feel abruptly hurled into action by an irresistible force, like an arrow out of a bow. The moralist and the physician, who claim to know everything, cannot explain the cause of this crazy energy which hits these lazy and voluptuous souls so suddenly, and how, incapable of carrying out the simplest and the most necessary things, one minute later they find an excess courage for executing the most absurd and often even the most dangerous acts.[43]

Primed by an "irresistible force," these lazy souls suddenly possess a "crazy energy" that is associated with beauty—the narrator shouts after the glazier, "Make life beautiful! [La vie en beau!]"—but also with danger. The narrator acknowledges this much when he says, "Such neurotic pranks are not without peril, and one can often pay dearly for them." But the awakening of the potential of the poor, it seems, is worth this risk.

In this passage, the focus remains on the narrator, his energy, and the thrill of provocation. Is his strategy of incitement only part of a larger strategy of containment in which the poor reflect or enable the narrator's excess courage? The reading of Foucault above would lead us to expect something else: that with the attempt at containment comes the risk of uncontainability—the possibility that the "crazy energy" will become more than one bargained for.

Baudelaire's Question: "What to Do?"

Le spleen de Paris repeatedly stages the transformation and release of energy in perilous encounters with the poor. Two prose poems in particular, "The Old Acrobat" and "Let's Beat Up the Poor!," allow for an investigation of the ways in which the power of the poor can be incited. They also reveal the double function of incitement and containment that Foucault assigns to modern literature. "The Old Acrobat" demonstrates the impact of poverty on its narrator while posing and leaving open the question of the correct mode of response to the poor, and in "Let's Beat Up the Poor!," this question finds an unexpected answer.

In "The Old Acrobat," the narrator recounts his holiday walk through a fair and describes the strongmen, dancers, and their audience before, at the end of the row of fairground stalls, he encounters "a poor acrobat, stooped, obsolete, decrepit, a human ruin."[44] Surrounded by "the joy, the profit, and the debauchery" of the performers and the crowd, the acrobat seems out of place:

> He was not crying, he was not dancing, he was not gesturing, he was not shouting; he was singing no song, neither joyful nor woeful, he was not beseeching. He was mute and immobile.

> [Il ne riait pas, le misérable! Il ne pleurait pas, il ne dansait pas, il ne gesticulait pas, il ne criait pas; il ne chantait aucune chanson, ni gaie ni lamentable, il n'implorait pas. Il était muet et immobile.]

The performer appears as a series of actions that he does not perform. The next paragraph continues the description by focusing on the acrobat's gaze:

> But what a deep, unforgettable look! It wandered over the crowd and the lights, whose moving waves stopped a few steps from his repulsive wretchedness!

> [Mais quel regard profond, inoubliable, il promenait sur la foule et les lumières, dont le flot mouvant s'arrêtait à quelques pas de sa répulsive misère!]

The mobile gaze seems to offer a stark contrast to the otherwise inert performer, but it would also be possible to understand the "deep look" and inertia of the old man as elements of a general receptivity.[45] Both the acrobat and the narrator are located for an instant in this shared space right on the edge of the crowd's "waves," on the threshold that Benjamin identifies as defining Baudelaire's relation to the crowd. Only in this location is such an encounter possible.

Mute, immobile, and exposed to the celebration around him, the *saltimbanque* has a paralyzing effect on the narrator:

> I felt my throat strangled by the dreadful hand of hysteria, and my sight seemed to be blocked by rebellious tears refusing to fall.

> [Je sentis ma gorge serrée par la main terrible de l'hystérie, et il me sembla que mes regards étaient offusqués par ces larmes rebelles qui ne veulent pas tomber.]

Another threshold appears here in the "blocked" moment right before crying, which is characterized by hysteria, impotence, and an aggressive, mimetic relation. He feels his throat being grasped by the "hand of hysteria," and, just as the acrobat does nothing, so too the narrator is reduced to inactivity, unable to respond or to narrate further the story of the encounter.[46]

This shared passivity then instigates a self-interrogation about activity. The next sentence reads "What to do?" and marks a transition from hysterical paralysis to hypothetical responses:

> What to do? Why ask the unfortunate man what curiosity, what marvel he had to display in that stinking darkness, behind his torn curtain? In fact, I did not dare; and, although the cause of my timidity might make you laugh, I admit that I was afraid of humiliating him. Finally, just as I had resolved to place in passing some money on part of his platform, hoping that he would

guess my intention, a huge backflow of populace, caused by some unknown turmoil, swept me far away.

[Que faire? A quoi bon demander à l'infortuné quelle curiosité, quelle merveille il avait à montrer dans ces ténèbres puantes, derrière son rideau déchiqueté? En vérité, je n'osais; et dût la raison de ma timidité vous faire rire, j'avouerai que je craignais de l'humilier. Enfin, je venais de me résoudre à déposer en passant quelque argent sur une de ses planches, espérant qu'il devinerait mon intention, quand un grand reflux de peuple, causé par je ne sais quel trouble, m'entraîna loin de lui.]

The narrator's encounter with the acrobat forces him to pose the question, "What to do?" He dismisses his first response, and when he finally makes up his mind to give the old performer some money, this seems to be only a halfhearted solution, which the crowd prevents him from carrying out anyway. Set off from the other entertainers and the crowd by doing nothing, the old acrobat confronts the narrator with the question of what to do. Swept from the threshold, his only reaction to the poor man remains the posing of his question. The nonperforming performer paralyzes the narrator, brings his speech to a stuttering halt, and, at the same time, demands action of some kind. Suspension and provocation coincide as the acrobat reduces the narrator to a state of potential action.

The final paragraph of "The Old Acrobat" contains the narrator's "analysis" of his encounter:

And, turning around, obsessed by that vision, I tried to analyze my sudden pain, and I told myself: I have just seen the image of the old writer who has survived the generation whose brilliant entertainer he was; of the old poet without friends, without family, without children, debased by his wretchedness and the public's ingratitude, and whose booth the forgetful world no longer wants to enter!

[Et, m'en retournant, obsédé par cette vision, je cherchai à analyser ma soudaine douleur, et je me dis: Je viens de voir l'image du vieil homme de lettres qui a survécu à la génération dont il fut le brillant amuseur; du vieux poète sans amis, sans famille, sans enfants, dégradé par sa misère et par l'ingratitude publique, et dans la baraque de qui le monde oublieux ne veut plus entrer!]

A comparison with the previously cited passages from "The Old Acrobat" reveals the extent to which this analysis aims to minimize and contain the disturbing encounter that has just taken place.[47] A disturbing moment of paralysis is interpreted as a kind of sympathetic identification, and the narrator domesticates the experience of shock as a helpful, if disheartening, lesson in these remarks that are explicitly distanced as something that "I told myself" and as an interpretation that he "tries" to undertake. The analysis also recasts the encounter as the sight of an image, but it would have been difficult for the narrator to have glimpsed "the image of the old writer" in the moment when his "sight seemed to be blocked." The encounter paralyzes the narrator, and its calamitous force reappears in condensed form in the final paragraph as a "sudden suffering" or "sudden pain" that the narrator's interpretation fails to explain and that points to an experience of passivity that is exposed to the possibility of action: "What to do?" The pain of this suspended relation to activity shows that the attempt to parry the shock comes too late, and the incongruity of the narrator's paralysis and his comforting analysis only highlights the disturbing force of the encounter with the acrobat.[48]

In his reading of "The Old Acrobat," Jean Starobinski repeats the final paragraph's misinterpretation of the encounter. The acrobat, he writes, "announces and prefigures in a prophetic manner Baudelaire's aphasia."[49] His emphasis on Baudelaire's future muteness distracts attention from the silence that the old man causes in the narrator, whose "strangled throat," lack of response to the crucial question "What to do?," and "sudden pain" can all be read as signs of paralysis already at work in the prose poem. For Starobinski, the *saltimbanque* is a "pure figure of failure" and "offers a spectacle of silent decline, the muting of energy and will, a fatal impotence," but the narrator's mimetic reaction cannot be reduced to what Starobinski calls a "symbolic and prophetic" anticipation of the fate of the prose poem's author.[50] Such a reading obscures the immediacy of the acrobat's effect on the narrator and the poem's language. In conventional reflections on mortality and aging, the narrator and, after him, Starobinski attempt to minimize the disturbance of being momentarily paralyzed.

In an article on narration in *Le spleen de Paris,* Cheryl Krueger criticizes readings of the prose poems that have taken at face value Baudelaire's declarations about the cycle, and her warnings also apply to the analysis that concludes "The Old Acrobat."[51] The narrator's interpretation can be read as a sign of the difference that separates him from the acrobat even in the moment when he seems so profoundly affected by their encounter, but the disturbance cannot be reduced to a prophetic sight of the "image of the old writer." Only when forcefully removed from the acrobat's immediate reach can the narrator perform the actions that the acrobat suspends and interpret the encounter in this way. Barely able to speak or see and unable to act, the narrator is carried away by the crowd, left only with the passivity or suffering that is caused by the performer and that recedes into the background of his interpretation.

Baudelaire's Answer: "Let's Beat Up the Poor!"

The question "What to do?" remains unanswered, but it is possible to read as a response the title of the penultimate prose poem of *Le spleen de Paris*, "Let's Beat Up the Poor!" The poem opens with a narrator relating how, after spending fifteen days confined to his room reading books on the problem of poverty, he has

> the dim seed of an idea better than all the old wives' formulas I had recently perused in the encyclopedia. But it was only the idea of an idea, something infinitely hazy.
>
> [le germe obscur d'une idée supérieure à toutes les formules de bonne femme dont j'avais récemment parcouru le dictionnaire. Mais ce n'était que l'idée d'une idée, quelque chose d'infiniment vague.][52]

So he goes out. He leaves his room with this "hazy" idea, which only becomes clearer after a double encounter with a gaze and a voice:

> As I was about to enter a tavern, a beggar held out his hat, with one of those unforgettable looks that would topple thrones, if mind could move matter, and if a hypnotist's eyes could ripen grapes.
>
> At the same time, I heard a voice whispering in my ear, a voice I knew well; the voice of a good Angel, or of a good Demon, who accompanies me everywhere. . . .
>
> This is what the voice whispered to me: "He alone is equal to another, if he proves it, and he alone is worthy of freedom, if he can conquer it."
>
> Immediately, I pounced on my beggar.

[Comme j'allais entrer dans un cabaret, un mendiant me tendit son chapeau, avec un de ces regards inoubliables qui culbuteraient les trônes, si l'esprit remuait la matière, et si l'œil d'un magnétiseur faisait mûrir les raisins.

En même temps, j'entendis une voix qui chuchotait à mon oreille, une voix que je reconnus bien; c'était celle d'un bon Ange, ou d'un bon Démon, qui m'accompagne partout. . . . Or sa voix me chuchotait ceci: "Celui-là seul est l'égal d'un autre, qui le prouve, et celui-là seul est digne de la liberté, qui sait la conquérir."

Immédiatement, je sautai sur mon mendiant.]

The narrator endows the beggar's gaze with hypothetical political powers, which, together with the voice of his demon, encourage the narrator to attack this figure, who in this moment becomes "my" beggar. The narrator proceeds to "beat him with the obstinate energy of cooks trying to tenderize a beefsteak," and the improper match of a singular tenor and plural vehicle draws attention to how this clash involves more than two individuals. The beggar's eyes and the narrator's demon also bear witness to the presence of other forces, and the first person plural imperative of the title "Let's Beat Up the Poor!" indicates the poem's "appellative character" that aims to present the action of a collective "we."[53] Just as in "To the Reader," poverty and beggars are intimately tied to an implicit appeal to a collective or fraternity. One is never alone in encounters with the poor.

The narrator recounts at length how he beats the beggar to a pulp with a tree branch until he solicits an equally violent reaction:

Suddenly,—Oh miracle! Oh delight of the philosopher who verifies the excellence of his theory!—I saw that antique carcass turn over, straighten up with a force [énergie] I would never have suspected in a machine so peculiarly unhinged. And, with a look of hatred that seemed to me a good omen, the decrepit bandit flung himself on me, blackened both my eyes, broke four of my teeth, and, with the same tree branch, beat me to a pulp.—By my energetic medication, I had thus restored his pride and his life.

[Tout à coup,—ô miracle! ô jouissance du philosophe qui vérifie l'excellence de sa théorie!—je vis cette antique carcasse se retourner, se redresser avec une énergie que je n'aurais jamais soupçonnée dans une machine si singulièrement détraquée, et, avec un regard de haine qui me parut de bon augure, le malandrin décrépit se jeta sur moi, me pocha les deux yeux, me cassa quatre dents, et avec la même branche d'arbre me battit dru comme plâtre.—Par mon énergique médication, je lui avais donc rendu l'orgueil et la vie.]

Just when the beggar comes to life, the narrator describes him as a carcass and as a machine on the blink; his energy is thus somehow dead and inhuman. He is metaphorically presented as *une machine* that is *détraquée*, a term that, according to Littré, can be used to describe a machine that has broken down or a mind that has gone mad.[54] And Baudelaire uses it in the moment when the beggar begins to act. This aspect of the incident reveals how ability and disability coincide in the understanding of the poor and their power; where nothing but "dead weight" (Marx and Foucault) and disability would be expected, the poor reveal a simultaneous activity and ability.

As the tide turns against the narrator, the beggar's gaze appears to the narrator to be a "good omen" ("de *bon augure*"), a phrase that complements with a divine sign the presentation of the hypothetical political powers of his eyes in the previous paragraph (and the hope that the old acrobat will guess or "divine" his intention). How can the beggar's "hateful gaze" be a "good omen"? Why would there be an omen for what happens immediately afterward? Since the gaze seems to bear a sign of the narrator's imminent defeat and surrender, the threat and the good omen appear to be almost identical, but, in fact, the omen inserts an indefinite temporal deferral into the immediacy of the threat, because the ensuing struggle may not be the event promised by the beggar's gaze, which, as "Let's Beat Up the Poor!" asserts, has only hypothetical force. Although the prose poem insists on the importance of action, what the narrator undergoes may be but a prelude to a more dramatic change to which the narrator and poetic language will be submitted.[55] The encounter with the beggar remains open and retains the character of an omen, and it thus undoes the narrator's apparent "appropriation" of the beggar in the service of his argument.[56]

Augury and Creation

The omen appears at the exact point in the text when the beggar turns on the narrator—just when the beggar's unsuspected, "miraculous" energy becomes active. The beggar's gaze demands close attention because of the importance given to the eyes of the poor throughout *Le spleen de Paris* and to this beggar's hypothetically powerful eyes earlier in the text. The coincidence of the actualization of the beggar's force with the appearance of the untimely sign of an omen should also shed light on the nature of the beggar's energy in its latent and active modes. The French term *augure* (omen) belongs to a group of words that is at once religious and political and whose traditional etymology Émile Benveniste famously submits to critique. He divides the group of Latin etymons into the three subgroups *augeo, auctor,* and *augur,* all of which emerged from *augeo,* whose conventional etymology argues for an original meaning of "to increase" or "to augment." Benveniste's discussion of *augeo* departs from a riddle that plagues this understanding: it is not clear how the modern terms "authority," "author," and "augury" could have a common origin in *augeo* if it is understood merely as augmentation. Benveniste looks to the earliest Latin texts and discovers that "*augeo* denotes not the increase in something which already exists but . . . a creative act which causes something to arise from a nutrient medium and which is the privilege of the gods or the great natural forces, but not of man."[57] *Augeo* is to create, not merely to augment, and the Romans also designated with the term *augere* the "benefits they expected from the gods, namely of 'promoting' all their enterprises."[58] With this sense of *augeo* in mind, it becomes clear how the later terms emerged from it. An *auctor* is someone who creates or founds something and, eventually, becomes what we know as an "author"; the abstract noun *auctoritas* is "the act of production" or the quality invested in an official; and the term "augur" is used to refer to "the 'promotion' accorded by the gods to an undertaking and demonstrated by an omen."[59]

Benveniste's examination of the vocabulary of authorship, authority, and augury reveals that the primary sense of their common root *augeo* is "to bring something into existence," and this can only be done with an "authority" that, according to Benveniste, is always associated with divinity. This is how Benveniste's conclusion condenses his argument concerning *augeo:*

> Every word pronounced with authority causes a change in the world, it creates something. This mysterious quality is what *augeo* expresses, the power which causes plants to grow and brings a law into existence. . . . Obscure and potent values reside in the *auctoritas,* this gift which is reserved for a handful of men

which allows them to cause something to come into being and literally "to bring into existence."[60]

In Benveniste's analysis, *augeo* indicates a force that enhances language's ability to effect change.[61] Authority appears here adverbially as a force that determines language, just as the gaze that augurs well in Baudelaire's text modifies the beggar's action as part of the adverbial phrase "avec un regard de haine qui me parut de *bon augure.*"

Beggarly Authority

The narrator of "Let's Beat Up the Poor!" awakens the beggar's energy and with it an ominous look, which the continuation of the poem shows to be necessary for the poem's composition, for its authorship. The beggar responds to the narrator's provocation by beating up the narrator, who interprets the response in this way:

> Then, I made a mighty number of signs to make him understand that I considered the discussion finished, and getting up with the self-satisfaction of a Stoic sophist, I told him, "Sir, *you are my equal!* Please do me the honor of sharing my purse. And remember, if you are a true philanthropist, you must apply to all your colleagues, when they seek alms, the theory that I had the *pain* to test upon your back."

> [Alors, je lui fis force signes pour lui faire comprendre que je considérais la discussion comme finie, et me relevant avec la satisfaction d'un sophiste du Portique, je lui dis: "Monsieur, *vous êtes mon égal!* veuillez me faire l'honneur de partager avec moi ma bourse; et souvenez-vous, si vous êtes réellement philanthrope, qu'il faut appliquer à tous vos confrères, quand ils vous demanderont l'aumône, la théorie que j'ai eu la *douleur* d'essayer sur votre dos."]

The beggar is the "equal" of the narrator's postpugilistic interpretation only if "equal" means participating in the same conflict and awakening of force—and not if "equal" is understood to designate the possession of the same privileges and rights.[62] It is the equality of belonging to the multitude invoked here: the demon, the magnetist, the cooks, and the collective "we" implied in the title. Only in this sense is there an equality established in the violent encounter, and the narrator can be seen to attack the beggar not only to make the beggar his equal but also to make himself the beggar's equal.

The narrator presents their bloody fight as a discussion—as linguistic—and then, as in "The Old Acrobat," he presents his surrender in the most recuperative terms before explaining his theory and its practice to the beggar, after which the beggar "swore that he had understood my theory and that he would comply with my advice." Here, too, the term *douleur* appears to disturb the moment in which the narrator interprets the encounter as pleasurable, as a "discussion" that he can emerge from with "self-satisfaction." In the expression "I had the pain of testing it out upon your back," he substitutes the term "pain" where convention dictates "pleasure," and this is the sole acknowledgment in the poem's conclusion of the violence that determines his theoretical proof.

In a text populated by demons, magnetists, alienists, and augurs, the beggar is revealed to be the bearer of a miraculous energy that verifies the narrator's argument; it is a painful, extrarational force that completes a rational demonstration, the second voice necessary for a violent "discussion" that is qualified no fewer than four times as "energetic"; that makes his "infinitely vague" idea explicit; and that allows his "dim seed of an idea" to come to fruition.[63] The beggar's contribution to the discussion gives it authority, because in him resides the energy necessary for the completion of the argument and the poem, a force that the narrator must beat out of him. The beggar is in a certain sense the coauthor of this prose poem, because he appears as the text's augural, authorial bearer of authority.

"Let's Beat Up the Poor!" seems to register the successful containment of the voice of the poor. It captures "the quotidian beneath the quotidian itself" and is able, by provoking the poor, "to cross boundaries, to ruthlessly or insidiously bring our secrets out in the open."[64] The association of the mendicant with authority and augury reveals how crucial he is to this poem's authorship, for the beggar and the narrator depend on each other for the productive act associated with augury. The narrator requires the beggar to prove his theory, and, according to the narrator, the beggar needs the narrator to provoke him to reveal his miraculous force. This reading could also be extended to "The Old Acrobat," in which the narrator's hysterical silence and paralysis, as well as his posing of the question "What to do?," depend on and originate in the encounter with the acrobat. The acrobat dictates the narrator's silence and then, as a reaction, his speech. In both cases, the "infamous" figure is mute and co-opted, even when the mendicant's voice finally appears, in the very last sentence. Besides his role in the "discussion," the sole instance of the beggar's voice is this reported oath of obedience quoted above: "He indeed swore that he had understood my theory, and that he would comply with my advice." "I swear" would have been a speech act, but, when reported as "he swore," it becomes a "description."[65] The beggar's voice remains distanced by citation. He never utters "I" in this poem, thus remaining dependent on the narrator's "I" to announce his presence, in third person, in the text.

In "Let's Beat Up the Poor!" the beggar utters an oath that in its content (an oath of obedience) and its form (reported speech) contains the beggar and his language within the realm delimited by the narrator, who, even when he is beaten up, speaks directly in the poem and never allows the beggar to speak.[66] One aspect of Foucault's infamy must thus be left behind. In the texts of Baudelaire, no longer does one lend "words, turns of phrase, and sentences . . . to the anonymous masses of people so that they might speak."[67] Or if one does, then these masses cannot speak directly. The beggar possesses a distanced authorship and a deferred force: distanced from enactment in a hypothetical force of the beggar's gaze, distanced temporally as an omen, and distanced linguistically in indirect quotation. "Let's Beat Up the Poor!" registers the attempt to force the beggar to show his energy, to participate in a debate, and to be "my equal," but his force remains hypothetical and deferred even when he attacks the narrator, for it is at that moment that the omen appears, thus registering a withdrawal from action even at the highest moment of activity and from the narrator even in the moment of submission and apparent containment in a theoretical proof.

In this poem, power "incites, provokes, produces," and "it makes people act and speak," but the mendicant's investment with power, which appears in this singular combination of activity and latency, manifests itself in the ability to remain distant from these provocations, to maintain an ominous potential even in his apparent domestication. His voice is not only contained. Even when he seems to be subsumed in the argument of the narrator, he disturbs it with his gaze that registers a kind of power that cannot be reduced to a proof for an already formulated theory. The omen's openness marks the uncanniness of his presence in the poem. If we follow Heidegger's claim that enactment cannot be the measure for the actuality of force, then not only is its nonenactment "not already its absence," but also, "vice versa, that enactment is not simply and solely presence."[68] This is the secret way in which the poor are present in Baudelaire's text. The beggar's force is there when he does not act, and its full actuality remains distanced and deferred even when it is enacted.

The reading of "Let's Beat Up the Poor!" gives a new resonance to Deleuze's claim, cited in chapter 1, that the texts of a minor literature speak with "the authority, the autonomy of the stammerer, of he who has won the right to stammer, as opposed to the 'proper speech' of the majority."[69] The beggar's voice is endowed with the authority not of an established power but of an alterity that appears only at a remove even in the heat of this encounter. This is what makes his presence uncanny. The beggar's cited response opposes the speech of the narrator, who needs the beggar to prove his theory even though the violence of his response and augural gaze threaten the narrator's very existence. The mendicant completes the argument by increasing its incompletion, by revealing the openness and wounding pain of any discourse or theory of poverty.

Submitting to the Poor

The title "Let's Beat Up the Poor!" seems to serve as an answer to the question "What to do?" posed in "The Old Acrobat," but, as Dolf Oehler has remarked, the actual relation to the poor suggested by the poem is closer to "Let's get beat up by the poor!"[70] At the end of the fight, it is the narrator who is pummeled and forced to surrender, and he awakens a power that overwhelms him. The mendicant compels the narrator to assume the passivity that at first was the domain of the poor, and the narrator's pain here mirrors the "sudden pain" in "The Old Acrobat," in which the narrator's dumbstruck passivity seems to mark a failure to answer the question "What to do?"[71] However, "Let's Beat Up the Poor!" shows how passivity is already a response to the poor. The question "What to do?" in "The Old Acrobat" can be reformulated after a reading of "Let's Beat Up the Poor!" as "What to undergo?" What should these narrators *suffer* when they encounter the poor? How should literary language expose itself to poverty? How should the stuttering force of the poor be made audible in literature?

Maintaining aspects of a collective relation even in this encounter with a sole beggar, "Let's Beat Up the Poor!" is the most extreme example in *Le spleen de Paris* of the "bath in the crowd," which Baudelaire presents in the prose poem "Crowds" as "that ineffable orgy, that holy prostitution of the soul which gives itself totally, poetry and charity, to the unexpected which appears, to the unknown which passes by."[72] The narrator of "Let's Beat Up the Poor!" gives himself up "totally," at least for a moment, just as the narrator of "The Old Acrobat" hysterically surrenders or is surrendered to the influence of the acrobat's paralyzing appearance and gaze. But even in this moment of surrender, the narrator seems to maintain a distance, to guard this "threshold" that Benjamin identifies in Baudelaire's poetry. This term could also be used to designate the way that the poor appear between present and future and force a transformation in the narrators who encounter them. *Le spleen de Paris* works "to liberate rebellion in even the weakest" and shows how this can occur in a relation of perilous nonidentical similarity, which allows poetry to participate—in disavowed and violent ways—in the forms of power and impotence that constitute poverty.[73]

The bath in poverty requires a similarity and a becoming poor, and the narrator's "energetic medication" awakens the beggar so that they might be equals in this orgy in which they meet as two forces and are active in a way that nonetheless reveals a kind of latency. The encounter with the poor begins as an experience of paralysis in "The Old Acrobat," but by the end of the collection, the relation to the poor appears as a productive, if violent, collaboration. We can read Baudelaire's collection as a literalization of Deleuze's statement that "a creator who isn't grabbed around the throat by a set of impossibilities is no creator. A creator is someone who creates his or her own impossibilities and thereby creates possibilities."[74]

Baudelaire's prose poems could be interpreted as provocations and experiences of impossibility followed by the containment of the newly awakened forces and possibilities, but such a reading would ignore the insistence in Baudelaire's texts on what cannot be contained even when the narrator seems to try: the hysterical paralysis of "The Old Acrobat" and the ominous energy of the beggar in "Let's Beat Up the Poor!" The poor exceed the theoretical apparatus that would contain or explain them, and this excess is at once as tumultuous as a street brawl and as silent as an augural gaze.

POETIC REBELLION
IN MALLARMÉ

An Ascetic Poet

The simultaneously paralyzing and energizing force of Baudelaire's beggars continues to determine their presentation in Mallarmé's poems,
which intensify the withdrawal that characterizes the poor in *Les fleurs
du mal* and *Le spleen de Paris*. If the beggar's true force appears in "Let's
Beat Up the Poor!" only as an ominous glint in the eye, the potential
of Mallarmé's beggars barely appears at all; in fact, his beggars hardly
come into view, except as indeterminate objects of address. This change
in the presentation of the poor bears witness to a general tendency in
Mallarmé's texts toward presenting a certain kind of virtuality or power.
This led many of his early critics to criticize or praise him as an arcane
poet of the negative. But one of his first readers resisted this trend and
interpreted his writing in terms of asceticism. Paul Valéry's writings about
his older friend insist that Mallarmé "gave those among his readers who
dared to think it a force, a faith, an asceticism, and a contempt for general opinions."[1] All of the elements in this phrase's enumeration are
estranged from their objects or from objecthood in general: force is distanced from actuality, faith is distant from what it believes in, asceticism
is distanced from what it renounces, and contempt creates distance
from "general opinions." Valéry describes Mallarmé's estranging gifts not
as themes, rules, or products but as potential objects that the daring
reader must realize by himself or herself.

Valéry refers elsewhere to Mallarmé's practicing "a type of asceticism," which implies that there can be different kinds of asceticism and
registers the necessity of defining the exact type that is appropriate for

discussing Mallarmé's poetry.[2] Valéry himself attempts to determine this in another text on Mallarmé:

Among the great men who were writers, some gratify us precisely by communicating the perfection of what we are. Others strive to lure us toward what we might be [séduire à ce que nous pourrions être], by means of a more complex intelligence or a readier wit or more freedom from habit and everything else that interferes with the broadest combination of our mental powers [nos puissances de l'esprit].[3]

Mallarmé's poetry is ascetic, because it does not offer satisfaction. Instead, it "lures" or "seduces" us into a state of possibility, "what we might be," which is not the same as leading us to actualize our possibilities. The conditional "might" remains and marks Mallarmé's "powers" off from an understanding of possibility as simply the potential for some act or realization. For Valéry, Mallarmé's poetry keeps its distance from every actualization.

Besides being distinct from actualization, Mallarmé's asceticism is not characterized by denial or renunciation. Valéry carefully avoids any formulation of Mallarmé's asceticism as a negation, because it is the other kind of poetry mentioned by Valéry, the poetry composed by "those great men," that is understood as negation, as that which "interferes with" the highest state of possibility. Mallarmé's poetry releases from restriction and allows for a "freedom" from prohibitions. In Valéry's account, his poetry is concerned with what could be and not with what is. Poetry has to do with powers, *puissances,* and moves away from the communication of what we are in favor of the presentation of the ability that allows us to be what we are and that could also allow us to be something else. To present power or "a force," Mallarmé's texts must distance themselves from what is, and this is the "type of asceticism" that Valéry finds in Mallarmé's poetry.

Mallarmé's poems on beggars offer an ideal corpus for investigating the coincidence of asceticism and power in his works, because they combine thematic treatment of poverty with formal, rhetorical, and linguistic devices that reduce literary language, at least for a moment, to the presentation of power. An indication of the general importance of poverty to Mallarmé's conception of literature can be found in his longest prose text, "Villiers de l'Isle-Adam," in which he criticizes his friend Villiers's relation to wealth: "He did not discern gold (which may be a consoling effulgence in its privation) from the true treasure, ineffable and mythic, with which it is forbidden to speculate, except in thought."[4] Villiers was unable to separate economic wealth and nobility from the gold of thought, but Mallarmé writes that Villiers eventually came to understand that there exist different kinds of poverty and wealth: "He who was fascinated with wealth understood at the end that the true state of the literary man, having all the rest, is poverty" ("le fasciné de richesses avait à la fin compris que l'état, en toute justice, de l'homme littéraire, ayant le reste, est la pauvreté").[5] Everything else accounted for, the state of literary man is poverty. Poverty is not the opposite of having, but something different from it. In "Villiers d'Isle-Adam," this poverty refers to Villiers's economic condition, as well as to his estrangement from the world, the present, writing, and life itself: "Did he live?" Mallarmé asks ("Véritablement et dans le sens ordinaire, vécut-il?").[6] But it remains difficult, within the text "Villiers de l'Isle Adam," to see why poverty is the exemplary literary state. To be able to understand Mallarmé's notion of poverty, one must look elsewhere.

In the following pages, I will argue that poverty belongs to a set of privative aspects of Mallarmé's writing, all of which bring about a distance from poetic language as it is in order to gesture toward a poetic language that remains absent. The first section of the chapter will analyze the role of money and privative figures in Mallarmé's poetics, especially in his key metapoetic text "Crisis of Verse"; the middle sections present readings of Mallarmé's poems in verse and prose that thematize poverty; and the final section interprets the impoverishing figures in "Un coup de dés" and "Ballets," two Mallarmé texts in which poverty does not appear as a theme. The goal will be to understand the place of poverty in Mallarmé's oeuvre as a whole and to determine the relation of poverty and privation in a wide range of his major texts.

Communication and Currency

Mallarmé often considers literary language in terms of economics, most notably in the well-known conclusion to one of his most frequently glossed texts, "Crisis of Verse," which begins with remarks about the historical crisis in French literature after the death of Victor Hugo and goes on to address more general questions about the nature of literature and literary language. It culminates in a discussion of the relation of "ordinary" language and poetry, and one passage seems to attempt to separate them:

> To tell, to teach, and even to describe have their place, and suffice, perhaps, in order to exchange human thought, to take or to put into someone else's hand in silence a coin, this elementary use of discourse serving the universal *reporting* in which, except for literature, all genres of contemporary writing participate.[7]

> [A] chacun suffirait peut-être pour échanger la pensée humaine, de prendre ou de mettre dans la main d'autrui en silence une pièce de monnaie, l'emploi élémentaire du discours dessert l'universel *reportage* dont, la littérature exceptée, participe tout entre les genres d'écrits contemporains.[8]

All kinds of writing "except for literature" are implicated in this understanding of language that Mallarmé presents as "l'universel *reportage,*" and it seems as if Mallarmé were participating in what he calls, in the previous paragraph, "an undeniable desire of my time . . . to distinguish two kinds of language according to their different attributes: taking the double state of speech—brute and immediate here, there essential." But, as Maurice Blanchot's commentary on this passage insists, the language of "exchange" or communication cannot be isolated from the more essential forms of speech:

> Mallarmé compared the common word to a currency of exchange. . . . But does he mean . . . that this language is worthless because, being in the service of understanding, it disappears completely in the idea it communicates? Quite the contrary. . . . In authentic language, speech has a function that is not only representative but also destructive. It causes to vanish, it renders the object absent, it annihilates it. . . . Mallarmé's position is, therefore, exceptional. The one who, more than anyone else, condemned discourse, which lacks common qualities—clarity, order, logic, that is to say, everything that matters to the universal and abstract character of language—is also the one who appreciates this character as its principal quality and the very condition of poetic form. If poetry exists, it is because language is an instrument of comprehension.[9]

Blanchot's analysis of the passage from "Crisis of Verse" identifies Mallarmé's double relation to the language of *reportage:* Mallarmé both "condemns" and "appreciates" the same element of discourse, abstraction, which Blanchot calls its "destructive" function. In Blanchot's reading, abstraction is at once the most deplorable element of language, because, by subordinating language to the task of comprehension, it can cause language to "disappear," and the most precious, because it also can turn the gaze from things to words and allow for the appearance of relations among words.[10] Literary language emerges from this tension within abstraction that can cause the word both to appear and disappear.

Literary language does not oppose itself to language understood, in Blanchot's terms, as an "instrument of comprehension," but the two languages are also not identical. How is one to understand the relation of literary language to the language of communication? In his essay "La musique et les lettres," Mallarmé describes the poet's relation to language as

> reverence for the twenty-four letters of the alphabet as they have fixed themselves, through the miracle of infinity, in some existing language, his, then a sense for their symmetries, their actions, their reflections, all the way up to a transfiguration into the supernatural endpoint, which is verse.[11]

> une piété aux vingt-quatre lettres comme elles se sont, par le miracle de l'infinité, fixées en quelque langue la sienne, puis un sens pour leurs symétries, action, reflet, jusqu'à une transfiguration en le terme surnaturel, qu'est le vers.[12]

The poet's attention to language as it is, to the letters as they happen to be "fixed" in his or her language, is carried to a point at which that language becomes the place of "transfiguration." Reverence is a means for transformation.[13]

The ordinary, monetary language of exchange is "the elementary use of discourse," Mallarmé writes, and poetry emerges from this element. The poet must sense certain "symmetries . . . , actions . . . , reflections . . ." within communicative language, because the language that Blanchot calls "authentic" is only a different relation to what could be called inauthentic language. In "Crisis of Verse," poetry is only "the surprise of never having heard that ordinary fragment of elocution."[14]

Poetry only modifies ordinary language and does not leave the language of communication behind or outside of itself, and this is why Blanchot writes, "If poetry exists, it is because language is an instrument of comprehension."

Everyday language plays an important role in Mallarmé's poetics, and often the language of journalism stands in for it in his texts. There are many passages in Mallarmé's writings that criticize the language of the newspaper, but, as Roger Pearson writes, Mallarmé often can be seen to be "testing the limits between poetry and journalism."[15] As many of Mallarmé's most expert readers have noted, everyday language and even the typographical practices of the newspaper appear regularly in his texts. Jacques Scherer, in his *Grammaire de Mallarmé,* has shown the centrality of argot as well as familiar and even vulgar language in Mallarmé's poetry and prose.[16] René Ghil reports a conversation in which Mallarmé insists that his vocabulary consists of "the same words that the bourgeoisie reads every morning [in the newspaper]—exactly the same! But then (and here his smile grew) if they happen to find them in this or that poem of mine, they no longer understand them."[17] Valéry describes how Mallarmé studied the distribution of print and spacing in newspapers and advertising posters "very carefully" as he wrote "Un coup de dés,"[18] and Walter Benjamin admired Mallarmé as a "pure poet" who, in "Un coup de dés," was the first to "make use of the graphic tension of the advertisement."[19] In 1874, Mallarmé founded, edited, and wrote most of the articles for a short-lived fashion magazine, *La dernière mode.*[20] Gilles Deleuze writes that, for Mallarmé, "the fold of the newspaper . . . is an occasional fold that must have its new mode of correspondence with the book."[21] If, as the reading above of "La musique et les lettres" shows and these Mallarmé readers argue, poetry does not define itself in opposition to everyday language, then what is their "new mode of correspondence"? What allows for the "transfiguration" that, according to Mallarmé, takes place within everyday language?

If poetic language does not leave communicative language behind, this is because communicative language always includes something other than communication. The first passage cited earlier from "Crisis of Verse" shows that the language of communication might never be simply a silent exchange of coins: "to tell, to teach, and even to describe have their place, and suffice, *perhaps,* in order to exchange human thought."[22] The hesitation of this "perhaps" points to the possible existence within communication of something else. Poetry brings out this element that may exist within language and that may exceed communication but whose existence can only be postulated and which takes form only in the "transfiguration" into verse. The next section attempts to determine what exactly this possible aspect of language might be.

Privative Concepts

Mallarmé writes in "Crisis of Verse" of the necessity of representation: "Nothing will remain without being proffered" ("rien ne demeurera sans être proféré").[23] Things must be represented to exist, but, for Mallarmé, this "proffering" is not the slavish repetition of something that already is. It also allows something else to become visible. It is possible to understand exactly what this something else is if the positive value of the word "nothing" or *rien* is read in the sentence "rien ne demeurera sans être proféré." The term *rien* occupies a special position in Mallarmé's writings, because its function can be reduced to neither affirmation nor negation. In *Grammaire de Mallarmé,* Jacques Scherer describes how, in Mallarmé's texts, words such as *aucun* and *rien,* used without the particle *ne,* regain their antiquated positive value.[24] Nothing can also be a "no-thing." Jacques Rancière insists on the liminal position of the "rien" in Mallarmé's poetry as "*rem,* something, a thing perpetually suspended, like Hamlet, between being and nonbeing."[25] The perpetual suspension of *rien* (even when accompanied by *ne*)—"this sweet nothing," as we read in "L'après-midi d'un faune"[26]—corresponds to the state suspended between presence and absence that we find in the final sentences of "Crisis of Verse":

> What good is the marvel of transposing a fact of nature into its vibratory near-disappearance according to the play of language, however: if it is not, in the absence of the cumbersomeness of a near or concrete reminder, the pure notion.
>
> I say: a flower! And, out of the oblivion where my voice casts every contour, insofar as it is something other than the known bloom, there arises, musically, the very idea in its mellowness; in other words, what is absent from every bouquet.[27]

A quoi bon la merveille de transposer un fait de nature en sa presque disparition vibratoire selon le jeu de la parole, cependant; si ce n'est pour qu'en
émane, sans la gêne d'un proche ou concret rappel, la notion pure.

    Je dis: une fleur! et hors de l'oubli où ma voix relègue aucun contour, en
tant que quelque chose d'autre que les calices sus, musicalement se lève, idée
même et suave, l'absente de tous bouquets.[28]

In the first paragraph cited here, writing appears as a "transposition" that
brings about a "near disappearance" of a natural object. This formulation is similar to the passage about transfigured letters cited earlier from
"La musique et les lettres." The result here is *la notion pure,* a phrase that
remains opaque until the next sentence's redescription of the process:
the poet says "flower" and there arises "what is absent from every bouquet." The *absente* is the name for something that exists within the
appearance of the bouquet but that exists as absent. It is neither a thing
nor an image; it is not an absence but a specific absent element that is
released in poetry.

    This absent element of poetry can be characterized more precisely.
In "Crisis of Verse," something similar to the *absente* is presented as a
relation to be established: "To institute an exact relation between images,
and let detach there a third, fusible, clear aspect, presented for divination" ("Instituer une relation entre les images exacte, et que s'en détache
un tiers aspect fusible et clair présenté à la divination").[29] The "absent"
notion cited earlier appears here as a "fusible" or "transformable" and
"clear" aspect that emerges from the relation established among images,
just as the relation among words ("a sense for their symmetries, their
actions, their reflections") brings about their transfiguration in "La
musique et les lettres." The emphasis on the institution of "a relation
between images" and a "sense" for the symmetries among words betrays
a shift of interest away from at least two fundamental poetic notions:

The pure work implies the elocutionary disappearance of the poet, who yields
the initiative to words, through the clash of their ordered inequalities; they
light each other up through reciprocal reflections like a virtual trail of fire across
precious stones, replacing the primacy of the perceptible rhythm of respiration or the classic lyric breath, or the personal feeling driving the sentences.[30]

L'œuvre pure implique la disparition élocutoire du poëte, qui cède l'initiative
aux mots, par le heurt de leur inégalité mobilisés; ils s'allument de reflets

réciproques comme une virtuelle traînée de feux sur des pierreries, remplaçant la respiration perceptible en l'ancien souffle lyrique ou la direction person-nelle enthousiaste de la phrase.[31]

Inspiration ("lyric breath") and the voice of the poet disappear, as the poet "yields the initiative" to words and the relations between them, which create a "virtual trail." The term *pure* that appeared in the phrase *la notion pure* resurfaces here in *l'œuvre pure*, which receives an explica-tion: in the pure work, inspiration and the poet have disappeared in favor of a virtual relation among words—just as, in the earlier quota-tion, the pure notion entails the disappearance *(sa presque disparition)* of an object and the appearance of an absent flower. In this and the earlier citation, something that exists as an object (a flower) or a sound (the poet's voice) vanishes and something else emerges as absent or virtual.[32]

In the relations among words and in the wake of the disappearance of the poet's voice and his or her object, literary language reveals a par-ticular kind of virtuality or absence. Mallarmé presents poetry not as representation or expression but as the poet's falling silent and, here, as a vanishing act in the service of virtuality:

> As opposed to a denominative and representative function, as the crowd first treats it, speech, which is primarily dream and song, recovers, in the Poet's hands, of necessity in an art devoted to fictions, its virtuality.[33]

> Au contraire d'une fonction de numéraire facile et représentatif, comme le traite d'abord la foule, le dire, avant tout, rêve et chant, retrouve chez le Poëte, par nécessité constitutive d'un art consacré aux fictions, sa virtualité.[34]

Poetry supplants any purely quantitative function that might be attrib-uted to speaking in favor of virtuality, because its operation is not one of substitution (of a word for a thing, of an absent language for a pres-ent one, of an essential for a frivolous language) but, as we have seen, of transposition and transfiguration that reveals something absent or virtual within what is present.

Based on Mallarmé's theoretical texts read so far, it is possible to draw some preliminary conclusions regarding his conception of the relation between everyday language and literary language and, in addition, his notions of virtuality, absence, and nothing or the "no-thing." Literary language allows the currency of communication to appear otherwise, because it suspends language's representative function. Literature shows that language can be something other than the exchange of fixed terms with fixed meanings and, thus, that it cannot be understood solely by means of the metaphor of the exchange of money. Literature can never only represent an object, because it always also could be something other than communication. It may also allude to something virtual or possible within communication that exceeds it and that only appears privatively—as absence or as a moment within an object's disappearance. All of these conclusions point to an impoverished language, stripped of its objects, its speaker, and its meaning and centered on its virtuality.

Giving Alms

The *rien* or "no-thing" that flashes forth in Mallarmé's writing depends on and suspends the communicative function of language; or, to use the poet's monetary terms, poetry emerges within the exchange of coins even as it transforms this exchange. In Mallarmé's poems, we will see how poverty allows for money to exceed its economic function and for language to allude to something other than communication. The following readings will develop the relation between thematic poverty and the forms of privation or impoverishment that the previous section discerned in Mallarmé's writings in poetics.

Two of Mallarmé's early poems in verse, "Hatred of the Poor Man" and "To a Beggar" ("Haine du pauvre" and "A un mendiant"), form a diptych spoken in the voice of an almsgiver and addressed to a beggar. "To a Beggar" was later titled "To a Poor Man" and was then included in Mallarmé's own edition of his poetry, the *Poésies* of 1887, as "Alms," a poem in terza rima composed of eight tercets and, as the verse form dictates, a final, isolated line.[35] In his address, the almsgiver insists on the possibility of a type of alms that would not be understood merely as useful. The coins that the donor throws to the beggar must be the source of a specific kind of pleasure, some "bizarre sin" to be extracted from the coin by the act of kissing it and breathing on it: "blow / An ardent fanfare till it writhe in the night [Souffles-y qu'il se torde!]."[36] The coins' *métal cher* must be twisted so that the alms may become something other than useful, a kind of gold that would not be exhausted by the process of circulation.

What would this other kind of gold *(or)* be like? It appears, at first, as a sound in the phrase "Souffles-y qu'il se torde!" This is the first time that the written unit <or> appears in the poem—at the moment when the donor tells the beggar to extract something other than economic value from the coins. The unit <or> appears once again in the word *oraison* (line 9), but the division of syllables between <o> and <r> means that the grouping of letters does not produce exactly the same sound as in *torde*. Then, in the sixth and seventh tercets, the written unit <or> occurs six times, three times in each tercet:

> Et quand tu *sor*s, vieux dieu, grelottant sous tes toiles
> D'emballage, l'aur*or*e est un lac de vin d'*or*
> Et tu jures avoir au gosier les étoiles!
>
> Faute de supputer l'éclat de ton trés*or*,
> Tu peux du moins t'*or*ner d'une plume, à complies
> Servir un cierge au saint en qui tu crois enc*or*.

Here, the unit <or> appears within the words that enumerate the extravagant pleasures that the donor's gold will permit. Only once do the graphemes <o> and <r> appear as the word "or." The unit <or> occurs in "Aumône" as a word, a phonetic unit, and a written unit, but all the occurrences of <or> in the poem can be grouped together only in terms of the written unit, because they cannot all be pronounced in the same way and because <or> only forms the word *or* in one instance.

Just as much as the word *or*, this written unit <or> could be read as the "alms" named by the title. The donor gives the beggar this <or> that includes within it the word "or." The unit <or> is neither meaningful nor meaningless; instead, it is potentially meaningful, able to be read as the word "or" but not exhausted in that reading. <Or> can become a word or a sound, but only on the condition that there exist the written unit <or>, which, by itself, is neither a word nor a single sound. Appearing within the words of the donor that plead for the overcoming of "useful alms,"[37] the unit <or> is a kind of gold that cannot be understood only as sound or meaning and thus cannot only be used in a significant utterance.

Although the almsgiver implores the beggar to extract nothing useful from the gold, the beggar must at the same time use the coins as a starting point for "bizarre sins," emblematized by the feather that he may procure: "you can at least adorn yourself with a plume [tu peux du moins t'orner d'une plume]." This feather is only a possible writing instrument, ornamental but always also potentially productive, like the unit <or>. Just as the language of communication serves in "Crisis of Verse" as the element in which poetry's transposition is accomplished, so too the coins' monetary value is the element that allows for something other than a monetary exchange to take place. The coins permit the beggar to have a relation to what exceeds their utility, and when they are spent extravagantly and bizarrely, their utility appears as just one among their many aspects. The coins can exceed their useful value just as the unit <or> exceeds its semantic containment within the word "or."[38] The bizarre pleasures to be bought with the coins correspond to the bizarre, meaningless appearance of the unit <or> throughout Mallarmé's poem.

Stripped of meaning and deprived of a single pronunciation, <or> is an impoverished form of the term for gold, and it is accompanied by another type of linguistic impoverishment in "Alms" that is implicit in the poem's central structure of address to the beggar. Although the address in "Alms" is strictly speaking not an instance of the related trope of prosopopeia, Paul de Man's discussion of prosopopeia is useful here both for his emphasis on the potential aspect of the addressee's speech and for his insistence on the purely negative understanding of this potential. In the Introduction, I discussed how de Man presents prosopopeia not as the projection of language but as the projection of the possibility of language, as "the fiction of an apostrophe to an absent, deceased, or voiceless entity, which posits the *possibility* of the latter's reply and confers upon it the *power* of speech."[39] Prosopopeia is thus a figure of power, concerned with the ability to speak, and the address in "Alms" presents a related gift of potential speech. The beggar's silence indicates the privative nature of prosopopeia. Prosopopeia, de Man writes, "means to *give* a face and therefore implies that the original face can be missing or non-existent."[40] In other words, the beggar would not need to have a voice created for him if he had one in the first place. The creation of a face is thus always also the acknowledgment of an original facelessness. De Man goes a step further and insists that to acknowledge facelessness is to create it, and this leads him to say that prosopopeia "deprives and disfigures to the precise extent that it restores" or instates the ability to speak.[41] De Man concludes by saying that, in prosopopeia, "we" are "silent as a picture, that is to say eternally deprived of voice and condemned to muteness."[42]

That the beggar is given the faculty of language does not, however, only imply his muteness, because this condition can also be understood positively, as an openness to receiving language. There is a potential for language that precedes the gift of language and that in the poem "Alms" also appears as the ability to be given alms, as an original exposure that must also be read positively. "Language, as trope, is always privative," de Man writes, but this privation must be understood as more than just an indication of being "eternally deprived of voice."[43] The figure of giving voice or creating a face necessarily implies the ability to receive a voice or to have a face created, and, in this case, the beggar is the recipient of a specific kind of linguistic element that exists in a virtual state.

The unit <or> is like what is absent in "Crisis of Verse," present in a way that is different from gold, the word "or" in the poem. This virtual element arises only as a relation among semantically unrelated instances of the graphic unit in the poem—and then between these instances and the word "or." Only in this set of relations does the new kind of quasi gold and quasi language appear; the poet "yields the initiative to words . . . ; they light each other up through reciprocal reflections like a virtual trail of fire." Less dramatic than a trail of fire, but no less important for Mallarmé's understanding of virtuality and absence is the trail left by the unit <or> in "Alms," a virtual relation that allows for the appearance of a new kind of gold given as alms to the beggar. "Alms" presents two kinds of poverty: the poverty of the unit <or>, deprived of sense, but able to be used as either a meaningful or sonorous unit; and the poverty that de Man reads as an original voicelessness but that must also be read as the ability that allows the beggar to receive language and the <or>. In "Alms," poverty characterizes both a potential linguistic unit and the beggar's speechlessness that allows for this unit—this alms—to be received.

The End of the Poem and a New Form of Poetry

Like "Alms," the prose poem "Poor Pale Child" is an extended address to a beggar, a child who sings for money in the streets and who, like Baudelaire's beggar in "Let's Beat Up the Poor!," is *énergique*.[44] The most surprising resemblance between the two poems, considering that "Poor Pale Child" is a prose poem, can be found in the terza rima form. It is made up of eight short paragraphs, and "Alms" has eight tercets. Both this prose poem and the poem in terza rima conclude with a single, typographically isolated final line. A single, isolated last line is necessary for the completion of a poem in terza rima, because it must respond to the middle, otherwise orphaned verse of the final tercet. Although "Poor Pale Child" has no rhyme scheme and thus no orphaned lines, its subject is—an orphan.[45]

Another prose poem by Mallarmé allows us to solidify the relation between the prose poem, the *rime orpheline,* and the orphan. Anne-Emmanuelle Berger calls the orphan the figure par excellence of poverty in the nineteenth century, because it signifies "painful privation . . . , weakness . . . , mourning, abandonment, and solitude."[46] But we will see how, for Mallarmé, the orphan also signifies the possibility of a new beginning, because, as Berger writes, the orphan can also "function as a sign and form of liberation and . . . mobility in the revolutionary imaginary."[47] The prose poem "Réminiscence," whose first published version was titled "L'Orphelin,"[48] is spoken in the voice of an orphan and refers to the history of the terza rima by mentioning its inventor, Dante: "I wanted to speak with an urchin too unsteady in his nightcap cut like Dante's hood."[49] The child who is too "unsteady" to "appear among his race" might be none other than the orphan rhyme, isolated from any rhyme fellows and vacillating between belonging to the rhyme scheme and being outside of it. Mallarmé's association of the prose poem and terza rima, as well as his wish to address a vacillating outsider, points to an operation at work on the border between literary genres that, as the next pages will show, also aims to transform poetry itself.

The narrator of "Poor Pale Child" imagines the future of the poor young singer and sees his eventual turn to crime and the resulting punishment of decapitation. For the narator, the orphan's body appears ready to be abandoned by the head:

> Your head straightens up continually and wants to leave you, as if it knew in advance, while you sing with an air that becomes menacing.
>
> When you pay for me, for those who are worth less than me, it will bid you adieu. That's probably why you came into the world and you are fasting from now on, we shall see you in the papers.
>
> Oh! poor little head![50]

The head, in its graphic separation from the body of the prose poem, is already prepared to be severed. The last line of any poem is always marked by a certain independence, not only from the poem, but from poetry itself. The prose poem attempts to mimic this aspect of poetry in verse. The linguist Jean-Claude Milner argues that the only mark of distinction between prose and poetry is the noncoincidence in poetry of metrical and syntactic divisions. An example of this is the possibility of enjambment, the potential noncoincidence of syntactic and metrical units at the end of a line.[51] Since enjambment is not possible in the last line of a poem, Giorgio Agamben, departing from Milner's analysis, concludes that the final line of a poem cannot be a verse.[52] For Agamben, the end of the poem is a zone of indetermination between poetry and prose.

The final lines of Mallarmé's poems take advantage of this indistinction. I would like to suggest that Mallarmé's poems seek to create a type of poetry that finds preliminary form in the no-man's-land of the *explicit* and that this attempt in his prose and verse poems inspires both hope and fear. The next few pages will explore this tension in readings of final lines that emphasize how they are simultaneously bound to and distanced from the poems they conclude. These readings aim to establish the link between the theme of poverty and the attempt to establish a new, impoverished literary language, whose possibility appears in the form of an isolated *explicit*. A poem composed of a single line would not already be a new kind of poetry, but the task of creating a new poetry in Mallarmé's texts takes as an image of its goal a poem made up of only an *explicit*.

"Un coup de dés," made up of a single sentence, could be read as the final attempt in a series of poems that begins as early as "L'après-midi d'un faune," which offers the image of a new poetry based on the final, separated line (the faun) rather than on the form of the couplet (the two nymphs). The metapoetic dimension of the faun's attempt to rape the pair of embracing nymphs appears when one considers the standard terms for the couplet: *rimes jumelles* and, in Italian, *rima baciata*. The faun attempts to separate one of the nymphs from the couple, which proves to be impossible, and he dreams of an art that would be "solo" (as opposed to the "duo"[53] of the nymphs) and that would create "a *[une]* sonorous, vain, and monotone line," a phrase in which the word "une" must be read as both as the cardinal number and indefinite pronoun. The poem's final line, "Couple, farewell; I'll see the shadow that now you are" ("Couple, adieu: je vais voir l'ombre que tu devins"), is isolated from the poem's body by a space, and this isolation finds analogous expression in the absent couple's abandonment of the present, single faun as well as in the final address that reduces the couple to a singular *tu*.[54] The faun functions as a figure for that line, a fantastic, hybrid man-animal that stands in for the new art that the poem proposes. He would be the speaker of some new, inhuman kind of language that appears only as the fantasy of this single monotone line.

But the faun does not give birth to a new genre. His final words, "Couple, adieu . . . ," separated from the body of the poem and from the couple, remain directed toward them. His distance from the poem and from the art of couplets consists only in an "adieu" and is thus only barely a separation. The unity of the single, final line is split, directed both toward and away from the poem. The same can be said of "Poor Pale Child," in which the child's head remains turned toward the body from which it has been separated and in which only one thing is said about the severed head: "It will bid you farewell." The head will still speak, but, like the final, separated line of "L'après-midi d'un faune," it only speaks about separation and is far from the institution of a new genre or language. Even when cut off, the head is connected to the body by this "adieu."

The Rhyming Cutlass

The isolation of the Mallarméan *explicit* is always accompanied by an insistence on its connection to the body of the poem. This is especially

visible in Mallarmé's poems in terza rima that thematize their dependence on the main body of the poem. In "The Jinx" ("Le Guignon"),
the final line hangs from the poem as the bodies of the poets hang from
the lamppost: "These ciphers call down thunderbolts—and then / Go
hang themselves from lampposts in the street" ("Ces héros excédés de
malaises badins / Vont ridiculement se pendre au réverbère").[55] "Alms"
ends with the fraternal call, reminiscent of Baudelaire's "To the Reader"
in its vocative, "And above all, brother, do not go to buy bread."[56]

In addition to the hanging or brotherly relation, all of these typographically isolated final lines remain connected to their poems by the
interlacing rhyme, *rime entrelacée*. The example that contains the most
striking coincidence of isolation and connection can be found in "Hatred of the Poor Man," which Mallarmé never published but which,
together with "Alms," forms a diptych on poverty. Like "Alms," the poem
is in terza rima and is addressed by an almsgiver to a beggar. It ends with
the donor telling the beggar that he could use the alms to buy a cutlass:

> Choisis.—Jetée? alors, voici ma pièce prise
> Serre-la dans tes doigts et pense que tu l'as
> Parce que j'en tiens trop, ou par simple méprise.
>
> —C'est le prix, si tu n'as pas peur, d'un coutelas.
>
> [Choose!—Wasted? All right, my coin has been taken. Grip it between your
> fingers and think that you got it because I wanted you to, or simply because
> of my contempt.—It's the price, if you're not afraid, of a cutlass.][57]

The almsgiver dares the beggar to use the alms to buy a weapon, pre-
sumably to use against the openly contemptuous almsgiver. In these
lines, the donor suggests the possibility of an indirect suicide, yet another form of potential "elocutionary disappearance" in Mallarmé's
texts.[58] But the hypothetical cutlass is not only threatening. The final
line is connected to the rest of the poem by means of the final rhyme:
that is, by means of the cutlass. The cutlass holds the poem together.
An intensified binding power of the sword can be seen if the end of
"Hatred of the Poor Man" is read together with the beginning of its
companion piece "Alms." The *explicit* "C'est le prix, si tu n'as pas peur,
d'un coutelas" would be followed by this tercet:

Prends ce sac, Mendiant! tu ne le cajolas
Sénile nourrisson d'une tétine avare
Afin de pièce à pièce en égoutter ton glas.

The first tercet of "Alms" continues the rhyme in /la/ that concludes "Hatred of the Poor Man."[59] In addition to binding the *explicit* of "Hatred of the Poor Man" to the body of the poem, the cutlass joins the poem to "Alms" and makes the two poems into a diptych.

The simultaneous binding and cutting power of the cutlass is analogous to a structure within the terza rima form. The chain of tercets in the terza rima "suggests processes without beginning or end, a *perpetuum mobile* in which linkage and continuation are seamlessly articulated."[60] This perpetual motion leads John Freccero to note that

> the rules for closure are not inherent in the form: the *terzina* as a metric pattern could theoretically go on forever and must be arbitrarily ended. . . . It is this openendedness that has moved some theorists to object that the pure terza rima does not exist, since it would have to violate its own rules in order to begin or end.[61]

The terza rima itself has no end and must "violate" itself to conclude, just as the poetic voice in "Hatred of the Poor Man" must appeal to someone else to bring about its own death. The poem must in some way include a relation to its own outside, to a force that exceeds it and that causes its demise. In Mallarmé's poem, this force appears as the possibility of stabbing, and his poems in terza rima thematize the necessarily violent end implicit in their verse form.

In the poems by Mallarmé discussed here, each final line serves as a marker for a force within the poem that gestures away from it. The cutlass in "Hatred of the Poor Man" would perform the same function, because it emphasizes the aggressive relation between the donor and the beggar even as it binds the final line to the preceding tercet and even ties together two poems. The cutlass emblematizes both a splitting and a binding force, and this double force offers another articulation of what is at stake in the <or> of "Alms." The cutlass would offer the beggar a chance to force the almsgiver into silence and possibly to speak by himself. In "Alms," the beggar could perform a similar usurpation, because his twisted gold could inaugurate a form of speaking that, although it has its origin in the voice and the gold of the almsgiver, could take over his speaking role. In both poems, this possibility of another kind of speech or writing remains unrealized—or only barely realized. The new kind of gold is already at work in "Alms," structuring the poem where it functions as a rhyme, and in "Hatred of the Poor Man," the force of the cutlass holds together the poem as a rhyme even as it threatens to silence the speaker.

In these ways, the virtual language of the beggar can be heard within the speaker's voice in Mallarmé's diptych. The abeyant power of the poor already has effects on poetic language. The cutlass remains virtual, but there are suggestions of its power in the graphic separation between the final line and the rest of the poem. With the dare to buy the sword, the poem is thus transformed into a text that can be cut up, into the place of origin of something that can already be intimated in the force of the beggar's cutlass and gold, as well as in the move toward independence inherent in the final line of a poem.

A Virtual Renegade

Mallarmé impoverishes his language as it is so as to prepare the way for a new language, and this intent can be seen in his texts' postulation of the possibility of a line breaking off and forming another kind of poetry. I am aware that this reading of Mallarmé's poetry might seem far-fetched, and I would hesitate to offer it if Mallarmé himself did not explicitly discuss its implications in at least two of his texts, including the well-known prose poem "The Demon of Analogy."[62] Mallarmé even acknowledges, in the prose text "Solennité," the possibility of the rebellion of a single line of poetry:

> [L]ines of verse go by twos or more, by reason of their terminal accord, that is, the mysterious law of Rhyme, which reveals itself with the function of guardian, and prevents any one of them from usurping, or peremptorily staying . . .[63]

The mysterious law of rhyme acts as a guardian to hold poetry together and to prevent the usurpation of a single verse. The fantasy of a single line of poetry bears witness to a fear of fragmentation (or "usurpation").

The rhyme schemes of both "Hatred of the Poor Man" and "Alms" are directed toward the containment of the rebellious cutlass of the beggar and its potential to cut into the body of the poem and usurp the power of the donor, but they also emphasize the risk of losing the unity of the poem by rhyming on the edge of the cutlass. Rhyme may be, according to one Mallarmé reader, "that which makes a virtue of duality and division," but for Mallarmé, it also guards against a more deeply incisive splitting of poetry.[64] The *rime entrelacée* is thus a *lacet,* a snare, but also the moment of a potential cut.[65]

The fact that Mallarmé conceives of the rhyme as a guardian indicates that the danger of a rebellious verse is as constant and banal as rhyme itself. The "mysterious law of rhyme," its role in impeding the usurpation of a single verse, is put to the test in the prose poem "The Demon of Analogy," which presents the scenario of a renegade linguistic fragment. Here, the speaker is haunted by a sentence that is repeated again and again in his mind: "The Penultimate is dead," which is described as "the damned fragments of a meaningless phrase." It is "the irrefutable intervention of the supernatural" that the poetic voice also presents as a daily occurrence in his work as a poet; it is only "the imperfectly abandoned residue of a linguistic labor on account of which my noble poetic faculty daily sobs at being interrupted."[66] The single, isolated phrase, unbound by rhyme, is a quotidian occurrence that emerges from within the poetic faculty. The movement of the "absurd" phrase is characterized as errant or wandering: "Harried, I resolved to let those words, by their nature so sad, wander on the lips of their own accord." Like the movement of the orphan described in the first sentence of "Réminiscence" as errant,[67] the phrase of "Le démon de l'analogie" neither circulates like a verse (*versus* comes from *vertere,* "to turn") nor walks forward like prose (*prorsum,* the origin of the term *prosa oratio).* It, like the final line of the poem, presents a zone of linguistic indeterminacy that is neither prose nor poetry. It is "virtual"—"The phrase returns, virtual" ("La phrase revient, virtuelle")—and a "sob," barely signifying.

Just as the faun lives under the shadow of the couple(t) of nymphs, so too poetry is haunted by the specter of the single line of poetry and the transformative cut it could inflict. "The Demon of Analogy" presents the virtual phrase as the cause of "that anguish tormenting my spirit that once was master." The independence of the phrase, like the "initiative yielded to words" in "Crisis of Verse," entails the poet's loss of mastery, his elocutionary disappearance. But this loss remains barely more than a possibility in Mallarmé's other texts. It is thematized in "The Demon of Analogy" and postulated in "Crisis of Verse," but this does not imply that Mallarmé's poetic program has already been realized. Just as the renegade phrase remains virtual in "The Demon of Analogy," the move presented in "Crisis of Verse" away from the author and toward a new kind of poetry is not complete in Mallarmé's œuvre. "Crisis of Verse" and the virtual poetry that it postulates remain prescriptive, and the carrying out of the essay's program appears in Mallarmé's poetry both as a task and as a cause of hope and fear. Future poetry is emblematized as gold, as a cutlass, and as a destructive single line of poetry, which appear as a virtuality within poetry as it is now. The final line of poetry emblematizes the possibility of another kind of writing, and, in Mallarmé's poems, the beggar is often the one who is able to receive this possibility. He is exposed to it and can receive it as alms or bring it about violently. Poverty is the state that enables the acceptance of this gift, and the power of the gift is itself impoverished, a hypothetical indication of something within poetry that promises and threatens to exceed it.

The Impoverished Throw of the Dice

Mallarmé's later writings move away from the theme of poverty, but, as the concluding pages of this chapter will argue, his texts continue to focus on hypothetical events, which are staged by means of an impoverished literary language. "Un coup de dés," a poem that one could be tempted to see as more than a hypothetical separation from the conventions of French poetry, is presented by Mallarmé in his preface to the poem as pure hypothesis: "Everything occurs, foreshortened, as hypothesis."[68] The hypothetical act in question in "Un coup de dés" is a single throw of the dice that would eliminate chance. The word "un," once again, should be read not only as the indefinite article but also as a cardinal number. Such an emphasis on the unity of the poem highlights the relation between "Un coup de dés" and the hypothesis of a single, isolated line of poetry. In his preface to "Un coup de dés," Mallarmé also insists that the poem be read and seen as a single unit. He writes that the "copied distance" that structures "Un coup de dés" makes possible "a simultaneous vision of the Page: the latter is taken as the basic unit, in the way that elsewhere the Verse or the perfect line is."[69] The preface emphasizes the unity of the poem, its simultaneity, and the perception of its pages as units.[70] Like the virtually separate *explicit*, "Un coup de dés" is intended as a single legible and visible unit.[71] The poem is dominated by a single sentence, "one central phrase introduced from the title and continuing onward," and even in his recitation of the poem to Valéry, Mallarmé's delivery was marked by tonal unity.[72]

The final pages of "Un coup de dés" spell out the results of an event, the throw of the dice that results in nothing.[73] But the dice throw is nothing only because it was stopped from being something else: "some splashing below of water as if to disperse the empty act / abruptly which otherwise / by its falsehood / would have founded / perdition." The act is abruptly "dispersed" by the "splashing" that surrounds and shoots through it. The final double page of the poem offers a more extended formulation of this dissolving, antifoundational force. Poetry counts out "the successive shock" within counting, the spacing between numbers, and thereby prevents the foundation to which the act aspired. "Un coup de dés" presents an act at the same time that it dissolves it by means of this spacing force, which does not emerge from elsewhere but which takes place within the event itself. The poem offers a conception of space and spacing in the sentence in capitals that dominates its final pages: "NOTHING / WILL HAVE TAKEN PLACE / BUT THE PLACE // EXCEPT / PERHAPS / A CONSTELLATION." The place is the only thing that may have taken place, but its virtual force is enough to stop the event from being foundational. The only thing that may emerge from this poem is a constellation, made up only of the "sidereal," spaced-out connection and separation of stars, which resemble the words on the page of "Un coup de dés."

"Un coup de dés" is relevant for a discussion of poverty in Mallarmé's poems because it presents both an act and its interruption, just as the poems on beggars at once postulate and work to prevent a new kind of poetic language. "Un coup de dés" represents a much later stage in

Mallarmé's writing, but his early poems' concern for "nothing" and its virtual taking place remains central. Jacques Scherer insists that the layout of "Un coup de dés" does "not contain any element that did not already appear in Mallarmé's earlier works."[74] The typographical and syntactical elements of "Un coup de dés" are only an intensification of elements that can be found in his earlier poems and prose writings. Recalling the formulation from "La musique et les lettres," one could read "Un coup de dés" as a transfiguration that results from Mallarmé's reverence for language and typography as it is. Just as "Alms" and "Hatred of the Poor Man" present hypothetical acts and pleasures of the absent, begging addressee, "Un coup de dés" focuses on a hypothetical event that "will not have taken place." Just as the specific kind of alms in "Alms" remains a wish, the throw of the dice remains only a "hypothesis."

Throughout his texts, Mallarmé pays attention to hypothetical, reduced, or absent events and figures. His writings on theater and dance share many of the terms and concerns of the poems on beggars and of "Un coup de dés." In "Ballets," Mallarmé presents a specific attitude necessary for properly watching dance:

> The only imaginative training consists, during the ordinary hours of attending Dance without any particular aim, in patiently and passively asking oneself about each step . . . , "What could this mean?" or, even better, from inspiration, to read it.[75]

The best possible way to watch the ballerina is to "read" her movements, and the mode of reading appropriate to dance aims to discern something other than significance—"to try and forget what the ballet might ostensibly be 'about' and just watch each step," as Roger Pearson writes.[76] Reading is different from and "better" than looking for significance. The move toward reading the ballet is accomplished by a progressive privation marked out in the following passage from "Ballets," in which dancer and spectator are joined by a "fundamental law" that decrees that

> dance, in its ceaseless ubiquity, is a moving synthesis of the attitudes of each group; just as each group is only a fraction, detailing the whole, of the infinite. There results a reciprocity producing the *un*-individual, both in the star and in the chorus, the dancer being only an emblem, never Someone . . .
> The judgment or axiom to be affirmed in the case of ballet!

> Namely, that the dancer *is not a woman dancing* [n'est pas une femme qui danse], for these juxtaposed reasons: that *she is not a woman* [n'est pas une femme], but a metaphor summing up one of the elementary aspects of our form: knife, goblet, flower, etc., and that *she is not dancing* [qu'elle ne danse pas] but suggesting, through the miracle of bends and leaps, a kind of corporal writing, what it would take pages of prose, dialogue, and description to express, if it were transcribed: a poem independent of any scribal apparatus.[77]

Dance is not the dancer, but the synthesis or reciprocity of the movements of the dancers, which makes each of them into something other than an individual.[78] In "Crisis of Verse," the words "light each other up through reciprocal reflections," and here the dancers bring about a similar reciprocity. In the final paragraph cited here, the impoverishment of the individual dancer takes place in a privative series in which the French structure of negation *ne . . . pas* is italicized and can also be read as a set of dance steps, of *pas,* that subtract characteristics from the dancer. "Reading" dance means paying attention to the progressive reduction of the dancer to a "reciprocity." "Ballets" circles around an object that disappears in favor of an un-individuality that resembles the absent flower in "Crisis of Verse."

The dancer's reciprocity and the "shock" of "Un coup de dés" join the ranks of hypothetical events and objects in Mallarmé's texts: the beggar's gold and cutlass in "Alms" and "Hatred of the Poor Man," the separation of the child's head in "Poor Pale Child," as well as the renegade phrase in "The Demon of Analogy." Mallarmé's most elaborate poems, lexically rich and syntactically complex, all contain moments that insist, even if only for a moment, on the impoverishing, suspending force of these hypothetical, absent objects or events at their center. The readings proposed here could be extended to other Mallarmé poems: the sonnet "Le vierge, le vivace et le bel aujourd'hui" ends with the immobilization of the swan; the sonnet "Ses purs ongles très haut dédiant leur onyx" closes with the fixating force of "oblivion contained by the frame" ("l'oubli fermé par le cadre");[79] and Hérodiade is barely a shadow, retreating from the scene and waiting: "J'attends une chose inconnue."[80] These privative moments emerge from within even the richest of Mallarmé's poems and reduce to a hypothetical state the wealth of their "décor."[81]

The poems on beggars occupy a privileged position among these texts, because their thematic focus corresponds to a series of linguistic and formal means of impoverishment. Privation and impoverishment appear in Mallarmé's texts as thematic poverty (beggars) and as forms of absence (the absent flower, the disappearance of the poet), as well as the effects or presuppositions of rhetorical devices (the facelessness of prosopopoeia), semantic and graphic operations (his use of *rien* and the graphic unit <or>), and poetic innovations (the spacing of "Un coup de dés," the theory and practices of the isolated final line). In these instances of privation in Mallarmé's prose and poetry, the possibility of a different kind of poetic language emerges, a possibility that is not actualized but that is indicated by an asceticism allowing for a withdrawal from enactment. Valéry writes that Mallarmé's writings offer "une force, un ascètisme," and this association of asceticism with power and not with surrender or transcendence anticipates the next chapter's discussion of Nietzsche's attempt to give asceticism another meaning. The force of Mallarmé's asceticism lies in its indication of possibilities such as the beggar's potential voice, which is the insistent and absent precursor of some other kind of poetic language. "Alms" and other Mallarméan texts continue Baudelaire's investigation of the effects of the poor and their power. When faced with the poor, the question, once again, is not "What to do?" but "What to undergo?" Mallarmé's almsgiver dares the beggar to purchase a cutlass that could inflict more damage than "my beggar" in "Let's Beat Up the Poor!," and the ominous glint in the beggar's eye in *Le spleen de Paris* becomes Mallarmé's "virtual trail of fire" that could consume poetic language from within.

THE TRANSVALUATION
OF POVERTY

Asceticism and Art

The move from Baudelaire and Mallarmé to Rilke must pass through
Nietzsche, because early-twentieth-century German-speaking writers
thought of Nietzsche when they wrote about poverty. Although Nietzsche shows little interest in the problem of socioeconomic poverty, his
creation of a new concept of poverty involves a critique of the notions
of difference and identity and a new understanding of the relation of
philosophical and literary language, and the twentieth-century writers
discussed in the next chapters couple their understanding of socioeconomic poverty with these philosophical concerns. The conclusion to
this chapter will show how Nietzsche's impoverished language is spoken by potential and not actual speakers, thus linking his concern with
poverty to the impoverished language of the French poets discussed in
the previous chapters. Nietzsche's impoverished language complements
the Mallarméan attempt to develop a transformative threshold within
language as it is.

Nietzsche's invention of a new concept of poverty takes place in the
context of his critique of asceticism, which crystallizes everything about
Christianity that he believes must be overcome. Deleuze shows how
asceticism appears in Nietzsche's texts as the term for Christianity's judg-
ing of human existence "according to values that are said to be superior to life: these pious values [that] are opposed to life, condemn it,
lead it to nothingness."[1] In Nietzsche's view of the dominant Christian
version of asceticism, men and women are bad copies of God, and our
world is a bad copy of paradise. His "transvaluation of all values" aims

to free humanity from this devaluation of existence that serves, according to him, as the foundation of all existing forms of morality.

The object of Nietzsche's critique seems to be Christianity, but the decline of religion and even its disappearance would not be enough. The death of God, "glamorous but insufficient," only makes asceticism change form.[2] The atheist claim "there is no God" is made in the name of truth, which serves as a new evaluating and degrading standard against which every act and utterance must be judged. Atheism's dependence on the opposition of truth and falsehood is only a newer version of the Christian opposition between this world and the afterworld. In a world governed by atheism and science, Nietzsche argues, only what is true has value. Truth simply takes over the place vacated by God, and it is no better than the previous occupant. Science's "will to truth," Nietzsche insists, is not simply the "remnant" of asceticism but "its kernel," asceticism and Christianity concentrated in a pure and poisonous "ascetic ideal."[3] The will to truth is nothing but "the *faith in the ascetic ideal itself.*"[4] In the wake of Christianity's decline, truth ascends the throne as the conclusion to what Nietzsche calls "the awe-inspiring *catastrophe* of a two-thousand-year discipline in truth-telling, which finally forbids itself the *lie entailed in the belief in God.*"[5] Atheism is the continuation of Christianity by different means.

If even science and atheism are only the newest versions of asceticism, how can one oppose the ascetic ideal's devaluation of human life? It seems that it has left nothing untainted, which requires Nietzsche to develop his struggle against asceticism from within asceticism itself. The search for an outside from which one could wage war on the ascetic ideal is futile, and the belief in an "elsewhere" is itself tainted, similar to the ascetic ideal's postulation of a better place where God or the truth exists.

A crucial advance has already been made, according to Nietzsche, when truth's intimacy with asceticism is revealed. The first step, he writes, is the identification of "the problem of the value of truth."[6] Nietzsche understands this "problem" as a task, and he approaches it as a philosophical and literary undertaking that he envisages as the beginning of "that great drama in a hundred acts reserved for Europe in the next two centuries, the most terrible, most dubious drama but perhaps also the one richest in hope."[7] The actors in this play will be truth and the only force that Nietzsche claims is capable of countering it: the "will to deception."[8] Instead of installing another unifying principle in the place of truth, Nietzsche proposes a form of dissimulation in which truth becomes just one mask among others. Such a summary statement of Nietzsche's will to deception risks becoming a meaningless slogan, but the following pages will ground it in readings of Nietzsche's texts.

The significance of the will to deception lies not in the move from truth to lie, but in its supplanting of all unifying principles with a form of multiplicity. Nietzsche's language itself must become multiple to allow the will to deceive to function, and one sign of this multiplicity can be found in the proliferation of modes of writing that Nietzsche introduces into his philosophy, from the aphorism to the poem to the dithyramb. The contestation of the will to truth takes place as a philosophical debate and as a literary drama in Nietzsche's texts, and the discussion of Nietzsche in this chapter will eventually focus on a conceptual struggle that takes place between Zarathustra and the personified Truth in the prototragedic genre of the dithyramb.

In this summary account of Nietzsche's critique of the ascetic ideal, he seems to pit an artistic will to deceive against the ascetic ideal and its will to truth, but to understand Nietzsche in this way would be to ignore the complexity of his thinking about asceticism and turn away from the necessity of finding resources for overcoming asceticism within asceticism itself.[9] An exclusively pejorative view of asceticism would have to ignore many laudatory passages in which Nietzsche even attempts to formulate his own kind of asceticism. In *Human, All Too Human*, Nietzsche praises the "noble poverty" of Greek orators, and, in *Daybreak*, he admires the "practical asceticism of all Greek philosophers."[10] In *On the Genealogy of Morality*, Nietzsche asserts that the ascetic ideal first made humans into "interesting" animals and gave them the ability to remember and to have a relation to the future.[11] Many pages of *On the Genealogy of Morality* are dedicated to the "cheerful asceticism" of philosophers, and, as early as *Human, All Too Human* and most explicitly in notes from the *Nachlaß*, Nietzsche presents asceticism as the affirmation of a life without morals.[12] A suggestive note from 1882 or 1883 reads, "asceticism—attempt to live without morality, . . . attempt to liberate oneself from morality."[13]

Nietzsche's texts search for something that both belongs to and undoes the ascetic ideal by submitting to critique each of what he calls the "three great catch-words of the ascetic ideal . . . : poverty, humility, and chastity."[14] He aims to find a force at work in them that could nourish the will to deception. Among these three catchwords, poverty figures most prominently in his texts, in which it appears as the virtue of an existence that can do without the ascetic ideal but that appropriates elements of asceticism in order to become what Pierre Klossowski calls an "existence without purpose, existence that suffices in itself."[15]

The pages that follow present Nietzsche's development of the virtue of poverty as a force that emerges from and calls into question the ascetic ideal. I will begin my reading with a presentation of his critique of Christianity and the Christian notions of virtue and asceticism before moving on to consider the two capital forms of poverty in Nietzsche's works: "the giving virtue" in *Thus Spoke Zarathustra* and the "poverty of the richest" in the *Dionysus Dithyrambs*.

Difference and Language

Since ascetic poverty, for Nietzsche, begins as a Christian virtue, an understanding of its Nietzschean version requires an explanation of the relevant aspects of his critique of Christianity, which can be summarized as an engagement with its understanding of relation and language.[16]

In *The Antichrist,* he writes about Christ: "to negate is the very thing that is impossible for him."[17] The impossibility of true opposition in Christianity can be seen in its failure to conceive of resistance, distance, and natural death.[18] Of course, there is something that appears to be difference in Christianity, but Nietzsche dismisses it in the first pages of *Thus Spoke Zarathustra,* as if he could not begin his major work without first criticizing it. When Zarathustra first emerges from the solitude of the mountains, he listens to a wise man teach that virtue consists of peace and reconciliation between different virtues ("Lest they quarrel with each other, the fair little women!") and with one's superiors ("Honor authority and be obedient!").[19] Virtue allows for a good night's sleep: "one must have all the virtues to sleep well." For Zarathustra, this man's wisdom ("to wake in order to sleep well") is "nonsense."[20] The wise man's lesson is nonsensical for Zarathustra, not because it is contradictory, but because it is not contradictory enough. From the beginning, equality governs the strife between the wise man's virtues. The differences among them exist only to be neutralized, to be subordinated to "sleep, the master of virtues."[21] Zarathustra wants to transform the notion of difference, but to do this he must first establish the possibility of differentiating himself from Christianity's preaching of a tranquilized difference. Later he declares, "I do not want to be mixed up and confused with these preachers of equality."[22]

The problem is clear: a new notion of difference requires precisely the difference that does not yet exist in order to differentiate itself from the old notion. Without overcoming the tranquilization of difference, Zarathustra's every word could be confused with the preacher's. To articulate his distance from Christianity, Nietzsche must thus offer a different understanding of difference—as well as a conception of language that would allow for this articulation.

Crucial to Nietzsche's critique of Christian understandings of language is the notion of *Gleichnis,* which means both parable and, less commonly, comparison:

> For this anti-realist [Christ], that not a word is taken literally is precisely the presupposition of being able to speak at all. . . . He speaks only of the innermost: "life" or "truth" or "light" is his word for the innermost—all the rest, the whole of reality, the whole of nature, language itself, has for him only the value of a sign, a parable *[Gleichnis].*[23]

In his understanding of Christianity, language functions only as a parable for "truth" and for "light," and such a linguistic understanding reduces language to a collection of symbols for something else. Language itself disappears in the face of its symbolic function. There thus appears to be no way for Nietzsche to articulate *difference,* because Christianity has put all forms of opposition to sleep; and there is no way to *articulate* difference, because Christianity has made language into a parable for another world.[24] Nietzsche approaches this double problem by exploiting a tension within the parable itself, in the *Gleichnis,* which, in addition to the acceptation of "parable," can also mean "similarity" or "likeness."[25] *Gleichnis* thus denotes both a type of relation and way of speaking. In the chapter "On the Tarantulas" in the first book of *Thus Spoke Zarathustra*, Zarathustra proposes *Gleichnis* as the relation and language that will supplant the Christian pseudo-opposition of equality and difference: "Thus I will speak to you in a parable *[Gleichnis]*—you who make souls whirl, you preachers of equality *[Gleichheit]*."[26] The shift from the preacher's speech to Zarathustra's first appears here in the slight, paronomastic move from *Gleichheit* to *Gleichnis*, "equality" to "parable" or "similarity." Zarathustra creates distance by means of a suffix in the change from *Gleichheit* to *Gleichnis;* he speaks in parables against equality.

In his adoption of parable, Zarathustra takes over and transforms Christ's favored means of teaching and thus the Christian form of speech par excellence. For Nietzsche, *Gleichnis* is neither difference nor identity, but similarity. Appearing as parody, paronomasia, and in other tropes and figures that rely on similarity, *Gleichnis* institutes a relation that allows Nietzsche's language to be both close to and opposed to Christian language. Such a relation is characterized by Nietzsche in *Thus Spoke Zarathustra* as "the smallest cleft": "Precisely between what is most similar, illusion lies most beautifully; for the smallest cleft is the hardest to bridge."[27] Intimacy and distance characterize this new kind of relation.

Zarathustra personifies this new relation because he is a transition figure. He repeatedly withdraws from and returns to his disciples; he moves toward being the overman and returns to humanity but never fully belongs to either.[28] He is only ever similar and never merely identical to humanity and the overman, because his place is "between." This is why Nietzsche, describing *Thus Spoke Zarathustra*, writes of the "distance . . . in which this work lives."[29] Elsewhere, Nietzsche describes distance as "artistic":

> Distancing oneself from things until there is a good deal that one no longer sees and there is much that our eye has to add if we are *still to see them at all*. . .—all this we should learn from artists.[30]

Nietzsche goes on to say that he wants to be wiser than artists and extend "this fine force" of distancing beyond art: "*We* . . . want to be the poets of our lives," and, in a draft, he writes: "Extend art's trick and make it into an art of living!"[31] Art transforms by means of estrangement, and

Zarathustra, as the inhabitant and representative of "the smallest cleft," emerges in and as distance.[32] *Gleichnis* is the term given by Nietzsche to this relation that supplants both difference and identity; it is the name for the distant intimacy that separates and joins man and over-man, the Christian understanding of poverty and Zarathustra's.

The precise nature of *Gleichnis* becomes clear in Zarathustra's presentation of the virtue that will allow humanity to overcome itself. This "Gift-Giving Virtue" emerges in an act of theft:

> Insatiably your soul strives for treasures and gems, because your virtue is insatiable in wanting to give. . . .
> Verily, such a gift-giving love must approach all values as a robber; but whole and holy I call this selfishness.[33]

The gift-giving virtue steals "all values" only to give them away.[34] The text goes on to make explicit that what is stolen is not owned, but becomes a gift: "You force all things to and into yourself that they may flow back and out of your well as the gifts of your love."[35] This giving virtue keeps nothing and gives away what it has stolen, and the only change that takes place is the slight modification marked here by the "as" *(als)*, which registers a transformation in which the "before" and "after" are neither opposed nor identical, but similar.[36] Virtue changes how things are, not what they are, and is nothing but this constant, minimal alteration that institutes a relation of similarity that cannot be subsumed under any understanding of identity.[37]

Zarathustra's desire "not to be mixed up and confused with these preachers of equality" takes on a specific form in his proposal of this new virtue in the chapter "On the Gift-Giving Virtue."[38] The sentences that open the second and third sections of the tripartite chapter "On the Gift-Giving Virtue" bear witness to the virtue's transformative power. The second part opens with these words: "Then he continued to speak thus *[also]*, and his voice had transformed itself."[39] And the beginning of the third part reads: "At last he spoke thus *[also]*, and his voice had transformed itself."[40] Zarathustra's voice changes as he continues to speak about the giving virtue, because, in its contact with virtue, his voice too is taken and given, marked by the change in his voice's "thus."

The "thus" and "as" that register the transformation effected by the giving virtue deserve close attention because of the title of the work in which they appear. The repetition of "thus" in the chapter "On the Gift-Giving Virtue," like the repetition of the sentence "Thus spoke Zarathustra" throughout *Thus Spoke Zarathustra,* emphasizes that and how Zarathustra speaks. The parodic, paronomastic operation at work in the text is this slight change that takes place within Zarathustra's speech. In *Thus Spoke Zarathustra,* Zarathustra speaks *thus,* as his voice and words have been taken from elsewhere (especially the Bible)[41] and then given as the gift of virtue. Most chapters of *Thus Spoke Zarathustra* end with the sentence, "Thus spoke Zarathustra," and the repetition of the title within the work traces out the constant alteration of the "thus" that makes Zarathustra speak thus, thus, thus, always differently. The "thus" acts as a linguistic anaphora and seems to refer back to what is most specific about a particular instance of Zarathustra's speech, but its formulaic function brings attention to the constant change that characterizes his voice, a change governed by the relation of similarity or "the smallest cleft," which separates his speech from the language of Christianity. The next sections of this chapter will present in more detail how Zarathustra's speech differs from the truthful language of the ascetic ideal.

Zarathustra's Shame

Despite the giving virtue's ability to expropriate "all things" and "all values" in *Thus Spoke Zarathustra,* it eventually encounters a limit to its thieving generosity. At the end of the second book, Zarathustra relates the "parable" *(Gleichnis)* of how he comes under the influence of the figure called "The Stillest Hour," who forces him to lament his miserliness: "Alas, my friends, I still could tell you something, I still could give you something. Why do I not give it? Am I stingy?"[42] She goes on to tell him that his problem is a kind of immaturity: "O Zarathustra, your fruit is ripe, but you are not ripe for your fruit."[43] In their sometimes vehement debate, the Stillest Hour insists that he "ripen" and bear a certain linguistic fruit: "Speak your word and break!" Zarathustra responds, "Alas, is it *my* word? Who am *I?*"[44] The Stillest Hour demands here that Zarathustra reveal "his" lesson of the eternal return, but there is a problem: it never appears as something that Zarathustra masters well enough to spell out, and, in fact, many critics have noted how the eternal return never appears as an explicit doctrine in Nietzsche's writings at all.[45] Zarathustra never offers a straightforward, discursive lesson of the "word" that is putatively his. The eternal return always takes the form of a parable, a vision, a parody, or, as Avital Ronell suggests, a rumor.[46]

Zarathustra is unable to give his final gift, to say the last thing that he must say, because he cannot conceive of the eternal return as a lesson that would be his. He gives and gives; he impoverishes himself but never performs the surrender and concomitant self-destruction demanded by the Stillest Hour in *Thus Spoke Zarathustra*. Instead, he insists on the distance from his word and on an essential doubt regarding his identity. In her demand that he recognize the eternal return as his, the Hour would require that he own himself before giving himself up. In her understanding of poverty, to give everything up means to have first owned everything and, above all, to have owned and been identical to oneself.

Zarathustra is never fully himself and thus cannot give himself up in the way the Stillest Hour demands. A willed act of self-surrender is still an act of the self, and the Hour's insistence on extreme allegiance to his virtue reveals her desire to implant a slavish attachment in Zarathustra, which he must avoid, even if it is an attachment to his own virtue of detachment.[47] According to the Stillest Hour, the final act of self-sacrifice is necessary and belongs to Zarathustra's task, the overcoming of humanity. The task she sets is deceptively similar to the demand that Zarathustra makes on himself to give everything and to the description of the final transformation in the series of camel, lion, and child described by Zarathustra in the chapter "On the Three Transformations."[48] However, the Hour's insistence on Zarathustra's "self," his word, and their surrender indicate the gap that separates her words from Zarathustra's presentation of transformation throughout *Thus Spoke Zarathustra*. This distanced similarity between them is the smallest cleft, which is especially apparent if one compares the vocabulary of the Stillest Hour with Zarathustra's praise of estrangement in the final paragraph of the chapter that precedes "The Stillest Hour": "And I myself want to sit among you disguised—*misjudging [verkennen]* you and myself: for that is the final instance of my human prudence. Thus Spoke Zarathustra."[49]

Although the comparison with a later text by Nietzsche cannot, by itself, justify this interpretation of *Thus Spoke Zarathustra,* the distance between Zarathustra and the Hour becomes even clearer when the understanding of shame in *Nietzsche contra Wagner* is considered. In "The Stillest Hour," Zarathustra says, "I am ashamed," to which the Stillest Hour replies: "You must yet become a child and without shame."[50] Far from praising a state without shame, *Nietzsche contra Wagner* inveighs against the shamelessness of the will to truth:

> No, this bad taste, this will to truth, to "truth at any price," this youthful madness in the love of truth, have lost their charm for us: for that we are too experienced, too serious, too gay, too burned, too *deep.* We no longer believe that truth remains truth when the veils are withdrawn. . . . One should have more respect for the shame with which nature has hidden behind riddles and iridescent uncertainties.[51]

Nietzsche would remain within the riddling veils that surround truth and even suggests that a truth without veils is not one. Within the text of *Thus Spoke Zarathustra,* and even more so in the perspective opened up by the place of shame in *Nietzsche contra Wagner,* the Hour's demand for shamelessness reveals her close ties to truth and the ascetic ideal— and her distance from Zarathustra.

Zarathustra impoverishes himself but never performs the task demanded by the Stillest Hour in *Thus Spoke Zarathustra.* He affirms his transitional state, but to do this by means of giving himself up would first require that he constitute himself as self-identical. In the Hour's demands, the complicity between total impoverishment and total plenitude appears. The notion of identity implicit in the Hour's demand is incompatible with the relation of *Gleichnis* or "the smallest cleft" that makes Zarathustra and his speech possible. Her deceptively similar trajectory of impoverishment requires a form of identity that would be inconceivable for Zarathustra.

The Voluntary Beggar

The entire text of *Thus Spoke Zarathustra* could be read as Zarathustra's creation of "smallest clefts" that distance him from figures and concepts that seem, at first glance, to be close to him. The difference between his impoverishing gift-giving virtue and the ascetic tradition of voluntary poverty becomes clear in the chapter titled "The Voluntary Beggar" in the fourth book of *Thus Spoke Zarathustra*. The beggar has given up everything to attain "happiness on earth" and, having been rejected by the poor, goes to live among a herd of cattle, because, he says, heaven no longer belongs to the poor—but to cows.[52] Zarathustra approaches him with the hope that the beggar, too, has learned the difficulties inherent in the gift-giving virtue. "You have learned," Zarathustra says, "how giving well is harder than receiving well, and that to give presents well is an *art* and the ultimate and most cunning master-art of graciousness."[53] At the end of their conversation, Zarathustra invites the beggar to come to his cave and join him in his task of overcoming humanity, even if it might be difficult for the beggar to leave his bovine companions behind: "For they are your warmest friends and teachers," Zarathustra says. The beggar responds, "You yourself are good, and even better than a cow, O Zarathustra," which incurs Zarathustra's wrath: "Away, away with you, you wicked flatterer!" he cries with malice. "Why do you corrupt me with such praise and honeyed flattery?"[54] Zarathustra's anger at the beggar's flattery (and, possibly, the comparison with a cow) betrays the existence of a conflict between the two figures and their respective understandings of poverty. The beggar gives everything up with the goal of finding "happiness on earth," while Zarathustra expressly rejects happiness as a goal at the beginning and again at the end of the fourth book of *Thus Spoke Zarathustra:* "What matters happiness! . . . I have long ceased to be concerned with happiness; I am concerned with my work [*Werk*]";[55] "Am I concerned with *happiness?* I am concerned with my *work!*"[56] His work is the overman: "I have the overman at heart, *that* is my first and only concern—and *not* man: not the neighbor, not the poorest, not the most ailing, not the best."[57]

The voluntary beggar is one of the "higher men" whom Zarathustra has lured or who are searching for Zarathustra. They would like, above all, to remain as they are. They aim to replace truth with their own values, such as happiness on earth, while Zarathustra seeks to overcome the need for any higher principle. His question is not "how to maintain humanity" but "how to overcome it."[58] The voluntary beggar gives up so as to be happy as he is; Zarathustra gives up to become something else or to prepare the arrival of something else. Zarathustra's specific art of giving depends on the continually renewed relation to the overman and the refusal of any form of identity that would supplant his transitional state.

My interpretation of the encounters with the Stillest Hour and with the voluntary beggar has emphasized how the Zarathustrian understanding of the overman differs from the deceptively similar conceptions of these other figures. In this context, it is also important to differentiate the concept of the overman from its common interpretation, according to which the overman comes after humanity. This understanding is thoroughly determined by the ascetic ideal and is thus a misinterpretation of one of Nietzsche's most important concepts. If the overman were to be imagined as coming "after" humanity and as the telos of humanity's "errant way," there would be no difference between Nietzsche's thought and the ascetic priest's conception of life followed by and opposed to an afterlife, according to which

> life counts as a bridge to that other existence. The ascetic treats life as a wrong path which he has to walk along backwards, till he reaches the point where he starts; or, like a mistake which can only be set right by action— ought to be set right.[59]

In the misunderstanding of the overman and in the ascetic view of life "as a bridge," this life and humanity's current form of life are bad copies of something else. Elsewhere, Nietzsche is explicit in his condemnation of any kind of "ideal type" of humanity.[60] The prefix *Über-* of *Übermensch* is not a marker for temporal succession. The overman must be understood to exist within humanity as it is, as its interruption or estrangement, as the result of the opening up within humanity of a cleft or difference from itself, which appears most prominently in *Thus Spoke Zarathustra* in the creation of new concepts that differ only slightly from the tradition that Zarathustra aims to undermine. Difference and parable become *Gleichnis;* poverty becomes the gift-giving virtue; and the overman supplants the notions of an afterlife and ideal man. In the next section, I turn to Nietzsche's final work, the *Dionysus Dithyrambs,* in which the encounter with the Stillest Hour occurs again, in a different and condensed form, in a debate with the allegorical figure of Truth. At stake is perhaps the most important differentiation, the difference between the place of truth in the ascetic ideal and its new, subordinated place in Nietzsche's overcoming of asceticism.

The Richest Poverty in the *Dionysus Dithyrambs*

In *Thus Spoke Zarathustra,* Zarathustra's relation to his word is not one of possession ("Alas, is it *my* word?"), and his relation to himself is not one of a secured identity ("Who am *I?*"). This makes it impossible for him to speak his word and "break" as the Hour demands, because he does not enter into relations of correspondence or identity without at the same time distancing himself from them. Zarathustra says "my word" and "I," but never without putting these terms into question. The ninth *Dionysus Dithyramb,* "On the Poverty of the Richest," restages the confrontation with the Stillest Hour as an encounter with truth. The preceding reading of *Thus Spoke Zarathustra* showed how the gift-giving virtue appeared as an expropriating, transforming force. The poverty of the richest is similar in its enabling of the expropriation of a number of kinds of speech, which occurs throughout the *Dithyrambs.* My readings in this section will examine a number of figures of the smallest cleft in the cycle as a whole, which will prepare for the next section's reading of poverty in the final dithyramb.

There are nine *Dionysus Dithyrambs;* three were originally part of the fourth book of *Thus Spoke Zarathustra,* and six were part of a cycle that was once called *Zarathustra's Songs.* Two of the *Dithyrambs* take over and modify fixed forms. The third dithyramb, titled "Last Will," is a version of a legal testament, and the seventh dithyramb, "Lament of Ariadne," adopts a genre from baroque opera, the "Lamento d'Arianna," and appropriates the juridical form of an accusation or complaint.[61] In the case of "Last Will," the poem as last will and testament is improper twice over, because of its literariness and because of its speaker, who, in the *Dionysus Dithyrambs,* is not the testator, as the form requires, but the heir. A juridical form becomes literary, and a living speaker takes on a role that is dictated by a living voice but whose full force is reserved strictly for the dead. In addition, "Last Will" presents appropriation as its theme: an act that should be taken as an example. The first and last stanzas begin with the lines, "To die / as I once saw him die."[62] The mode of exemplarity of this death is carefully circumscribed. The lines are not "I want to [or will] die as he did" but "To die as I once saw him die." Since the initial clause, "To die," remains an infinitive without a grammatical subject, the "I" sees a death that becomes exemplary, but not for any subject. The poem thus presents a doubly improper form—a literary will spoken by the heir—and a way of dying that is exemplary in a way that does not require or even permit an imitating subject.

"Last Will" takes and gives a fixed linguistic form and estranges it from the traits that define it, especially from the prescribed speaker and addressee. This act of expropriation reduces the importance of the self in the speaker and in the voice that is assumed, and this distancing (but not total dissolution) of the identity of what is expropriated extends, in the other dithyrambs, to Zarathustra himself. How can Zarathustra "himself" be characterized? As one of the central figures in the dithyrambs, Zarathustra is always caught between roles, speaking in a voice at the same time that he is distanced from it. In the fourth dithyramb, "Among Birds of Prey," Zarathustra's "between" position can be seen in the thematic and rhetorical aspects of a series of alliterative lines that includes his name. All of the words that begin with "z" in "Among Birds of Prey" characterize Zarathustra as occupying a liminal position: he "zögert an Abgründen . . . zwischen der Ungeduld / wilden Gerölls . . . zwiesam im eignen Wissen . . . zwischen zwei Nichtse / eingekrümmt, / ein Fragezeichen" (hesitates on the edge of abysses . . . amid the impatience of wild boulders . . . twofold in self-knowledge . . . between two nothings / contorted / a question mark).[63] He also appears as estranged from himself: "among a hundred mirrors / false before yourself" (zwischen hundert Spiegeln / vor dir selber falsch).[64] The alliterative effect here emphasizes the link between Zarathustra, the question mark, and the words *zwiesam* ("twofold") and *zwischen* ("between"), but it also brings attention to the fragility of this link, because the figure of alliteration establishes a relation between two words based on a merely phonetic link. The tie could not be more tenuous between these words, just as the tie between Zarathustra and his many voices is characterized as much by distance as it is by intimacy.

"Among Birds of Prey" also assigns Zarathustra to a "between" space by the use of another device: the anagram. The fourth dithyramb presents a divided Zarathustra in the anagrammatical couplet repeated twice in the poem: "Self-knower! / Self-executioner!" (Selbstkenner! / Selbsthenker!).[65] These two words are almost identical, distinguished only by two letters, and the exclamation "Self-executioner!" presents an antagonistic relation to the self that is also a pejorative rephrasing of the exclamation "Self-knower!" The two words are similar, inseparable in any reading of the poem despite their divergent meanings; both describe a relation to the self as other, and they are almost the same word, alike and different.

A similar relation can be read within the doubly pleonastic title *Dionysus Dithyrambs*. The dithyramb is a genre originally associated with Dionysian rites and thus always contains an implicit reference to Dionysus. A dithyramb is always a Dionysus dithyramb. The phrase "Dionysus dithyramb" is as redundant as "Bacchus Bacchanalia" would be, and the title thus calls attention to itself and demands interpretation. The redundancy is intensified when one takes into consideration that the term "Dithyramb" is also an epithet for Dionysus himself: "'dithyramb' is also an old name for Dionysus; i.e. the god is identical with the dithyramb, the hymn of praise in his honor."[66] More than redundant, the title *Dionysus Dithyramb* is a stuttering repetition of Dionysus's own name.

The relation between the words "Dionysus" and "Dithyrambus" is reinforced once again in the seventh dithyramb, "Lament of Ariadne," when Dionysus himself speaks up. In the first part of the poem, Ariadne laments her martyrdom at the hands of Dionysus and insists that Dionysus surrender himself to her. When he refuses and withdraws, she begs him to return. Dionysus responds with an encomium of distance that concludes the dithyramb:

Be clever, Ariadne!
You have little ears, you have my ears:
stick a clever word inside!—
Must we not hate one another if we are to love one another?
I am your labyrinth . . . [Ich bin dein Labyrinth . . .][67]

These lines offer another term to be considered along with the words "Dionysus" and "dithyramb." Since there is no direct mythological or literary evidence to explain the identification of Dionysus and the labyrinth (besides the shared link to Ariadne), we are forced to consider what their relation could be within the dithyrambic cycle. Dionysus says that his word is "clever," and he then offers his parting bon mot and word of advice. What is clever about his word? Dionysus, here, insists that he *is* a "labyrinth": or, if Dionysus's other name is substituted, then Dithyramb is a labyrinth: dithyramb = labyrinth. The words are anagrammatical, close to each other in the same way that "Self-knower / Self-executioner" are.

These three anagrammatical or pleonastic pairs ("Selbstkenner/ Selbsthenker," *Dionysus Dithyrambs,* "Labyrinth/Dithyramb") present a doubled, split self that is always different, a self that can be said to be neither one nor the other but that occupies a position between the two— between the lines, in a hyphen, between a name and an epithet, or between a name and its anagram.[68] In the *Dionysus Dithyrambs,* identity is a riddle, and Zarathustra is always only an approximation of himself, a quasi identity that makes possible a renaming that Nietzsche's handling of linguistic clefts permits: Parathustra.

The Will to Deceive

I have emphasized these gestures of linguistic self-estrangement in the *Dionysus Dithyrambs* to prepare for the reading of the role of Zarathustra in his final encounter with a personified Truth, which, as in his meeting with the Stillest Hour, centers on conflicting notions of the self and the nature of Zarathustra's poverty. The poem "On the Poverty of the Richest" is made up of seventeen stanzas of unequal length; the first ten are spoken by Zarathustra, who presents his virtue of poverty and attempts to lure the figure of Truth into his poem. Truth appears, and Zarathustra introduces her with the isolated single line, "Silence! My Truth speaks!" Then, in the following six paragraphs, Truth describes Zarathustra's poverty with a markedly different vocabulary— and demands, as the Stillest Hour does, that Zarathustra give himself up. The poem then concludes with the single, isolated line "—I am your Truth . . . " (Since all nouns are capitalized in German, it is impossible to distinguish when the term *Wahrheit* refers here to the speaking figure of Truth or to the concept of truth. When referring to the poem's use of the term, I will capitalize the "t" to indicate that it could be a common noun or a proper name.)

It is not clear who speaks these closing words, but the stakes of their attribution are high, especially if one considers the following passage from *The Gay Science:*

> The ultimate question about the conditions of life has been posed here, and we confront the first attempt to answer this question by experiment. To what extent can truth endure incorporation? That is the question, that is the experiment.[69]

Avital Ronell concludes her reading of Nietzsche's "experimental disposition" with this passage from *The Gay Science,* and the ninth *Dionysus Dithyramb* is exemplary for Nietzsche's drive to test himself and the limits to which he can bring himself in his dealings with truth. In fact, Nietzsche once intended for the ninth dithyramb to appear as the closing poem of *Nietzsche contra Wagner,* where he writes of the poem as a "test" for "a second taste" and "a different art."[70] This text is a test, and we must submit the final line to examination, because it is there that "the" question and "the" experiment are decided. To what extent can Zarathustra incorporate and thus eviscerate Truth?

The trick question that, according to Deleuze, determines all of Nietzsche's philosophy is decisive here. Any reading of the poem is forced to consider in the most concrete way the question "Who is speaking?," a variant of the question that, for Deleuze, marks the difference between metaphysics and Nietzsche, who asks not "What?" (What is truth? What is beauty? What is wisdom?) but "Who?" The essence of a thing, for Nietzsche, is determined not by *what* it is but by "the force that possesses it and that is expressed in it," the *who* that has appropriated it.[71] If it is Truth who speaks, the dithyrambic cycle ends with the assertion of her domination of Zarathustra. If the poem closes in Zarathustra's voice, this means that Zarathustra adopts the voice of Truth and speaks in her name. Critical engagement with this dilemma of attribution is crucial, and not only for any interpretation of the *Dionysus Dithyrambs.*

Since the *Dithyrambs* are Nietzsche's last completed work, the concluding sentence of "On the Poverty of the Richest" could be said to contain nothing less than Nietzsche's last words, the final words that he
destined for publication.[72]

"On the Poverty of the Richest" tests the limits of good taste with a
very mixed metaphor:

> My soul,
> with its insatiable tongue,
> has licked every good and terrible thing,
> dived down into every depth.
> But always, like a cork,
> always it surfaces again,
> it flickers like oil on the surface of brown seas:
> on account of my soul I am known as: the happy one.[73]

Zarathustra's language appears incarnated as a tongue that is constantly
changing and never only itself. Like a cork, though, it always resurfaces;
it separates out from the voices he takes on. Zarathustra speaks in the
voices he expropriates, but he also exceeds these voices, and this excess
moves him to take over more voices.[74] If anything can be isolated as the
floating cork or the resurfacing layer of oil, as Zarathustra "himself,"
within the many voices of the *Dionysus Dithyrambs,* it is this constant
movement of expropriation and estrangement.[75]

Truth sees things differently. According to her, Zarathustra takes like
a thief—and keeps things for himself, thus impoverishing others. For
Truth, it could be said that Zarathustra's virtue is "the wealth of the
poor," a phrase that does not appear in the text but that is suggested by
this line: "you *poorest* of all the rich! / You sacrifice yourself, your wealth
torments you."[76] In her version, he has wealth but is the "poorest,"
because his excess is a taxing burden, which must be offered up as a sacrifice. Truth conceives of his excess as a torment that he must own up
to and then give up.

Besides this conceptual disagreement, there is a crucial linguistic
difference between Zarathustra and Truth. Zarathustra's lines do not
contain a single reflexive verb, whereas Truth's speech is dominated by
the repeated, reflexive imperative "Give yourself!" The accumulation

of reflexive verbs in this invective stanza characterizes her understanding of Zarathustra's poverty:

> You sacrifice yourself, your wealth torments you—,
> you surrender yourself,
> you do not spare yourself, you do not love yourself . . .
>
> *first give yourself,* O Zarathustra!
>
> [Du opferst dich, dich quält dein Reichthum—,
> du giebst dich ab,
> du schonst dich nicht, du liebst dich nicht . . .
>
> *Verschenke dich selber erst,* oh Zarathustra!][77]

Nowhere in "On the Poverty of the Richest" does Zarathustra use reflexive verbs or speak about "torment," "sacrifice," or "giving yourself." In *Thus Spoke Zarathustra,* he specifically opposes his excessive wastefulness to the notion of sacrifice: "Why sacrifice? I squander what is given to me, I—a squanderer with a thousand hands: how could I call that sacrificing?"[78] Nietzsche's critique of sacrifice runs through his works and culminates in the opening pages of *On the Genealogy of Morality,* where the "self-sacrificing instincts" are equated with another object of Nietzsche's scorn, the "unselfish."[79] *Beyond Good and Evil* specifically warns philosophers not to martyr themselves for truth: "Be on guard, all you philosophers and lovers of knowledge, and beware of turning into martyrs! Beware of suffering 'for the sake of truth'!"[80]

The terms of Zarathustra's encounter with Truth in "On the Poverty of the Richest," and especially the vocabulary of sacrifice, appear in Nietzsche's texts that precede the *Dionysus Dithyrambs* and point to the difficulty of their reconciliation.[81] Antagonism characterizes their relation from the beginning, when Zarathustra summons Truth not so that he can surrender himself to her, but so that he can "pluck" her:

> With gilded smiles
> let Truth draw near me today,
> sweetened by the sun, tanned by love,
> I will pluck only a *ripe* truth from the vine today.[82]

These lines show how he reaches out to perform further acts of expropriation. If his soul allows him "to lick every good and terrible thing," it may permit him to lick Truth herself—to take over and transform her voice.

He attracts her, and she approaches with her reflexive imperatives. Zarathustra's luring of Truth requires that he appear needy and eager for surrender, and he succeeds in convincing not only Truth, but also many critics, that he is ready to sacrifice himself. Clemens Heselhaus writes of the *Dithyrambs* as "the project for a new ideal of a good death," and Philip Grundlehner states in *The Poetry of Friedrich Nietzsche* that "the poverty of the richest is that condition of giving oneself in an act of sacrificial suffering."[83] Even such a sensitive reader of Nietzsche as Michel Haar can write about the dithyrambs as a celebration of the flight of Zarathustra's soul into the sun, but Zarathustra, even though he sometimes may resemble Empedocles, never takes the final leap or wishes for what Haar presents as "l'union avec l'être universel."[84]

How does Zarathustra respond to Truth's demands? It seems at first that he does not respond at all. After he introduces her in the poem with the words "Quiet! My Truth is speaking!" it seems that he never speaks again, unless he is the speaker of the isolated final line, "—I am your Truth . . ." The rest of this chapter will be dedicated to a discussion of this possibility. This is a crucial issue, because the line concludes Zarathustra's struggle with Truth; because it is a rewriting of the earlier encounter with the Stillest Hour; and because it is the final Nietzschean statement about poverty and asceticism.

An examination of the text in isolation reveals little about the speaker of the final line. A few signs support an attribution to Zarathustra. Only he begins his stanzas with a dash (stanzas 8, 9, 10); only he says the word "Truth" (lines 18 [in the plural], 23, 25, 59, 64, 66, 75); and the only other isolated line in the poem is spoken by him (stanza 10). But such evidence is not sufficient to attribute the line to Zarathustra.[85] We are left only with the possibility that Zarathustra may be speaking.

The critical edition of the manuscripts shows how the final line developed and how the problem of attribution appears even as Nietzsche wrote the poem: Nietzsche first wrote "you are mine *[meine]*" but immediately changed it to "I am your Truth," and the final version reads:

"—I am your Truth . . ."[86] The first version seems to have been spoken in the voice of Zarathustra and could have been a confirmation of Truth's dominant position, but, like his introduction in line 75 ("Quiet! My Truth is speaking!"), the line could be read with emphasis on "mine" and thus as insisting on Truth's subordination to Zarathustra. When changed to "—I am your Truth . . . ," it could be spoken by Truth and thus be either a confirmation of Truth's rule ("—*I* am your Truth . . .") or of Zarathustra's domination of Truth ("—I am *your* Truth . . ."). In the third and final version, the addition of the dash and the capitalization of the "i" in the first person singular pronoun *ich* (which, unlike the English "I," is not capitalized in German) isolate the sentence from Truth's speech and either make her finale more insistent or mark a change in speakers.

Nietzsche's revision of the text hesitates between "you" and "I" being identified with Truth and reveals a tendency toward the further isolation of the final line from the body of the text by means of capitalization and the dash. The concerns of my reading are reflected in the changes considered by Nietzsche, which affect the identification of the speaker and addressee as well as the connection of the final line to lines that precede it. Although the manuscripts reveal nothing decisive about the attribution of the final line, they do show that, in each of its three versions, Nietzsche's text scrupulously maintains the impossibility of definite attribution. We learn from the critical edition only that Truth and Zarathustra are difficult to tell apart at every stage of the poem's composition.

Nietzsche's earlier texts offer some assistance in interpreting the encounter between Truth and Zarathustra in his final work. In the well-known aphorism "On the Problem of the Actor" in *The Gay Science,* Nietzsche discusses the problem of dissimulation and takes advantage of the polysemy of the verb *sich geben,* which can mean "to surrender" and "to pretend":

> Listen to physicians who have hypnotized women; finally, one loves them— one is hypnotized by them! What is always the end result? That they pretend even when they surrender themselves [Dass sie "sich geben", selbst noch, wenn sie—sich geben. . . .]. Woman is so artistic.[87]

The crucial moment of supposed surrender is more than just another instance of mimicry, because mimicry is at its strongest here, able to turn against the very authority that attempts to make it show itself and surrender. The same model of mimicry may be operative in "On the Poverty of the Richest," because Zarathustra may be acting at the moment when he seems to give in either by submitting to Truth (if we read the final line as hers) or by assuming her place (if we read him as the final line's speaker). He fakes surrender or he fakes being Truth. The final line would be a masquerade, just as Wolfram Groddeck reads the final lines of the seventh dithyramb as farcical, burlesque, and "like an operetta."[88]

If we read Zarathustra as the speaker of the final line, this means that poverty's generous and expropriative force allows Zarathustra to take over Truth's role. But such a switching of roles would mean that Truth's role would simply be extended under another name, just as truth, as the kernel of the ascetic ideal, takes the place left vacant after the demise of Christianity. When truth is contested, Nietzsche tells us that it can no longer be decided who is speaking:

> The problem of the value of truth came before us—or did we appear before it? Who of us is Oedipus here? Who the Sphinx? It is a rendezvous [Stelldichein], so it seems, of questions and question marks.[89]

This passage from the opening paragraphs of *Beyond Good and Evil* could be read as a description of the attempt to identify the speaker of the *explicit* of "On the Poverty of the Richest." The encounter between Zarathustra and Truth becomes something other than the meeting of two discrete figures, and even the seductive aspect of their meeting, implicit in Zarathustra's talk of licking and plucking, is mirrored here in Nietzsche's choice of the term "rendezvous." The final line leaves us with a speech that is neither only truthful nor only Zarathustrian but that wavers between the two. We must understand it as the coming together of a series of "questions and question marks," the most important of which is the question "Who is speaking?" The question of attribution is not exterior to the *explicit*, because the final line is itself nothing other than an identification: "—I am your Truth . . ." The insistence on identification coincides with its near impossibility, provoking the question "Who is speaking?" while precluding any definitive response.

The appearance of Oedipus in the passage cited from *Beyond Good and Evil* reveals a link between the problem of truth and tragedy. In

The Birth of Tragedy, the Apollonian finds itself cornered by the Dionysian after having served as the necessary veil for the Dionysian throughout the tragedy, which

> ends by forcing the Apollinian drama itself into a sphere where it begins
> to speak with Dionysian wisdom and even denies itself and its Apollinian
> visibility. . . . Dionysus speaks the language of Apollo; and Apollo, finally,
> the language of Dionysus; and so the highest goal of tragedy and of all art is
> attained.[90]

Tragedy is a genre in which it is impossible to decide who is speaking at the moments of most intense conflict. Nietzsche presents tragedy as a sustained skirmish between two forces that "in the end" speak each other's language, even as each is unable to speak its own.[91] The dithyramb, whose importance as the predecessor of tragedy is noted throughout *The Birth of Tragedy,* stages a similar conflict between Zarathustra and his Truth.

The final *Dionysus Dithyramb* offers its own partial response to the question posed by the title to the third essay in *On the Genealogy of Morality:* "What is the meaning of ascetic ideals?" In "On the Poverty of the Richest," poverty always means at least two things, even when the dithyramb seems to say only one thing and to insist on identity ("I *am* your Truth"). The dithyramb stages an encounter of two forces that are as inextricably linked as the "brotherly bond" of Apollo and Dionysus in *The Birth of Tragedy.* Zarathustra is similar to Truth, so similar that he may become "your Truth" but so opposed that he must pluck her. They are bound together and kept apart by the "smallest gap" or *Gleichnis* that is neither difference nor identity but an intimate conflict and an antagonistic proximity that also mark the ways in which they speak. Truth speaks the language of Dionysus, and Zarathustra may end up speaking in her name. As they vie for the right to define poverty, their vocabularies are deceptively similar. Their tongues are locked, like the snake and the shepherd in Zarathustra's parable of the eternal return.[92] But Zarathustra's understanding of poverty as an expropriating virtue that allows him to take over other voices may permit him, in the end, to transform the voice of Truth, and truth is nothing less than the "kernel" of the ascetic ideal and thus also of the concept of poverty under the ascetic ideal. My reading reveals the conclusion of "On the Poverty of the Richest" to be a concrete example of the statement in this chapter's introduction: Nietzsche proposes a proliferation of masks in which truth is just one mask among others. The virtue of poverty allows for this to occur. Zarathustra's coup would not be the assumption of Truth's voice or even a definitive hold on the virtue of poverty. Instead, his success would lie in effecting an estrangement of truth and poverty by means of a kind of ventriloquism that may be able to split them from within. "To what extent can truth endure incorporation?" Nietzsche asks, and the ninth dithyramb attempts to answer this question. Truth is no longer just the kernel of asceticism, but a mask that can be worn, a form of dissimulation within a multiplicity that no unity or truth can master. The new virtue of poverty would not depend on an identity that must be assumed before being surrendered; instead, it would be the virtue that allows for everything, including truth, to be "taken," in every sense of the word, and transformed.

These conclusions must remain hypothetical, because their foundation is shaky, the mere possibility that Zarathustra is the speaker of the final line of "On the Poverty of the Richest." The postulated wandering of the *explicit* between the mouth of Truth and the mouth of Zarathustra corresponds to the more general hesitation and estrangement brought about by Zarathustra's conceptual and linguistic operations. Truth, her voice potentially mimicked by Zarathustra, may no longer only be herself, and poverty is at once the virtue proposed by Truth as the justification for Zarathustra's self-sacrifice and the virtue proposed by Zarathustra as the foreclosure of the possibility of ever fully being a self. At every moment, the virtue of poverty in the ninth dithyramb both belongs to and undoes the ascetic ideal. Nietzsche's last words, as clever as Dionysus's, insist on this doubling, revealing within the ascetic ideal and the will to truth the possibility of their destruction.

RILKE AND THE AESTHETICIZATION
OF POVERTY

La comparaison n'est pas toujours recherche d'une
correspondance, mais souvent plutôt un moyen de tenir
à distance.
—HENRI MICHAUX, *L'infini turbulent*

Rilke as Reader

Critical discussions of Rilke's relations to his literary and philosophical
predecessors usually begin with remarks on his attempt to efface the
marks of influence on his writing. Erich Heller's formulation, in his
classic essay on Rilke and Nietzsche, is typical: "Rilke was in the habit
of suppressing . . . acknowledgment of his intellectual debts."[1] The Italian Germanist Furio Jesi goes so far as to say that "the only books that
we know with absolute certainty that Rilke read are those that he translated."[2] Of course, Jesi notes, this is an exaggeration: Rilke's letters mention and comment on many books, and he wrote a number of book
reviews, especially between 1893 and 1904. It does seem, however, that
Rilke hides his indebtedness, especially to German writers and especially in the texts published in his lifetime, but it would be wrong to
reduce this phenomenon to a mere coquettishness or desire to appear
original. Instead, Rilke's relation to his predecessors reveals something
essential about his conception of reading as a kind of impersonal sub-
jection to overpowering forces.

Rilke presents his relations to other authors in a response to a literary survey from 1907, in which he names several authors whom he read
and admired, including Dostoyevsky, Ibsen, and Jens Peter Jacobsen.
In this short text, it becomes clear that the question of influence, even
of reading in general, is difficult for Rilke to answer:

> Even now my relations to books are not without a kind of nervousness, and
> it can happen that, in large libraries, I feel as if I had been handed over to a
> superior, enemy force against which any kind of individual resistance would
> be useless.[3]

He then writes that books "refer beyond themselves" and offer him "the openness to a non-selective vision and the determination to admire."[4] The state that Rilke describes as being "handed over to a superior, enemy force" reappears here in much more positive terms, but both phrases present Rilke in a passive relation to what he sees and experiences. In all these cases, the work itself—its narrative, form, figures, style—disappears, and what matters is not the text but the openness that it makes accessible and that can appear either as being "handed over" or as "admiration." If this is Rilke's relation to books in general, then what can be inferred about his relation to the authors discussed in the first chapters of this book? What kind of openness does Rilke find in Baudelaire, Mallarmé, and Nietzsche?

These questions can be only partially answered; my responses will be limited in this chapter to the possible connections between the treatment of poverty in Rilke and in Nietzsche and Mallarmé. I will defer discussion of Baudelaire's presence in Rilke's writing to the next chapter, because Baudelaire is cited and submitted to critique in *The Notebooks of Malte Laurids Brigge.* The most direct testimony to Rilke's reception of Nietzsche can be found in his marginalia to *The Birth of Tragedy,* an incomplete set of notes found among the papers of Lou Andreas-Salomé after her death.[5] In these notes, Rilke conceives of a poetics of comparison based on the relation of Apollo and Dionysus, and in this crucial sentence, he reformulates the relation between the Apollinian and the Dionysian:

> Since we are unable to endure unapplied force *[unangewandte Kraft]* (i.e.
> God himself), we relate it to images, destinies, and forms, and we place ever
> new comparing things along its way, because it passes by appearances, proud
> like a conqueror.[6]

The attempt to bear Dionysus (or God) requires that "comparing things" be placed along his way, and the simile "proud like a conqueror" already offers one comparing thing to present the god.

Rilke's marginalia eventually become more precise about the relation of Dionysus and his images. In what must be a response to the fifth chapter of *The Birth of Tragedy*, Rilke writes that "lyric creation" begins with listening to the "primary rhythm of the background," which he later calls "those Dionysian sounds of the background."[7] In roughly contemporaneous texts on the visual arts, Rilke discusses background and landscape as the hidden location of a community that remains invisible in the foreground: "We *are* there, while we come and go in the foreground."[8] These texts are worth focusing on for a moment to discern the role of Nietzschean vocabulary in Rilke's texts on painting and sculpture. In his book on the artists' colony at Worpswede, he writes that its residents are taking part in the "transvaluation of all values," and he describes the landscape in Dionysian terms as "without a face" and "frightful and oppressive."[9] In his "Notes on the Melody of Things," he presents the landscape as the attempt to show a "mood" *(Stimmung)*, a central concept for Nietzsche in the fifth chapter of *The Birth of Tragedy*.[10] The landscape, as something "foreign" and "general," is for Rilke only one form of a "background" that can also appear in literature.[11] In a text on Maeterlinck's drama, Rilke writes:

> [Maeterlinck] thus strives to give to the attentive and gazing [audience] a second, deeper community behind the action. However, such an involuntary meeting is only possible in a great, primary feeling.[12]

The emphasis on the background rephrases a similar passage from Rilke's notes on Nietzsche, in which he writes that the drama "creates a unity out of hundreds, i.e. an instrument for those Dionysian sounds of the background," and the "great, primary feeling" of Maeterlinckian drama is close to the Dionysian "primary rhythm of the background" in the marginalia. For Rilke, Maeterlinck's drama aims to create a "unity" of its audience brought together not by any shared identity, but in an "involuntary" Dionysian feeling.

In his texts from the period of his notes on Nietzsche and in the notes themselves, Rilke uses *The Birth of Tragedy* to develop a poetics of similes and a notion of a community based on a shared exposure or instrumentalization in the service of Dionysus. This is the specific kind of openness that Rilke finds in Nietzsche. In his works on the poor,

Rilke emphasizes some of the same characteristics that chapter 4 identified as signs of an impoverished language of similarity in *The Birth of Tragedy* and in the *Dionysus Dithyrambs*. Like a Rilkean version of Dionysus, the poor appear in the 1903 cycle "The Book of Poverty and Death" primarily as an object of comparison, as an "unapplied force" that must be related to "images, destinies, and forms." This chapter will show how the similes that dominate the cycle are a response to the shock of encountering the poor. Chapter 5 will then demonstrate how the community in the "background" of *The Notebooks of Malte Laurids Brigge* joins the narrator to the destitute outcasts whom he meets on the streets of Paris.

Since Rilke left nothing like the marginalia on Nietzsche to establish his relation to Mallarmé, the presence of the French poet in Rilke's writings is more difficult to distinguish. Rilke knew Mallarmé's poetry well and even translated several of his poems, albeit many years later than the poetry that will concern us here.[13] Already, though, at the beginning of the twentieth century, there are signs of Mallarmé's importance for Rilke. A transformed citation of the well-known *incipit* of Mallarmé's "Brise marine" ("La chair est triste, hélas! et j'ai lu tous les livres") figures prominently in the original conclusion of the *Notebooks* ("Wenn Gott *ist*, so ist alles getan und wir sind triste").[14] In addition to these verifiable relations of translation and conscious appropriation, Beda Allemann writes that there are "surprising connections" between Rilke and Mallarmé that exceed "influences," and he argues that Rilke was an attentive reader of Mallarmé and that he developed many of Mallarmé's figures and themes; he sees their common ground in the "phenomenon of muteness that surrounds their poetry."[15] He finds correspondences between the two poets' understandings of absence, as demonstrated by strikingly Mallarméan phrases such as "quasi-name of millenary absences" ("presque-nom d'absences millénaires") in one of Rilke's French poems and "known figure" ("gewußte Figur") from one of his German poems, which is an adaptation, according to Allemann, of Mallarmé's phrase "known calyces" ("calices sus") in "Crisis of Verse."[16] Blanchot also asserts a resemblance based on the two poets' emphasis on absence.[17] Despite the difficulty of establishing a direct link between the presentation of poverty in Mallarmé and Rilke, the chapters on Rilke that follow will show how something similar to Mallarmé's attention to virtuality reappears in Rilke's attention to the powerful silence of the poor.

Rilke continues the engagement with poverty that takes place in the writings of Nietzsche and Mallarmé, adopting elements of their texts and developing new ways of responding to the exigencies of representing the poor. In Rilke's poems and prose, Baudelaire's question "What to do?" as well as the Nietzschean "Who is speaking?" surface again in new contexts and with different emphases and responses.

"The Book of Poverty and Death"

"The Book of Poverty and Death" is the third and final cycle in a larger collection of poetry titled *The Book of Hours*.[18] The cycle's thirty-four poems are addressed to a central figure called "the Poor One," and, in the first poems of the cycle, the poetic voice assumes a mediating position, calling for the Poor One to help the urban poor. The following poems enumerate the problems of the poor: city life is described as inauthentic and city dwellers as so destitute that they do not even die a death that could properly be called their own. The Poor One then appears as the savior of the poor, endowed with the ability to replace their mass urban poverty and impersonal deaths with an authentic poverty and a death that is truly theirs.

The genesis of the poems can be traced to the first of Rilke's many extended stays in Paris. From August 1902 to March 1903, he lived in the French capital under conditions that put an increasing strain on his physical and mental health. A letter to Otto Modersohn from December 31, 1902, succinctly records Rilke's reaction to the city:

> Paris is a difficult, difficult, frightening city. And even with their beaming eternity, the beautiful things that are here cannot make up for what one must suffer from the oppressiveness [*Grausamkeit*] and confusion of the streets and the unnaturalness of the parks, people, and things. For my anxious senses, Paris has something unspeakably frightening.[19]

After seven months, an overwhelmed Rilke fled Paris for Viareggio, Italy, where he wrote "The Book of Poverty and Death" in seven days, between April 13 and 20, 1903. The conflict between the difficult experiences

of Paris and Rilke's retreat to Italy is registered in the cycle as the opposition of the disturbing urban poor and the consoling Franciscan figure
of the Poor One. "The Book of Poverty and Death" is only the first chapter in Rilke's confrontation with urban poverty in the first decade of
the twentieth century. His letters testify to a sustained engagement with
the poor that leads almost without interruption from "The Book of Poverty and Death" to the composition of *The Notebooks of Malte Laurids
Brigge,* which he begins to write in 1904 and completes in 1910; poems
in *The Book of Images* and *New Poems* also testify to this interest in poverty. A letter to Lou Andreas-Salomé from July 18, 1903—only three
months after the completion of "The Book of Poverty and Death"—
already contains early versions of key scenes from the *Notebooks.*

The critical reception of "The Book of Poverty and Death" has until
now been dominated by readings that focus almost exclusively on Rilke's
calls for a proper death and real poverty. Interpretations of the cycle,
for this reason, have tended to concentrate on one line in particular:
"For poverty is a great luster from within" (Denn Armut ist ein großer
Glanz aus Innen). It is understandable why this line attracts attention.
It seems to be a glorification of poverty, and, indeed, it reflects one
aspect of Rilke's cycle that has been described as an aestheticization of
socioeconomic poverty.[20] I will argue that such a reading does not do
justice to the complexity of Rilke's text, because a close look at these
poems reveals how their language calls into question any aestheticization of the poor and, indeed, the very possibility of representing them
at all. The first part of my reading of "The Book of Poverty and Death"
will focus on the presentation of the Poor One and, then, of the urban
poor. In the second part, I will situate my analysis with respect to the
Rilke interpretations of two major twentieth-century writers, Robert
Musil and Gottfried Benn. Finally, in the third part, I will offer a new
reading of the cycle's most famous—or infamous—lines.

Without Qualities

The Poor One combines aspects of St. Francis and Orpheus but bears
no name.[21] According to Beda Allemann, the Poor One belongs to the
group of Rilkean figures such as the angel and the future beloved who

are "figurations of the border of what is poetically possible," occupying a position "at the transition point into the invisible."[22] This liminal position takes at least three forms in Rilke's cycle: the Poor One's location, his relation to his name, and his relation to his attributes. The first two poems of "The Book of Poverty and Death" address the Poor One in the second person even as they present the difficulty of identifying or even locating the "you" and thus the speaking "I": "Am I walking inside you now? / . . . Or is it fear in which I live, / the deep fear of monstrous cities."[23]

The Poor One's particular kind of namelessness also exemplifies his indeterminate state. He is "as if without a name" (wie ohne Namen). He has been expropriated of his name, but this expropriation is not his; he is only "*as if* without a name." He is thus, strictly speaking, not nameless.[24] Distanced by the simile, even his namelessness has been deprived of any constancy. The problem of the Poor One's name appears in the poem that presents him at length and that will also allow us to investigate the Poor One's relation to his attributes:

> Du bist der Arme, du der Mittellose,
> du bist der Stein, der keine Stätte hat,
> du bist der fortgeworfene Leprose,
> der mit der Klapper umgeht vor der Stadt.
>
> Denn dein ist nichts, so wenig wie des Windes,
> und deine Blöße kaum bedeckt der Ruhm;
> das Alltagskleidchen eines Waisenkindes
> ist herrlicher und wie ein Eigentum.
>
> [You are the poor one, the one without means,
> you are the stone without a resting place,
> you are the outcast leper,
> outside the gates with a rattle in hand.
>
> For yours is nothing, just as the wind [has nothing];
> and praise barely covers your nakedness;
> the workaday clothes of an orphan are more
> magnificent and like property.][25]

These two stanzas are crucial for an understanding of Rilke's cycle, because they offer the most extended presentation of the Poor One. The

first stanza's series of metaphorical designations of the Poor One represents an insistent attempt at identification. But each attempt to name
the Poor One also emphasizes the difficulty of this project. In a line that
echoes Luther's translation of the First Letter to the Corinthians, we
read that the Poor One has "no place" and, in these lines, no single,
binding name or attribute.[26] In this accumulation of metaphors, an excess of identification and lack of attributive force coincide.

Instead of continuing the first stanza's enumeration of attributes,
the second stanza seems to acknowledge the failure to name in the first
stanza and begins by asserting that the Poor One has nothing and is
almost naked—and goes on to describe this destitution by means of similes. The negative comparison with the wind gives an image for the central figure's poverty, and, like the metaphors in the first stanza, the
negative comparison with an orphan's clothing stresses once again the
inadequacy of the poem's description of the Poor One. The first stanza's
metaphors present the difficulty of saying what or where the Poor One
is, and the second stanza intensifies this questioning of the poem's ability
to identify the Poor One, who remains free of any definitive attribute
except "poor," which may be nothing but a term for his being without
attributes.

From Metaphor to Simile

The laconic "For yours is nothing" punctuates the transition from one
stanza to the next and the move from one rhetorical figure to another:
nothing is "yours," despite the previous stanza's enumeration of characteristics; nothing is "yours," because nothing can be said to belong to
you: no property, no attribute.[27] The second stanza's similes follow and
take account of this insistence on the Poor One's being without qualities.
The move from metaphor to simile belongs to a progressive impoverishment of the central figure, because the simile assigns characteristics
and, at the same time, emphasizes the estrangement from them with
its "like" that separates vehicle and tenor.[28] The simile creates more distance between vehicle and tenor even as it asserts their similarity. Unlike
the first stanza's metaphors, which appear as identifications ("you are
. . . you are . . ."), the similes in the second stanza appear as negative

comparisons that highlight their own inability to name both in their assertions and in the form of the simile.[29]

The impoverishing aspect of the simile figures even more prominently in the cycle's presentation of the urban poor:

> Zu ihnen drängt sich aller Staub der Städte,
> und aller Unrat hängt sich an sie an.
> Sie sind verrufen wie ein Blatternbette,
> wie Scherben fortgeworfen, wie Skelette,
> wie ein Kalender, dessen Jahr verrann . . .
>
> [All the city's dust presses onto them,
> and all the refuse clings to them.
> Disdained like smallpox beds,
> cast away like potsherds, like skeletons,
> like last year's calendar . . .][30]

In the first sentence of this quotation, the poor are attached to and removed from the garbage that covers them. The poor are then presented by means of similes that compare them to different kinds of refuse: a smallpox bed, discarded shards, skeletons, and an out-of-date calendar. The term used here for refuse, *Unrat,* can also mean "loss, wastefulness, excess, damage, squalor, helplessness, lack, need, confusion."[31] *Unrat* thus means both excess and lack; it is associated with damaged goods, things that cannot be used or recuperated.[32] The poor are like trash, the similes tell us, reformulating the assertion made in the first two lines of this quotation by means of the simile. Garbage hangs off them, and the simultaneity of distance and sticky intimacy reappears in the form of the simile, which both attributes and estranges. The poem's first lines retreat from naming the poor at all and limit themselves to describing what clings to them.

A similar distancing from naming appears in the two lines that precede the stanzas about the urban poor: the poor are "marked by the mark of ultimate fears, / and disfigured all over and stripped bare [or exfoliated]" (gezeichnet mit der letzten Ängste Zeichen / und überall entblättert und entstellt).[33] The poor are marked *(gezeichnet) and* stripped bare *(entblättert),* written upon and deprived of any surface (such as a *Blatt*) that would allow for writing. The "and" must strain to join two irreconcilable assertions.[34] In Rilke's cycle, this difficult syncategorematical position is often occupied by the simile. In later poems that introduce the urban poor to the Poor One, comparison's weakness takes on a different form: "Observe them and see what would resemble them" (Betrachte sie und sieh, was ihnen gliche); "they almost resemble things" (fast gleichen sie den Dingen).[35] In these lines, the comparisons associated with the urban poor are accompanied by an even stronger insistence on their tentative nature. The subjunctive "would resemble" *(gliche)* and the qualification of "almost" *(fast)* before the second instance of "resemble" *(gleichen)* both weaken comparison's already fragile grasp; they *would* resemble this and that, they *almost* resemble things.

At this point, it should be clear that the simile plays an important role in the presentation of the poor in "The Book of Poverty and Death." In fact, these poems often seem to be nothing but an enumeration of similes—and, in this matter, Rilke's critics have responded with something like disgust. The excess of similes in *The Book of Hours* leads one critic to condemn its "schematic poetics" of "almost infinite enumerations";[36] and another critic writes:

> And that . . . is *The Book of Hours:* an uninterrupted surge of ecstatic fits
> and anxieties, raptures and secretive whispers, excessive comparisons,
> circumlocutions, and paradoxes.[37]

This criticism is useful, because it points to the centrality of the simile to *The Book of Hours,* but its negative judgment closes off the possibility of considering the function of the simile in Rilke's poetics. It is precisely this function that Gottfried Benn and Robert Musil—in different and yet related ways—recognized in their remarks on Rilke.

A Great LIKE-Poet

On August 21, 1951, at the University of Marburg, Gottfried Benn delivered a lecture titled "Problems of Lyric," which quickly became what has been called "an *ars poetica* for the younger generation" of German poets.[38] A long list of prominent critics and poets (including Beda Allemann, Ernst Robert Curtius, Hugo Friedrich, and T. S. Eliot) praised Benn's speech, which was immediately published and went through a new edition almost every year for the next decade.[39] In his lecture, Benn gives three "symptoms" of "unmodern" poetry; "the second symptom," he writes, "is 'LIKE.'"[40] Benn criticizes the "like": it is "a break in vision, it fetches from somewhere else, it compares, it is not a primary positing."[41] Begrudgingly, he then goes on to exempt Rilke's similes from his critique of comparison:

> Rilke was a great LIKE-poet; admittedly, Rilke could do that, but, in principle, LIKE is always the intrusion of narrative or journalism into lyric poetry, an abatement of lyrical tension, a weakness of creative transformation.[42]

For Benn, Rilke is not a great poet, but only a great "LIKE-poet." The importance of the simile and its estranging effects on Rilke's poetry was evident to Benn, whose dislike of the simile belongs to a tradition that considers the explicit comparison with "like" or "as" to be awkward or "less elegant" than metaphor.[43] "For the simile . . . is a metaphor differing only by the addition of a word, wherefore it is less pleasant because it is longer," we read in Aristotle's *Rhetoric*.[44] The "like" appears in many accounts of simile as a useless addition to the more economic metaphor—or, as Derrida has it in his summary formulation of Aristotle's differentiation of metaphor and simile, "metaphor sets before us, vivaciously, what the comparison more haltingly reconstitutes indirectly."[45] There is something deadening about simile that interferes with the conception of poetry as a lively, enlivening "primary positing." Benn's text also belongs to a specifically modern aversion that can be found in other poets, especially Claudel, Marinetti, and, perhaps, Mallarmé, who is reported to have said to a friend and follower, "I am erasing the word 'like' from the dictionary."[46] And like many other readers, Benn is irritated by a "weakness" that he says Rilke avoids "in principle" but that he nonetheless associates with him. This, too, is a commonplace in critiques of Rilke; one critic identifies Rilke's "basic mood" as "an emotional state that merely questions, a fickleness and sliding, like jelly," an insecurity and excess of which the simile seems to be a mere symptom.[47]

One aspect of Benn's lecture can help us determine more precisely the function of "like" in Rilke's poetry. Benn tacitly registers the transformation that the simile undergoes in Rilke's texts by carefully avoiding the use of traditional rhetorical terms to describe what he repeatedly identifies simply with the word "LIKE," written in capitals. Only once does he even use the verb "to compare" *(vergleichen)*. For Benn, "LIKE" is barely associated with the function of comparison and has become, in modern poetry, the agent of "intrusion" or "idleness" *(Einbruch* or *Leerlauf)*.[48] Benn's attempt to erase the word "like" is preceded by the silent elision of its conventional rhetorical function and accompanied by its jarring capitalization. Simile is no longer, or not only, a weak metaphor.

In a text written twenty-four years before Benn's speech, Robert Musil pays close attention to many of the same characteristics of Rilke's poetry. He too reads Rilke's poetry as marked by interruption, and in his "Address at the Memorial Service for Rilke in Berlin" he goes so far as to say that Rilke's poetry "signifies . . . , in short, an interruption and an exclusion *[Unterbrechung und Ausschaltung]*."[49] For Musil, the simile is the central figure of Rilke's poetry: "We might say: In the feeling of this great poet everything is likeness, but nothing is *only* likeness" (Man kann sagen: im Gefühl dieses großen Dichters ist alles Gleichnis, und—nichts mehr nur Gleichnis).[50] Musil's unqualified use of the term *Gleichnis* leaves it open here to the polysemy (comparison, simile, parable, similarity) discussed in the reading of Nietzsche, but Musil eventually makes it clear that he is talking about Rilke's similes:

> The spheres of the different orders of being, separated from ordinary thinking, seem to unite in a single sphere. Something is never compared *[verglichen]* to something else—as two different and separate things, which they remain in the comparison—for, even if this sometimes does happen, and one thing is said to be like another, it seems at that very moment to have already been the other since primeval times. The particular qualities *[Eigen-schaften]* become general qualities *[Aller-schaften]!* They have detached themselves from objects and circumstances, they hover in fire and in the fire's wind.[51]

This discussion of Rilke's similes begins with the breakdown of what simile requires: the separation of "different orders of being" into vehicle and tenor.[52] Like Benn, Musil distances the simile from the function of comparison, because Rilke's simile does not compare "two different and separate things," because nothing remains standing in the moment of comparison, especially not the two things that are being compared. For Musil, comparison is a moment in which characteristics "have been removed" from "things and conditions" and enter into a state of becoming and suspension.[53]

A close look at Musil's own language reveals how it takes on the characteristics of Rilke's similes as it describes them. The first sentence's assonance insists on "oneness" to the point of stuttering: "sch*ein*en sich zu *ein*er *ein*igen Sphäre zu ver*ein*en" ("seem to unite in a single sphere"). This sentence itself seems to be in the process of becoming a single sphere in its alliteration and the repetition of the syllable *ein*. The next sentence offers a more precise description of the simile's unification and significantly avoids the present tense. Even when one thing is compared to another, "it seems at that very moment to have already been the other since primeval times." In Musil's text, the present tense is absent, except in the verbs "to compare," "to seem" (or "appear"), "to become," and "to hover": "so scheint es schon im gleichen Augenblick seit Urzeiten das andere gewesen zu sein. Die Eigen-schaften werden zu Aller-schaften." There is only a semblance *(scheinen)* of presence in the simile, which effects a "having been other" that is historical or even prehistorical but which cannot be said to exist in the present, except as an "appearance" or *Schein.*

For Benn, Rilke's simile is a sign of his potential failure as a modern poet; for Musil, by contrast, his identification of the simile as the distinguishing feature of Rilke's poetry is accompanied by his hyperbolic claim that Rilke is "the greatest lyric poet the Germans have seen since the Middle Ages."[54] Although the texts of Benn and Musil lead to critical evaluations that could not diverge more, their characterizations of Rilke converge at a crucial point: Rilke's "like," a term that, according to both writers, brings about an interruption in literary language and exceeds its traditional role of comparison.[55]

In "The Book of Poverty and Death," the poor appear not as themselves but as a series of similes—and, I would argue, as the simile itself—as the "LIKE" that has irritated a century of Rilke criticism. "LIKE" is a weakness, an abatement, an interruption, and thus a linguistic approximation of the way in which the power of the poor remains distanced from enactment even as it appears as a potential. The poor are like "LIKE." They do not appear to fit into the system of economic production that they make possible, just as the "like" of the simile appears, from

Aristotle to Hegel to Benn and recent Rilke readers, as a useless, embarrassing device that the more elegant, economic metaphor can do without. Benn and other Rilke readers mechanically repeat a rhetorical commonplace that excludes the simile, just as the poor, in Rilke's cycle, are excluded.[56] The poor and the simile are *Unrat,* excessive and impoverished, but their apparently exterior position does not keep them from playing an essential role in the systems—economic and rhetorical—that insist on their superfluity and that are threatened by their interrupting force.

Losing Mastery

The break in the poetic voice effected by "like" calls into question the reading of "The Book of Poverty and Death" as an aestheticization of the poor, which has become a commonplace in Rilke scholarship, appearing in the work of such critics as Reinhold Grimm, Andrea Pagni, Peter Por, and August Stahl. Such interpretations are based on lines and stanzas in "The Book of Poverty and Death" that, taken separately, appear to glorify economic poverty and the urban poor. It is true that, taken in isolation, lines such as these that present the bodies of the poor as "so beautiful . . . so passionate and miraculous" (so schön . . . / so leidenschaftlich und so wundersam) can be interpreted in this sense.[57] But even these moments in which the poor appear as "beautiful" are countered by the cycle's foregrounding of its own inability to present the poor at all, and every attempt at stylization or metaphorization of the poor is marred by the breaks and hesitation identified by Benn and Musil in the very processes of figuration. In these poems, Rilke achieves anything but the aesthetic perfection that his critics often want to see in his poetry.[58]

In "The Book of Poverty and Death," the complexity of the Rilkean "like" belongs to a more general transformation of the poetic voice in its encounter with the poor. The cycle's second poem prays for a change in the voice as it comes into contact with the "you":

Und willst du jetzt von mir: so rede recht,—
so bin ich nichtmehr Herr in meinem Munde
der nichts als zugehen will wie eine Wunde . . .

If you would like to enlist me, tell me now—
so I will surrender the right to my mouth
and have it seal up like a wound . . .[59]

In these lines, the poetic voice is confronted with a possible loss, which appears here in the dominance of the sonorous aspect of language. These lines contain alliteration ("meinem Mund," "will wie eine Wunde"), homoioteleuton ("nichtmehr Herr"), assonance ("ich nichtmehr"), and an approximation of a rich rhyme that, the "m" and "w" sounds excepted, extends four syllables ("meinem Munde," "eine Wunde"). The phonetic exception of the "m" and "w" from the rhyming elements is even compensated for by the graphic mirroring of "m" by "w" projected across the space that separates the lines. Losing mastery over his mouth, his voice glides toward the nonsemantic, sonorous, and graphic aspects of language.[60] Such a loss of mastery comes about in the poetic voice's contact with the Poor One and his sonorous qualities: "You are the quiet one without a home / . . . You wail in the storm" (Du bist der leise Heimatlose . . . / Du heulst in Sturm).[61] These lines complete the enumeration of direct attributions that marked the first stanza on the Poor One quoted earlier; they close that poem by insisting on his connection to both silence and inarticulate noise.

At one point in the cycle, the poetic voice emphasizes the distance that separates it from an adequate presentation of the poor: "And if there be a mouth for their protection, make it mature and set it into motion" (Und giebt es einen Mund zu ihrem Schutze / so mach ihn mündig und bewege ihn).[62] The mouth described here, which would protect the poor, is a purely hypothetical one. It is by no means certain that there could be a mouth that would be able to master this task and fill the position envisaged by this poem; it voices a doubting hope that some other voice will be able to speak for the poor. The cycle emphasizes its wounded inadequacy and its inability to speak about the poverty that figures in its title.

Critiques of Asceticism

Rilke's insistence on the challenge posed to representation by poverty must be taken into account when considering a common charge leveled against representations of the poor in general: that of converting poverty into a kind of wealth. In one of Rilke's favorite books, Jens Peter Jacobsen's *Niels Lyhne,* a character declares his poverty and the wealth that compensates for it:

> I'm not forgetting that I am poor—yes, you must hear this—so poor that I
> have to let my mother live in a poor house, and I must, yes, I must, I am
> that impoverished. . . . and yet there is a world where I am ruler, with power—
> proud, rich, I tell you.[63]

Such claims are the object of critique of many of Rilke's contemporaries, including Georg Simmel, who, in an article from 1899 titled "Über Geiz, Verschwendung und Armut" (On Miserliness, Squandering, and Poverty), writes:

> In this way, the Franciscans are characterized as "having nothing and possessing
> everything." Poverty has lost its ascetic essence. It was the negative condition
> for the acquisition of inner goods, which, however, descended to it of their
> own accord. The renunciation of the means that are the ultimate purpose for
> the rest of the world itself became elevated to the highest value.[64]

For Simmel, asceticism is itself a kind of wealth, and his critique seems to be appropriate at several moments in "The Book of Poverty and Death," including this one:

> Denn selig sind, die niemals sich entfernten
> und still im Regen standen ohne Dach;
> zu ihnen werden kommen alle Ernten,
> und ihre Frucht wird voll sein tausendfach.

> For blessed are those who never distanced themselves
> and stand calmly outside in the rain, without a roof;
> to them will come all harvests,
> and their ripe fruit will be numerous.[65]

This stanza, written in the manner of the Beatitudes, seems to be the perfect example for Simmel's equation of poverty and wealth, for the poor "without a roof" over their heads will one day receive "all harvests" and "fruit." But these new Beatitudes do not present the poor as they are; instead, they emphasize the hypothetical and prayerlike aspect of their presentation with their formulaic *incipit* "blessed are those who . . ." These lines must be considered in the context of a cycle that often prays for deliverance from poverty and the city and simultaneously insists on the poor becoming as poor as the Poor One. The cycle creates a complex concept of poverty in which this seeming pleonasm is not one.

The poor are not who they should be. Rilke's definitive estrangement of the poor from their own poverty as well as his presentation of the Poor One's indeterminacy allow for "The Book of Poverty and Death" as a whole to avoid the accusation of such a conversion of poverty into wealth, even if certain isolated passages might seem to illustrate well Simmel's criticism of the notion of poverty.

Simmel's essay, which Rilke may have known, criticizes the kind of discourse on poverty that can be found in many devotional and literary texts, including Kierkegaard's *Christian Discourses,* a text Rilke read and discussed with Clara Rilke.[66] *Christian Discourses* contains a text titled "The Care of Poverty" that ends with the following enumeration of types of poverty:

> The bird is poor and yet not poor; the Christian is poor and yet not poor, rich; the heathen is poor, and poor, and poor, and poorer than the poorest bird. *Who* is *that* poor man who is so poor that this is the only thing that one can say about him, just as it is the only thing he himself can talk about? It is the heathen. According to the teaching of Christianity, no one else, no one is poor, neither the bird nor the Christian. It is a long road—in poverty to desire to be rich. The bird's short cut is the shortest, the Christian's way the most blessed.[67]

Rilke's poor are in no way rich—neither like the bird, which Kierkegaard says is rich without knowing it, nor like the Christian, whose wealth in Heaven increases as his poverty on earth intensifies. This last kind of poverty is a classic example of the kind of impoverishment Simmel criticized. In "The Book of Poverty and Death," Rilke's poor are even poorer than the birds: "And what are freezing birds compared to you?" (Und was sind Vögel gegen dich, die frieren?)[68] The only position in Kierkegaard's text that can be related to Rilke's poor is that of the heathen. Rilke's poverty appropriates elements of the Christian doctrine of spiritual poverty but also distances itself from the recuperative elements that characterize a simplistic understanding of Christian doctrine. Rilkean

poverty in "The Book of Poverty and Death," inseparable from the interrupted language of similes that presents it, cannot be transformed into
a possession or into a new kind of wealth.

Poverty's Luster

"The Book of Poverty and Death" closes with the Poor One's dispersal
that the poetic voice makes into its object and that ultimately characterizes the poetic voice itself. The larger collection *The Book of Hours*
opens with a symmetrical dispersal in the first poem of the first cycle,
"The Book of Monkish Life":

> Nichts ist mir zu klein und ich lieb es trotzdem
> und mal es auf Goldgrund und groß,
> und halte es hoch, und ich weiß nicht wem
> löst es die Seele los . . .

> There's nothing too small, I can still find its charm
> and paint it in gold and quite big,
> I hold it up high without even knowing
> whose soul will be freed by it . . .[69]

The person who is to be dissolved in these lines loses his or her substance
and identity even before being dispersed; he or she is only described as
"I do not know who." The cycle ends with the dispersal of something,
though—of seed, a metaphor of beginning and potential. A poem in
"The Book of Poverty and Death" closely circumscribes the potential
of the poor as it compares it to "the strength of a seed" (eines Keimes
Kraft) growing in the womb of a mother who tries to "strangle it."[70]
This poor seed is a power that its bearer strives to suppress: not growth
and new beginnings, but a specific kind of power that is threatened with
extinction. In Rilke's monograph on Rodin, poverty also appears as the
suppression of an ability; Rodin "had to suppress innate know-how to
begin poor" (mußte angeborenes Können unterdrücken, um ganz arm
zu beginnen).[71] The Poor One and Rodin are associated with a specific
kind of impotent possibility; the Poor One, like the "like," appears as
a "standstill" whose force Rilke's cycle registers with its excess of similes and insistent lack of mastery.

I began my reading of *The Book of Hours* by mentioning that the Poor One has the ability to restore a proper death and a real poverty to the urban poor—that he will be able to respond to the demand to give them their own death and to allow them to experience poverty as a "great luster from within." Now it is possible to return to those claims and investigate them in the perspective opened up by my reading of the cycle. What are the poor now and what would the intervention of the Poor One make of them? The poor in Rilke's poetry are simply "those who are not wealthy" and who appear as the object of prayer: "make the poor, finally, poor again."[72] They only need "one thing—to be allowed to be as poor as they really are."[73] These prayers are immediately followed by the poem on the Poor One that I discussed earlier and whose attributive first line "You are the Poor One" (Du bist der Arme) identifies him as what the urban poor are not and should become.[74] The Poor One's status as a guarantor of identity should be surprising given the ways in which he is a figure difficult to identify. These lines make sense only if we read "poor" here in the specific context of the cycle. "Making the poor poor" means to approximate the Poor One's poverty, which I showed to be not a condition characterized by identity but a state of becoming without attributes. The desire for the poor to be made poor thus aims not to restore identity but to become like the Poor One and to lose any form of identity. Making the poor poor does not entail their assumption of their proper state but, on the contrary, the intensification of their poverty through their adoption of the impropriety of the Poor One.

The second central demand of "The Book of Poverty and Death" is the call for a proper death that would overcome the mass-produced, inauthentic death of the big city: "O Lord, give each of them his own death" (O HERR, gieb jedem seinen eigenen Tod);[75] "Because this makes dying foreign and hard: that it is not *our* death" (Denn dieses macht das Sterben fremd und schwer, / daß es nicht *unser* Tod ist).[76] In Rilke's collection, the proper death belongs to the Poor One in the final poem of *The Book of Hours*. And, yet, if one examines the text closely, it becomes clear that his death, too, is marked by impropriety in this line that I have already partially cited: "And when he died, as light as if he had no name . . ." (Und als er starb, so leicht wie ohne Namen . . .).[77]

The exemplary proper death releases from any kind of belonging and is suspended between anonymity and being named. In the poems' call for one's own death, what seems to be a demand for propriety actually calls out for the assumption of impropriety. The same is true of the demand for a proper death in *The Notebooks of Malte Laurids Brigge,* in which the exemplary proper death is that of Malte's paternal grandfather. Walter Sokel writes that this excessive death "is the force that originates within the self, yet transcends and annihilates it," and Sokel concludes from this that "the culmination of what is most 'our own' is at the same time a falling asunder of ourselves."[78] One's own death is the death that overcomes one.

It is from the perspective opened up by this properly improper death that one must read the scandalous line "For poverty is a great luster from within." In the poem that precedes it, we read that the poor are

. . . so naïve and eternally Yours,
desiring nothing and needing only one thing:

being allowed to be as poor as they really are.[79]

The poor are helpless, fully "Yours" and without a will of their own; it is with this dependency that the "luster" or *Glanz* of the next single-line poem should be understood. *Glanz* can mean the "brilliance" of a light source, but it primarily means "luster" or "the glow of reflected light." This dependence on a foreign light source allows Goethe to write the maxim: "Dirt glitters *[ist glänzend]* when the sun happens to shine."[80] Two other appearances of the noun *Glanz* and the verb "to shine *[glänzen]*" in *The Book of Hours* are clearly meant to indicate the reflection of light,[81] which, according to the Grimms' dictionary, is the dominant acceptation in modern usage.[82] If *Glanz* is understood as reflection, poverty must be understood to come from elsewhere, even as it emerges "from within." It is like the Dionysus of Rilke's notes on Nietzsche, because it can never appear as itself and must instead be presented with "ever new comparing things." In these figures marked by poverty, the innermost comes from elsewhere.

The poor reflect a poverty that is not their own.[83] The very line that appears to glorify and aestheticize the poor insists in the final analysis that the poor cannot be seen for what they are but are instead to be understood as reflective—and blank. The luster is "great" in its overpowering of the surface that reflects it and that appears only as this surface. The surface itself, a figure for the poor, is only a suppressed power that makes other appearances possible. The flash of poverty, the privation of identity that coincides with socioeconomic poverty, recalls the privative moments in Mallarmé when virtuality appears (such as the "virtuelle traînée de feux sur des pierreries") as well as the glow in the eyes of Baudelaire's beggars.

Rilke's "Book of Poverty and Death" is not what it has been taken to be. Its poems constitute not an aestheticization of poverty but, rather, a complex testament to the difficulty of representing poverty at all. In "The Book of Poverty and Death," Rilke not only attempts to present the poor, he also emphasizes their resistance to presentation by creating a language in which attributes, in Musil's terms, "detach themselves" from their would-be bearers and in which representation interrupts itself in a luminous, blinding moment that highlights the impotence and withdrawal of the poor. The poor, in short, are themselves impoverished in and by this cycle. The figures who inhabit "The Book of Poverty and Death" cannot even be called "poor," for they are deprived of the attribute that would describe their destitution.

AN OUTCAST COMMUNITY

Malte's Calm, Malte's Vehemence

Rilke's "prose book" *The Notebooks of Malte Laurids Brigge* records the changes effected by life in Paris upon a young Danish poet named Malte Laurids Brigge.[1] The seventy-one notebook entries cover topics ranging from Malte's Danish childhood and episodes in the history of France to his Parisian neighbors and, most important for the reading of poverty in Rilke's texts, Malte's troubled relations with the "outcasts" *(die Fortgeworfenen)* whom he encounters on the Parisian streets. Malte runs into them in the hospital, on the street, in the park, and in his favorite *crémerie,* and he even fearfully speculates about their imminent appearance in his room.[2] The Poor One's disappearance at the end of "The Book of Poverty and Death" is definitive, and there is little hope in the *Notebooks* for an intervention from elsewhere that would resolve the tensions caused by poverty.

Malte's notebooks register his attempts to understand his disturbing relations with the outcasts, and many critical accounts of the *Notebooks* concentrate on the threat that the outcasts pose to Malte. Andreas Huyssen writes about Malte's "anxiety-ridden identification" with the outcasts and insists that it "is displaced by his joyful identification with *die grossen Liebenden* [the grand lovers] in the second part of the book," in which the attention is shifted away from the city and toward childhood memories and reflections about a hypothetical love without object.[3] Malte's supposed turn to an "identification" with the lovers in the second part of *The Notebooks of Malte Laurids Brigge* belongs to what Huyssen interprets as an evasion of the problems faced by Malte in Paris.[4] Huyssen considers the relation to the outcasts to belong solely to the first part of the book, and their putative absence in the second part brings Huyssen to this conclusion: "What Rilke had to offer modernist prose, I would argue, is all in the first part, which focuses radically and uncompromisingly on the truth of an unreconciled and antagonistic present."[5]

Another reader of the *Notebooks*, Ernst Fedor Hoffmann, faults the outcasts for exactly what Huyssen praises in them:

> Despite the intensity and strength that Malte ascribes to the impoverished characters, it is evident that [the outcasts] do not succeed in the fundamental transformation of their misery. And it is thus more understandable why they present a temptation and even something like a danger for Malte. . . . For Malte's task is also the formation of his own feeling.[6]

In his summary interpretation of the outcasts, Hoffmann offers no textual evidence that the *Notebooks* propose the "transformation of misery" as a task, nor does he indicate why he thinks Malte's goal is the "formation of feeling." While Huyssen would exclude the second part of the book because of its supposed movement toward a false reconciliation, Hoffmann's insistence on "formation" leads him to remove the first third of the novel:

> For heuristic reasons, it is appropriate to leave aside the first third of the book along with its vehement [*ungestümen*], almost hectic experiments. Only after the series of family memories begins in the twenty-seventh section can one sense a calmer way of proceeding, and the text seems to open itself up more easily to an eye looking for externally recognizable lines of development.[7]

Hoffmann's excision of twenty-six sections of the *Notebooks* corresponds to the general goal of his reading: to establish a "general structure" of the *Notebooks*, whose progress he conceives of as a "reflection of Malte's simultaneous development."[8] Only with the appearance of "family memories" can Hoffmann's enterprise begin. His "formation" of the *Notebooks* as well as his conception of Malte as "developing" and "forming" himself depend on Hoffmann's own deformation of Rilke's text, just as, in his understanding of Malte's character, his conception of the "formation of feeling" requires the marginalization of the outcasts and the obfuscation of their close relation to Malte.

Despite their differences, Hoffmann's reading of the *Notebooks* as a bildungsroman-like narrative of formation and Huyssen's theory of fragmentation in the *Notebooks* are perfectly complementary, because they both rely on the book's dismemberment. In their accounts, the text as a whole is not given full consideration, and the force of the outcasts is restricted to the first part of the novel. Both Huyssen and Hoffmann characterize the novel as tracing out Malte's process of overcoming fragmentation and moving from the "vehemence" of the early entries to the "calm" of the later ones. Hoffmann praises this process and sees its culmination in the telling of the parable of the Prodigal Son at the end of the book, which appears in his reading as the overcoming of the "confusion" of Malte's Paris experiences.[9] Huyssen sees the "mystificatory use" of the Prodigal Son as the culmination of the "flight from the reality of his experiences and his subjectivity."[10] Both critics agree that the *Notebooks* present a development characterized by increased formation and the repair of fragmentation inflicted upon Malte during his Paris stay. Only their evaluations of this trajectory differ.

The Parisian outcasts appear in both critical accounts as the embodiment of fragmentation and formlessness.[11] For Huyssen and Hoffmann, the outcasts are, respectively, repressed and overcome as the book progresses toward greater order and form. The understanding of Malte's relation to the outcasts has effects upon the conception of the *Notebooks'* form and, according to Huyssen, "what Rilke had to offer modernist prose." What if the relation to the fragmented, fragmenting outcasts were important to the entire text of the *Notebooks* and not merely one stage of Malte's "development"? In the pages that follow, I will argue that Malte's bond to the outcasts presents the exemplary notion of relation in the *Notebooks* as a whole and show that the impoverishment that characterizes this tie involves conceptions of community, language, and form that determine the entire text of the *Notebooks*. The poetics of the simile in "The Book of Poverty and Death" unfold here in a more sustained consideration of the new forms of relation that poverty makes possible.

A Sign Only Outcasts Would Recognize

Although earlier entries in *The Notebooks of Malte Laurids Brigge* include figures who could be outcasts (the first entry's baby with a rash, the poor woman whose "non-face" shows through her face in the fifth entry), Malte's first extended encounter comes in the sixteenth entry, in which he poses questions about their insistent presence. "They look at me and know. They know that in reality I belong to them," Malte writes, but he hesitates to specify precisely what form this belonging takes (*Notebooks*, 39). Malte wonders in particular about a woman who shows him a pencil:

> And how did that small, gray woman come to be standing at my side for a whole quarter of an hour in front of a display window, showing me an old, long pencil. . . . I felt that it was a sign, a sign for the initiated, a sign only outcasts could recognize; I sensed that I was supposed to go somewhere or do something.[12] (*Notebooks*, 40–41)

Seeing and belonging appear together in this scene that mixes two gazes that are central to life in the modern city: window shopping and looking at the poor. Malte understands the woman's "sign" as a summons or a command that has a temporal effect: "And the strangest part was that I couldn't get rid of the feeling that there actually existed some kind of secret appointment which this sign belonged to, and that this scene was after all something I should have expected" (*Notebooks*, 41). The sign makes Malte's encounter with the woman into an "appointment," and his relation to her becomes something that also belongs to his past. In this primal scene of community with the outcasts, belonging emerges first of all as the awareness that this bond predates their meeting. The emergence of this awareness occurs simultaneously with the implied desire to "get rid" of it, but the flight from the outcasts, for Malte, can only be a privative mode of belonging that depends on him already having been "initiated" into the outcast community.

Malte's recognition of the alterity of the outcasts determines his relation to their signs as something that he can only sense and not understand. But this recognition is accompanied by his acknowledgment of the fact that he belongs to them and that he is also run through with something that is not him, this "strange" feeling that he should have known about this meeting and the awareness of this community in the background that, as chapter 5 showed, Rilke associates with Dionysus.

These pages of the *Notebooks* are full of similar recognitions of alterity and of the self as folded into that alterity. In the next three sections, I will focus on a long entry that follows closely upon Malte's retroactive appointment and that juxtaposes three relations: the relation to the city (being-in-the-world), to the outcasts (being-with), and to writing (being-written).

Being-in-the-World

On a day when Malte is forced to leave his apartment because of his smoky stove, he wanders the streets rather than visiting places such as the Louvre where he knows he will encounter the outcasts. He knows that they would greet and watch him: "they watch me, they keep watching, with their cloudy, multiple gaze" (44). During his wanderings, he runs into a blind cauliflower vendor, and then, in a well-known episode, he sees the exterior of a building that reveals traces of the demolished building that once stood next to it. He recognizes there "the stubborn life of those rooms" and immediately flees. A long passage that describes the lives of the demolished building's residents concludes with these sentences:

> It is this wall that I have been talking about all along. You would think I had stood looking at it for a long time; but I swear I began to run as soon as I recognized this wall. For that's what is horrible—that I did recognize it. I recognize everything here, and that's why it passes right into me: it is at home inside me *[zu Hause in mir]*. (*Notebooks,* 47–48; *Aufzeichnungen,* 43)

Malte's flight in no way allows him to escape the consequences of this recognition, because what he has come to know in this encounter is not a fact about the wall but the fact of the building's relation to him and to its former residents. Such a recognition cannot be escaped, because it is "at home inside me." The relation of Malte's vision and his feeling is closer in German, because the same term denotes the building *(Haus)* and appears in the expression "at home" *(zu Hause).*

Like the encounter with the outcast woman, the sight of the building wall awakens something that seems already to have been present in him. Just as much as the statement that the recognition is "inside me," the immediacy of Malte's reaction shows us how the terror emerges less from the wall itself than from the realization of the intimacy of the relation to the wall that somehow seems to predate its actual sighting. In a 1927 lecture course, Heidegger cites the entirety of Malte's description of the wall to illustrate how being-in-the-world "leaps toward us from things."[13] Malte's account of the wall and, indeed, much of his *Notebooks* register his recognition of an implication in his world, which, as Heidegger insists in the lecture course and elsewhere, is not added to Dasein but belongs fundamentally to its existence.[14]

From the moment when he encounters the woman showing him a pencil, the outcasts belong to Malte's past and future, and he can avoid them as little as he can overlook how close he is to them:

> That was two weeks ago. Since then, hardly a day has passed without a similar encounter. Not only in the twilight, but at noon, in the busiest streets, a little man or an old woman will suddenly appear, nod to me, show me something, and then vanish, as if everything necessary were now done. (*Notebooks*, 41)

Here, as in the scene in front of the shop window, the change effected is hypothetical, presented in the subjunctive: earlier, there was "the feeling that there actually existed some kind of secret appointment" and now Malte leaves "as if everything necessary were now done." A few pages later, during his visit to the Salpêtrière, comes what Malte calls "the first official confirmation that I belonged to the outcasts" (*Notebooks*, 55). But his belonging, despite the confirmation, remains hypothetical. He insists on this belonging, but his interactions are limited to these "sudden" encounters that consist solely of a hasty display and that testify to a relation Malte understands neither as difference nor as identity: "No, it's not that I want to distinguish myself from them; but I would be overvaluing myself if I tried to be like them [wollte ich ihnen gleich sein]. I'm not" (*Notebooks*, 212; *Aufzeichnungen*, 167).

Malte and the outcasts never speak to one another, and there is never even the fantasy of speech between them or of a conventional resolution of the relation in familial or amicable terms as there is in Thomas Mann's story "The Starvelings," in which the central character Detlef sees in a beggar a "comrade" to whom he cries out, in an imagined dialogue, *"We are brothers, after all!"*[15] There is no address or dialogue as there is in Baudelaire and Mallarmé. Similar to the "like" discussed in chapter 5 and to other Rilkean syncategoremata, the bond with the poor remains estranged. In *The Book of Hours,* the "like" stands in for a relation or the possibility of a relation but leaves open the question of what this relation might be and includes within itself the possibility that the relation might be a nonrelation. So far, in our reading of Rilke's *Notebooks,* it is only possible to say that Malte's belonging to the outcasts consists in showing and seeing, which Malte presents here as "everything necessary" for indicating this new awareness of community.

Being-With

The notion of "community" *(Gemeinsamkeit)* lies at the center of Rilke's reflections on art and love and plays an important role in a wide range of Rilke texts, from his notes on *The Birth of Tragedy* to his book on the Worpswede artist colony to his *Letters to a Young Poet,* but Malte's mode of "belonging" to the outcasts remains unexplicated in his first encounters with them.[16] One reason for this obscurity may lie in the general disintegration of relations in the *Notebooks.* A contemporary reviewer of the *Notebooks* wrote that Malte "suffers from every kind of community [leidet unter jeder Form der Gemeinsamkeit]," and a more recent critic states that, for Malte, "every form of community" is "excluded from the outset."[17]

At first glance, it does seem that *The Notebooks of Malte Laurids Brigge* registers nothing but Malte's *loss* of every kind of belonging. Malte is in exile in Paris and thus estranged from his homeland. He is separated from his family and from his own name: "Today Brigge and nevermore," he calls out as he stands watch over his father's corpse (*Notebooks,* 159). And he describes in great detail the loss of his aristocratic past, most vividly in the image of his furniture that he was forced to leave behind in Denmark and that is now rotting away in a barn (*Notebooks,* 43). These unraveled bonds have in turn taken away the possibility of being a poet: "And to think that I too would have been a poet" (*Notebooks,* 43). Malte writes, but it is as if he were writing in the place of someone else; he is only "the first one to turn up," "just anyone" who writes but not "the most suitable person" (*Notebooks,* 24; *Aufzeichnungen,* 25). Writing is something that he does but that does not belong to him, because he has been separated from the identity of a writer just as he has been cut off from other forms of identity and belonging.

The *Notebooks* thus present the narrative of Malte's impoverishment: the loss of his home, his name, his family, and his class, as well as the loss of identity as a writer. This leads Maurice Blanchot to write about Malte's "vagabond existence" and to say that Malte is "banished from his station in life."[18] He has been displaced from these positions of belonging and is now only permitted to be an approximation. Like the poor in *The Book of Hours,* he is estranged from his attributes, but I will argue here that this new distance leads beyond the solitude that some critics see in the *Notebooks* to a new form of community.[19] The emergence of his awareness of a preexisting relation to the outcasts occurs simultaneously with the undoing of every other kind of bond.

Walter Sokel suggests that the outcasts offer the possibility of a new kind of community. In a reading of Malte's encounter with an epileptic, Sokel writes that, as the man collapses and a crowd encircles his twitching body, "he has become one with the multitude, and no distinction is left between the self and mankind."[20] As soon as the epileptic is taken over by his seizure and stops trying to create an image of "normality," Sokel sees "a much more real relationship between the self and the others."[21] The scene comes to an end when the man collapses and onlookers gather around him: "for he was already surrounded by people, and I could no longer see him" (*Notebooks,* 71). The man is obscured from vision as the crowd envelops him, but, instead of showing a new kind of belonging, as Sokel argues, the elimination of distance and the disappearance of the epileptic make relationship impossible. Sokel's two statements regarding the epileptic's fate are contradictory: that there is no distinction between the man and the crowd and that this finale allows for a closer relationship. Where there is no distinction, there can be no relation and only a fusional communion that would rid its members of the distance that in the *Notebooks* seems to be essential to the notion of community.

No new bond arises in the moment of communion between the epileptic and the crowd, but I would argue that there is still the possibility of a form of community in this scene. Sokel's account assumes that Malte appears as a removed spectator, a role that he is unable to occupy.[22] Malte is drawn into what he sees as he notices the epileptic's loss of control, as his tic becomes a seizure and eventually a collapse:

> A cold twinge shot down my spine when his legs suddenly made a small, convulsive leap. . . . I knew that as he walked and with infinite effort tried to appear calm and detached, the terrible spasms were accumulating inside his body; I could feel the anxiety he felt as the spasms grew and grew. . . . I gathered my little strength together like money and, gazing at his hands, I begged him to take it if it could be of any use. I think he took it. (*Notebooks*, 68–70)

As soon as Malte notices the man's twitching, a tie is established: "From this moment on, I was bound to him" (*Notebooks*, 68). As in all of Malte's interactions with the outcasts, their relationship is marked by distance and the lack of communication. There is only the fact of being "bound," just as the woman showing him the pencil meant only that he belonged to the "initiated."

The beggars in Malte's account are isolated and never appear as a group. In fact, this isolation seems to be a central part of the relationship that binds them. Malte writes about a single beggar feeding birds: "And the more people gather around him . . . , the less he has in common with them" (*Notebooks*, 79). Their community is based upon a bond that requires distance. Besides the figures of the beggars that appear in Baudelaire, the presentation of the outcasts' community could be compared to Baudelaire's poem "A une passante," in which the poet takes pleasure in the fleetingness of his encounter with the passing woman, whose appeal exists only as *fugitive beauté*.[23] Fleetingness is essential to the Baudelairean encounter, of which Benjamin writes, "Fulfillment is not so much denied as spared."[24] Like Malte's relation to the outcasts, the experience of the passing woman is both intimate and estranged, and Malte's bond with the poor cannot be understood as a shared identity or purpose, but as a shared estrangement or exposure.

A similar bond emerges when Malte flees the scene of the building wall and runs to his favorite *crémerie*, where he finds, in his preferred seat, an outcast whom he senses is dying: "Yes, he knew that he was now withdrawing from everything in the world, not merely from human beings. One more moment, and everything would lose its meaning. . . . So he sat there, waiting for it to happen" (*Notebooks*, 51). Malte sits down next to him and, with no exchange of words or glances, a relationship immediately emerges: "The connection between us was established" (*Notebooks,* 50–51). Malte goes on to explain the nature of the bond. They are connected "because inside me too something is taking place that is beginning to withdraw and separate me from everything" (*Notebooks,* 52). The man is only separated by "one moment" from a total estrangement from his surroundings or from death. This realization leads Malte to flee once again.

Malte's relation to the outcasts is based on such a shared estrangement, which is frightening because of its association with death. It is as if he were beginning to experience the estranging force of the simile that the last chapter identified in *The Book of Hours*. The community with the outcasts seems to correspond to what Rilke writes in a book review: "there are no common experiences, and one can share only separations and farewells," and Malte shares with the man only the farewell and separation that death "is."[25]

Malte flees the building wall only to find that what he flees is in him, just as he runs from the *crémerie* even though the reason for his flight is the fact that something in him is like the dying man. Once at home, he considers how he could have avoided the man, and he repeats to himself the phrase "if I weren't poor . . ." If Malte were not poor, he could afford to eat in restaurants where dying men would not be admitted, and he would be able to afford wood that would not make his room too smoky to stay at home. But Malte *is* poor, as he insists in these sentences that appear earlier in the same entry that introduce the sight of the wall:

> Will people believe that there are buildings like this? No, they'll say I am not telling the truth. But this time it *is* the truth; nothing has been left out, and of course nothing has been added. Where would I get it from? People know that I'm poor. People know it. Buildings? But, to be exact, they were buildings which no longer existed. (*Notebooks,* 45)

Poverty is the state that forces him to leave his house and see the wall and the dying man. It also precludes the addition of anything to the barren, witnessed scene. Heidegger reads this passage as a "testimony" to being-in-the-world and to the function of literature: "Poetry, creative literature, is nothing but the elementary emergence into words, the becoming-uncovered, of existence as being-in-the-world."[26] To take account of the ineluctable presence here of the remarks about belonging to the poor, Heidegger's phrase can be expanded to include the claim that literature is also the emergence into words of "being-with," existence as always already an existence shared with others.[27]

In *Being and Time,* Heidegger presents being-with as one of the fundamental modes of being of Dasein, an "existential" that takes account of how "Dasein in itself is essentially being-with."[28] The relation to others is not a simple relation of isolated selves to a group, nor is it the "summative result of the occurrence of several 'subjects.'"[29] Instead, Dasein only ever exists in relation to others, just as it only ever exists in relation to its world. This structure of Dasein explains how Malte's experience of the wall is in him and how he senses that the encounter with the beggar woman should have been expected and that there is a connection with the dying man. His relation to them reveals something essential about relation in general, something that Malte should have known and which the contact with the outcasts reveals to him again and again. He shares something with the poor, even though they share no attributes and exchange no words, and this sharing exists even before his first encounter with them. There is something about the reduced state of the barren, husklike outcasts that allows for them to realize what this sharing is and to provoke an explicit awareness of it in Malte. He experiences this bond in all of its estranged purity; he adds nothing to it—no words and no identity: "Where would I get it from? People know that I'm poor."

Being-Written

Even if he were able to avoid the outcasts and the wall, Malte would still have this irreducible relatedness "in him." He tries to console himself: "If my fear weren't so great, I would find some consolation in the thought that it's not impossible to see everything differently and still remain alive" (*Notebooks,* 52). His fear registers an alienating change that has already taken place: "But I am frightened, I am unspeakably [*namenlos*] frightened of this change" (*Notebooks,* 52; *Aufzeichnungen,* 46). In the idiomatic German expression used here, he fears "namelessly," which indicates that the feared loss of identity is already present in his fear. "This change" appears in the next pages of the same entry, but not in the form of another encounter with the dying man or the building wall; instead, it is a transformation that occurs within Malte's writing. He sketches out what this new kind of writing would be like:

> For the time being, I can still write all this down, can still say it, but the day will come when my hand will be distant, and if I tell it to write, it will write words that are not mine. The time of the other interpretation will dawn, when there shall not be left one word upon another, and every meaning will dissolve like a cloud and fall down like rain. In spite of my fear, I am still like someone standing in the presence of something great, and I remember that I often used to feel this happening inside me when I was about to write. But this time I will be written. I am the impression that will transform itself. It would take so little for me to understand all this and assent to it. Just one step, and my misery would turn into bliss. But I can't take that step; I have fallen and I can't pick myself up, because I am shattered. (*Notebooks,* 53)

This passage proposes a future model of writing that, together with the nostalgic passage later in the book about a lost mode of "true story-telling," negatively frames Malte's own writing and reinforces the lines cited earlier about his only ever approximating the identity of a writer. Blanchot goes so far as to say that the final sentence cited here is the "hidden center" of the book, and he equivocates, saying that it presents "the death of Malte, or the instant of his collapse."[30] For Blanchot, Rilke placed this passage toward the beginning of the *Notebooks* "to demonstrate to himself that after this end something remains possible, that it is not the frightful final line after which there is nothing more to say."[31]

But what remains possible for Malte after this death or collapse? It comes as the final catastrophe in this long notebook entry: he flees the wall, the man in the *crémerie,* and ends up facing something that he cannot run from so easily. My reading here will focus on the "time of the other interpretation" in its relation to the encounters with the wall and the dying man. As in those earlier encounters, the relation to this future writing is a disturbing, fearsome proximity. Only "one step" separates Malte from it, and when this time comes, writing will emerge from his own hand, which, however, will be alienated from him. Just as Malte already becomes anonymous in his "nameless" fear, here too he appears only as similar to himself, fearing "like" an impersonal "someone *[einer]* standing in the presence of something great." Malte's text remains similar to this future writing, related to it in a way similar to the relation of *Gleichnis* discussed in chapter 4's reading of Nietzsche. He is "shattered," but this broken state is already close to that future time, because, in the many relations of similarity in this passage, he constantly shifts positions and attributes. In a way, the condition described in this sentence has already come to pass: "I am the impression that will transform itself." Already in this sentence's combination of the first clause's present tense and the second's future, Malte *is* this impression, and even as he fears this future, he hopes for something that will help him reach it:

> Until now I have always believed that help would come. There it is, in my own handwriting, the words that have been my prayer, evening after evening. I copied them from the books I found them in, so that they would be right in front of me, issued from my hand as if they were my own words *[wie Eigenes]*. (*Notebooks*, 53; *Aufzeichnungen*, 47)

Malte goes on to quote from Baudelaire's prose poem "Une heure du matin" and from the book of Job, approximating the "time of the other interpretation" by already writing words that are not his. The entry closes with these citations.

This notebook entry presents Malte's triple exposure: to the wall, to the dying man, and to writing. The interest of the *Notebooks* for the current study lies not merely in the fact that Malte realizes this interpenetration of self, other, world, and language, a banality to which every work of literature attests. Instead, what sets *The Notebooks of Malte Laurids Brigge* apart is the way in which it proposes poverty as the exemplary state for the emergence of an awareness of these forms of belonging, which appear here as a kind of impoverishment of the self. Being-in-the-world, being-with, and being-written appear here as forms of exposure that are thematized in Malte's relation to the outcasts. In his relation to them, he is infected by their decomposition of identity, by a becoming poor that is experienced as threatening and promising. The poor expose him to transition states that are without duration or constancy and that approximate another, coming condition.

For Malte, poverty is a transitional exposition to alterity, and it is painful and terrifying, making him seek help in the form of citation and copying, which expose him to exactly that alterity. The outcasts embody alterity throughout Malte's *Notebooks,* and the community that he involuntarily becomes aware of is the model for a loss of self in writing that first appears in the novel after an encounter with the dying man. Shielding himself at first from the relation to the outcasts and from a form of writing without mastery, Malte tries to console himself with the reminder that it is "not impossible to see everything differently and still remain alive," but the fear remains (*Notebooks,* 52). His notebooks take as their object this "seeing everything differently" that Malte associates with the outcasts, because they are the last thing he wants to see. But he must see them if he is to see everything differently and if, as Blanchot writes, something is still possible after Malte's collapse. The task of seeing differently is as central in his memories of his family in the second half of the book as it is for his Paris experiences. Without the city and the outcasts, there would be no memories of childhood and no retelling of the parable of the Prodigal Son in the final pages of *The Notebooks of Malte Laurids Brigge.* The next sections of this chapter will show how the return to Malte's childhood and the turn to historical, biblical, and literary episodes do not constitute an escape from the difficulties of his Parisian experiences but a discovery of what, in these other events and texts, remains disturbing or unexplained.

There Is No Choice, No Refusal

The new bond with the outcasts arises along with a new way of seeing, and to see everything differently, Malte must first see everything and not turn his gaze from even the most disturbing sights. After his father dies, he insists on watching as the doctors puncture his father's heart to ensure that he will not be buried alive:

> Besides, I had never seen what it is like when someone's breast is perforated. It seemed appropriate not to reject [*abzulehnen*] such a rare experience. . . . Now the heart had been perforated, our heart, the heart of our family [*das Herz unseres Geschlechtes*]. (*Notebooks,* 157–59; *Aufzeichnungen,* 126–28)

Malte experiences his father as a corpse and his father's fate as his own. The pierced heart is "ours" not only because of the blood relation but also because, as Malte watches the procedure, he is once again absorbed in what he sees. Earlier in his notebooks, Malte writes about such attention to the corpse as Baudelaire's task in the poem "Une charogne": "It was his task to see, in this terrifying and apparently repulsive object, the being that underlies all individual beings. There is no choice, no refusal [Ablehnung]" (Notebooks, 72; Aufzeichnungen, 62).[32] Just as it appears proper to Malte not to "reject [abzulehnen] such a rare experience" as his father's heart perforation, so too he sees in Baudelaire's gruesome poem about a rotting corpse the refusal to reject and indeed the laconic imperative of an aesthetic task with a wide scope: "there is no refusal." The close relation between Malte's understanding of Baudelaire's poem and his father's corpse demands a reconsideration of the split between Malte's memory and his Paris experiences; his account of his father's heart perforation and his implication in it is anything but what Huyssen calls "evasions" of the splits and tensions of his Paris stay.[33] If anything, it is an intensification of the breakdown brought on by his urban experiences.

The poetic program outlined in the pages of the Notebooks that discuss Baudelaire shows a development in Rilke's relation to Paris and its outcasts. In a letter to Heinrich Vogeler from September 17, 1902, Rilke writes: "Paris? Paris is difficult. A trial. I cannot even tell you how much everything here is disagreeable to me—nor can I describe the instinctive rejection [Ablehnung] that I feel when I walk around." Rilke's "instinctive rejection" of Paris becomes, in the Notebooks, Malte's insistence that there can be no rejection, no refusal. He now knows that what he flees is "at home" in him.

Love

In Malte's reading of Baudelaire's poem, it becomes possible to discern the shortcomings in critical accounts of the Notebooks as a narrative of formation. Baudelaire's poem "Une charogne" is programmatic in this respect for Malte.[34] After presenting the vermin-infested corpse, the poem seems to turn away from its horror and idealize it. Malte insists on the process of deformation described earlier in the poem and criticizes Baudelaire's attempt to present art as the preservation or memory of form. Malte writes about Baudelaire and "Une charogne": "It was his task to see, in this terrifying and apparently repulsive object, the being that underlies all being" (*Notebooks*, 72). But Malte criticizes what he calls "Baudelaire's incredible poem": "Except for the last stanza, he was in the right" (*Notebooks*, 72). In the last stanza, Baudelaire intensifies the recuperative dimension that was already explicit in the description of the "sketch" of the corpse just cited:

> But as your kisses eat you up
>   my beauty, tell the worms
> I've kept the sacred essence, saved
>   the form of my rotted loves![35]

> Alors, ô ma beauté! dites à la vermine
>   Qui vous mangera de baisers
> Que j'ai gardé la forme et l'essence divine
>   De mes amours decomposés![36]

For Malte, "the being that underlies every being" or "the divine essence" is not form, as Baudelaire might be read to say in these last lines, but decomposition. In the *Notebooks*, the poet's duty is not, as Baudelaire writes, to "[keep] the sacred essence of . . . my rotted loves," but to maintain an intimacy with the process of decay. Malte makes this task explicit as his attention moves, in the same entry, from Baudelaire to Flaubert, whose tale "Saint-Julien-l'hospitalier" Malte brings into relation with "Une charogne": "This, it seems to me, is the test: whether you can bring yourself to lie beside a leper and warm him with the heart-warmth of lovers' nights" (*Notebooks*, 72). Love is thus already implicated here in the relation to the leper, which makes it difficult to argue, as Huyssen does, that Malte's theories of love only appear later in the notebooks as a repression of the relation to the outcasts. In the *Notebooks*, as well as in Rilke's letters and other literary texts, love is only "joyful" insofar as it is a kind of isolation or destitution.[37] A question posed by Beda Allemann is relevant here: "Who knew better than Rilke himself that the term 'love' is not a solution to an artistic problem but, at best, the same problem posed more clearly?"[38]

Love in the *Notebooks* is first of all love for the leper and the outcast. This is even clearer in a more developed reflection on the same concerns in a letter to Clara Rilke from October 19, 1907:

> This lying down beside the leper and sharing all one's own warmth, including the heart warmth of lovers' nights: this must at some point be a part of the artist's existence as the overcoming that allows for a new bliss.

Flaubert made his decision with St. Julien to lie down with the leper, and Rilke, too, "must" go through this identification with Malte as he examines his intimacy with the outcasts. Rilke presents this relation as "love," which means that love is there from the beginning in Malte's exposure to the horrors of urban life and is far from being a hollow, recuperative cliché that would cover up the experience of the city.

Seeing the corpse—both in "Une charogne" and in the scene with Malte's father—is equated with St. Julien's lying with the leper. In the *Notebooks,* "seeing" comes to mean something new:

> I am learning to see. I don't know why it is, but everything enters me more deeply and doesn't stop where it once used to. I have an interior *[ein Inneres]* that I never knew of. Everything passes into it now. I don't know what happens there. (*Notebooks,* 5; *Aufzeichnungen,* 10)

To see is to be penetrated—and to be exposed to something inside the self that Malte did not know about and that, even now, remains unknown except for the fact of its existence. He wonders at the end of his reflection on Baudelaire and Flaubert whether what he has experienced can be communicated: "My God, if only something of this could be shared" (*Notebooks,* 73). This question is present from the beginning of his *Notebooks.* Right after he realizes that he is being changed by what he sees, he expresses a doubt about the possibility of writing about it:

> What's the use of telling someone that I am changing? If I'm changing, I am no longer who I was: and if I am something else, it's obvious that I have no acquaintances. And I can't possibly write to strangers, to people who don't know me [Und an fremde Leute, an Leute, die mich nicht kennen, kann ich unmöglich schreiben]. (*Notebooks,* 5–6; *Aufzeichnungen,* 10–11)

Malte's statement "an fremde Leute . . . kann ich unmöglich schreiben" can be read not just as the idiomatic "I could not possibly write" but also, literally, as "I can write impossibly"—and this would be a good description of the writing that we read in his notebooks. It is impossible because of its refusal to abandon for safer ground the constant, insistent awareness of being-with, being-in-the-world, and being-written. Malte writes from the position of a constant transformation and exposure, and it is impossible for him to write anything more than brief entries in a notebook. This short notebook entry opens with "I am learning to see" and closes with the identification of an impossible writing to which his new kind of vision has exposed him and which allows him, in the later entry on Flaubert and Baudelaire, to write in a way that neither rejects nor idealizes decomposition. The notebooks do not attempt to "keep the sacred essence" of his experiences but, instead, offer an account of the decomposition and emergence of forms of community that first appear in the encounter with the poor.

Facelessness and Whatever Being

Malte's absorption in what he sees changes him in ways that he does not understand, but the incidents of absorption never last very long. The notebook form precludes extended reflection; few entries exceed three pages. The absorption in an event or a person overwhelms Malte, and then the entry breaks off, and the next entry presents yet another episode of absorption. It is as if Malte had replaced other kinds of belonging—national, familial—with a series of episodic absorptions in which he is almost completely drawn into what he sees.[39] Theodore Ziolkowski writes that, in the course of the notebooks, "Malte has been absorbed wholly by the metaphors of his own self. . . . [B]y the end of the notebooks, . . . Malte has vanished behind the projections of himself."[40]

It is important to emphasize how Malte's identity recedes and to show how the notebooks' excesses are inseparable from this impoverishment. The accumulation of events and experiences occurs simultaneously with Malte's replacement of an identity with a form of exposure that approximates the "whatever being" proposed by Giorgio Agamben in his *Coming Community*.[41] In every form of belonging, Agamben argues, there is the fact of belonging itself. Being Catholic, being communist, and being Armenian all assume a being-such (or being-thus) that is a kind of original openness to belonging, similar to Heidegger's being-with: I can only be Armenian because I am exposed in the first place in my being-such to the possibility of being-x and being-y. This being-such follows Heidegger's explication in *Being and Time* of Dasein's existence as its essence, as Agamben insists that the impropriety of being-such should be appropriated and not replaced with the search for a lost propriety or identity.[42] The exemplary coming communitarian in Agamben's text is Robert Walser, but *The Notebooks of Malte Laurids Brigge* shows, with a pathos and fear that are absent in Walser, how Malte works to understand and appropriate his being-such: his exposure to the world, to the outcasts, and to writing.

Being-such appears as being-faceless in the *Notebooks*. In the entry that comes after his declaration that he is learning to see, Malte describes what he is learning to see: faces. According to him, people have a definite number of faces, and, when the supply is exhausted, "the foundation shows through, the non-face" (*Notebooks*, 7). He then presents an incident in which he disturbs a poor woman, who looks up so suddenly that her face remains in her hands while her nonface is exposed. Malte concentrates on the face in her hands, because, he writes, "I shuddered to see a face from the inside, but I was much more afraid of that bare flayed head waiting there, faceless" (*Notebooks*, 7). As the *Notebooks* progress and Malte adopts Baudelaire's task of seeing "that being that underlies every being," Malte increasingly turns his gaze to the nonface. The most brutal example of facelessness comes in the fifty-fifth entry, which centers on Carl the Bold's corpse and its ripped-off face, but the notebooks contain other, less explicit considerations of phenomena that are similar to facelessness.[43] The interest in the nonface is similar to the love for the leper's decomposition.[44] Malte comes to focus on the nonface as what allows for faces to be worn, and his learning to see becomes learning to see the nonface. Walter Sokel describes the nonface not as a mere lack but as an ability to bear a face:

> This real self behind the mask is not an identity, an unchanging substance. Rather it is that which assumes identities. . . . The real self is that which gives rise to identities and then seeks to liberate itself from them.[45]

What Sokel calls the "real self" exceeds every identity and allows for identities to be assumed and discarded. Sokel goes on to call it "the hidden power that shapes the ego as a mask prepared for social uses and destroys it when it has become too confining."[46] For Malte, the nonface eventually loses some of its horror and becomes envisaged positively as the source of transformation. The possibility of an anonymous, faceless writing is posited in the *Notebooks,* but the *Notebooks* is not yet this writing. Malte is not properly a writer, and his writing neither follows the model of true "narration" that belongs to the past nor does it correspond to the frightening "time of the other interpretation."[47] Instead, Malte occupies a middle position. He is an exposed nonwriter engaged in an impossible writing that is caught between a lost propriety and a future impropriety.[48]

Malte's writing becomes increasingly bound to the nonface of the outcasts. Instead of attempting to avoid or overcome the "failed formation" that Hoffman sees in the outcasts, Malte attempts to appropriate their failure for himself. What attracts Malte to the outcasts is precisely the formlessness that leads Hoffmann to consider them as mere steppingstones on Malte's path to formation. Malte sees their inability to be presented as a kind of ability—the ability not to have a face, not to be formed, and to acknowledge a relation based on impropriety and not on identity.

St. Francis

One of the possible sources for describing, in Rilke's own vocabulary, the improper bond based on exposure would be his admiration for St. Francis. More than the other authors treated in this study, Rilke's texts demonstrate a sustained interest in the figures and doctrine of the Franciscans. The fact of Rilke's debt to the Franciscan tradition has been established: Rilke made several trips to Assisi, admired Paul Sabatier's biography of St. Francis, and often read the *Fioretti* and other texts from the Franciscan tradition.[49] Rilke's interest belongs to a wider nineteenth-century German revival of Franciscanism, which included new translations of Franciscan poems, starting in 1842 with J. F. H. Schlosser's edition.[50] The first modern German biography of St. Francis was published in 1840, and Francis was for many nineteenth-century German poets the "Orpheus of the Middle Ages."[51] Furio Jesi calls St. Francis a "recurrent topos of so-called European decadent literature, to the point that it causes one of Huxley's characters to complain."[52] This revival had effects long into the twentieth century. Hermann Hesse's engagement with Franciscanism, for example, can be seen in *Peter Camenzind,* the story "The Beggar," and, of course, "From the Childhood of Saint Francis of Assisi."[53] In the Dada Manifesto of 1918, the "true Dadaist" is "half Pantagruel and half Francis." In 1929, Hofmannsthal was buried, according to his wishes, in a Franciscan habit, and, in the 1920s, Heimito von Doderer planned a book on St. Francis and chose him as his patron saint when he converted to Catholicism in 1940.[54]

In *The Notebooks of Malte Laurids Brigge,* the outcasts are depicted in the traditional Franciscan activity of feeding the birds, and the thought of St. Francis is inseparable in the text from the ideal of fraternity (*Notebooks,* 78–79). Malte's connection to the outcasts responds to the Franciscan imperative to be similar to "vile and dejected persons, the poor and the weak, the sick, the leprous, beggars and vagabonds."[55] As in the Franciscan concept of fraternity, Malte's new bond with the outcasts is accompanied by the dissolution of other bonds.[56] Despite these similarities, it would be difficult to argue for a Franciscan Malte. Unlike the Franciscans, Rilke does not present the community of outcasts as a new "family" bound by a mission. In the *Notebooks,* the poor are abandoned by Christ: "I think only Jesus could endure them, who still has resurrection in all his limbs; but he can't be bothered with them" (*Notebooks,* 214). The critique of Christianity in the *Notebooks* (and in *The Book of Hours*) claims that Christ intervenes in the relation between God and humanity and makes the relation to the divine more difficult because of a deceptive intimacy with humanity (*Notebooks,* 250). The suggestion of a community based on Franciscan ideals is accompanied by the critique of much of the foundation of a Franciscan community. Rilke's Franciscanism can be seen in the refusal to turn away; the imperative of community, too, is Franciscan for Rilke, even if the principles that organize it are not.

Malte's Indifferent Writing

The relation between Malte and the outcasts is paradigmatic for relation in general in the *Notebooks.* The similarity and distance that join and separate Malte and the Parisian poor also characterize the relation between the notebook entries. What links the many entries together, especially in the second part, is a similarity between certain figures: Carl the Bold, the teacher who translates Sappho, "the lonely one," "the false czar," the neighbor. They are similar to Malte, but, like the attributes given to the poor in "The Book of Poverty and Death," these figures in Malte's notebooks are also distanced from him.

The final entry of the *Notebooks* retells the parable of the Prodigal Son. In Rilke's version, the son leaves home to escape his family and their love, which he experiences as the fixation of an identity that suppresses the freedom of facelessness. The son is similar to the outcasts: he lives in abject conditions after he spends his inheritance, and "poverty terrified him every day with new hardships" (*Notebooks*, 255). Like the poor in "The Book of Poverty and Death," whose qualities include being "lost," the Prodigal Son's epithet in German is *der verlorene Sohn* ("the lost son"). Like the poor of *The Book of Hours*, he is almost anonymous. He seeks what Malte calls "inner indifference" *(innige Indifferenz)* or the indistinction that allows him distance from his family and the identity that they would impose on him (*Notebooks*, 251; *Aufzeichnungen*, 195). He first does this in his brief afternoon excursions away from the house, but he must definitively leave home to achieve a more complete anonymity, to avoid the "shame of having a face" and to feel "general and anonymous" (*Notebooks*, 255–56).

Malte's Prodigal Son wants to love and not be loved; he serves as the example for the theory of love developed in the second part of the *Notebooks,* in which love is impoverished and stripped of its object. The notebooks' entries on such an intransitive love develop earlier passages on facelessness, and the parable of the Prodigal Son presents Malte's final attempt to understand or occupy the place of the outcast. The estrangement of attribution and identity in *The Book of Hours* and the rest of the *Notebooks* is complemented in the retelling of the parable by a distancing from narration. After a list of strangers' accounts and possible stories about the Prodigal Son, the narrator asks how the story should be told and then answers the question:

> Strangers saw him on the Acropolis, and perhaps for many years he was one of the shepherds in Les Baux. . . . Or should I imagine him at Orange, resting

against the rustic triumphal arch? Should I see him in the soul-inhabited shade of Alyscamps where, among the tombs that lie open as the tombs of the resurrected, his glance chases a dragonfly?

It doesn't matter. I see more than him: I see his whole existence, which was then beginning its long love toward God, that silent work undertaken without thought of ever reaching its goal. (*Notebooks*, 256–57)

The parable of the Prodigal Son appears in this passage as a hypothetical series of events that are inessential to the son's "silent work," which I will discuss in a moment.[57] A similar suspension of the parable takes place in Malte's interpretation of the gesture made by the Prodigal Son when he returns to his family:

It is easy to understand how, of everything that happened then, only this has been handed down to us: his gesture, the incredible gesture which had never been seen before, the gesture of supplication with which he threw himself at their feet, imploring them not to love. . . . They interpreted his vehemence *[sein Ungestüm]* in their own way, forgiving him. (*Notebooks*, 259–60; *Aufzeichnungen*, 201)[58]

Malte disagrees with the interpretation of the gesture as a request for forgiveness. He offers his own interpretation and, at the same time, presents the gesture's resistance to interpretation, its *Ungestüm*, which means "violence" or "vehemence" and can characterize a movement with or without a goal.[59]

It is this vehemence that causes Ernst Fedor Hoffmann to exclude from his analysis the first third of Malte, "with its vehement, almost hectic experiments" (mit seinen ungestümen, fast überstürzten Versuchen). We can see here that vehemence plays a central role even at the end of the *Notebooks,* in the episode in which, according to Hoffmann, Malte's process of formation overcomes his disturbing Paris experiences. Malte insists on the violence of the Prodigal Son's gesture even as he interprets it, just as he narrates the parable while simultaneously distancing himself from narration and just as his notebooks could be thought of as exactly that writing to strangers that would be impossible.

These estrangements are among the effects of Malte's rethinking of identity and community, and the final form that this distance takes in the *Notebooks* can be found at the center of the retelling of the parable of the Prodigal Son, as Malte relates in an extended simile how the Prodigal Son learns to love:

> He was like someone who hears a glorious language and feverishly decides to write poetry in it. Before long he would, to his dismay, find out how very difficult this language was; at first he was unwilling to believe that a person might spend a whole life putting together the first, short sham sentences without meaning. He threw himself into this learning like a runner into a race; but the density of what had to be mastered slowed him down. It would be hard to imagine anything more humiliating than this apprenticeship. (*Notebooks*, 257)

> Er war wie einer, der eine herrliche Sprache hört und fiebernd sich vornimmt, in ihr zu dichten. Noch stand ihm die Bestürzung bevor, zu erfahren, wie schwer diese Sprache sei; er wollte es nicht glauben zuerst, daß ein langes Leben darüber hingehen könne, die ersten, kurzen Scheinsätze zu bilden, die ohne Sinn sind. Er stürzte sich ins Erlernen wie ein Läufer in die Wette; aber die Dichte dessen, was zu überwinden war, verlangsamte ihn. Es war nichts auszudenken, was demütigender sein könnte als diese Anfängerschaft. (*Aufzeichnungen*, 199)

This is his silent work. The Prodigal Son is "like someone who hears a glorious language," and this "someone" *(einer)* is at first distinct from the Prodigal Son, but the continuation of the sentence speaks of the difficulty of learning this new language as if it were the Prodigal Son's activity, whereas it should be, strictly speaking, the work of the vehicle, the impersonal "someone" of the simile. There is no clean break between the vehicle and the tenor of the simile, and the Prodigal Son achieves his goal of "inner indifference" and becomes, for a moment at least, indistinct from the masculine, impersonal "someone."

This is a crucial moment for my reading of Rilke, because it brings together chapter 5's thesis of an impoverishing simile in "The Book of Poverty and Death" and the reading of an impoverished bond with the poor in the *Notebooks*. In this simile used to describe (and estrange) the Prodigal Son, there emerges a moment in which the Prodigal Son is indistinguishable from "someone." In this moment of indistinction, a "marvelous language" appears. The parable *(Gleichnis)* of the Prodigal Son becomes the occasion for a simile *(Gleichnis)* that simultaneously allows for the Prodigal Son's striving for indifference and the emergence of a new kind of language that is impoverished, because, in it, one can only write "short sham sentences without meaning." Malte's *Notebooks,* which begin as the project of depicting his encounter with the Parisian poor, closes with this brief hypothesis of a new language that still has to be learned but that already appears as a language in which "someone" indistinguishable from and yet not identical to the Prodigal Son decides to write. This is the final formulation of Malte's hypothetical, impossible language.

Like Malte, the Prodigal Son is distant from the many personae he assumes in his childhood games as well as in his adult search for anonymity. Like Nietzsche's virtue of the richest poverty, the poverty of Malte and the Prodigal Son allows for a masquerade that estranges its masks, an indifference that appears in Malte's reduction in the book's second part to little more than a being-exposed or being-such, amid an excess of shifting personae. The irreconcilable elements that Andreas Huyssen saw in the urban poor have not been repressed in the second part of *The Notebooks of Malte Laurids Brigge.* Instead, they have taken on new forms in the Prodigal Son's indifference as well as in the violence of his misinterpreted gesture. In Malte's retelling of the parable, the Prodigal Son's linguistic abilities are reduced to creating a misinterpreted gesture and, in an unstable simile within a parable, writing sham sentences in a foreign language.

Who speaks in these forms of speech? Malte shows that, in the gesture and in his learning to love and to write, it is the inner indifference that speaks. It drives him to escape from his family and then to return to them; it determines his actions and the course of the parable. At the same time, indifference alienates the Prodigal Son from who he is; it seizes him "with such purity that he had to start running, in order to have no time or breath to be more than a weightless moment in which the morning becomes conscious of itself" (*Notebooks,* 251–52). In the Prodigal Son and in his future language, what is most proper and most improper coincide, and in this way he is exemplary for Rilke's presentation of poverty.

Rilke's Untimely Modernity

My reading of *The Notebooks of Malte Laurids Brigge* opened with a consideration of two critics' assessments of the threat posed to Malte by the outcasts. Malte's experiences in Paris, and especially his encounters with the outcasts, result in the unraveling of his relations to his past, his family, his identity, and his writing, and the awareness of a bond with the outcasts emerges simultaneously with the dissolution of these other ties. In his *Notebooks,* Malte's attention to the outcasts estranges him from every form and every identity; like the Prodigal Son, Malte's impossible writing and Malte himself become marked by indifference, an inability to be and to write as merely oneself.[60] This indifference appears as the potential to assume personae and to become anonymous. It is the place of intersection of the Prodigal Son and "someone" else, and in this way it is similar to Baudelaire's incognito, the impoverished speech of the *The Birth of Tragedy* and the *Dionysus Dithyrambs* as well as the virtual language of Mallarmé. In the Prodigal Son's indifference we can hear Zarathustra's cry "Oh, is it *my* word? Who am I?" and Mallarmé's insistence on "the elocutionary disappearance of the poet." Rilke's similarity to Nietzsche and Mallarmé makes the exclusion of the second part of the *Notebooks* from "modern prose" by Andreas Huyssen as well as Rilke's omission from Hugo Friedrich's once canonical *Structure of Modern Poetry* surprising.

The proper response to Rilke's exclusion from modern poetry or modern prose may not be the reactive insistence that Rilke *is* modern after all but, perhaps, the emphasis on Rilke's withdrawal from what is merely modern. In Rilke's writing, the simultaneity of modernity and a retreat from modernity can be read in such dissonances as the contrast of the modern city of Paris with the figure of St. Francis as well as the meeting of Malte's aristocratic Danish past with the bleak, anonymous present of his Paris experiences. The centrality of the beggar, too, is a sign of Rilke's untimeliness.[61] This heterogeneity has long posed problems for his readers. Rilke's contemporaries who found in *The Book of Hours* the work of a great devotional poet were disturbed by the "psychopathology" of the *Notebooks,* and readers of the novel are at a loss when it comes to *The Book of Hours* and its religious content.[62] Many Rilke readers attempt to take account of such dissonances by creating a "good" and a "bad" Rilke. Reinhold Grimm's reading of Rilke's relation to the poor concludes with the decision that his poetry aestheticizes the poor while his prose represents a faithful engagement with their plight.[63] Paul de Man's reading of Rilke in *Allegories of Reading* separates out "messianic" and "demystifying" dimensions in Rilke's poetry, and Heidegger asserts that, among Rilke's collections of poetry, only the *Duino Elegies* and *The Sonnets to Orpheus* are "valid" *(gültig)*.[64] For Blanchot in *The Space of Literature*, the good, later Rilke denies the possibility of a death that could be mastered, while the bad, early Rilke insists on such a death.[65] But Blanchot himself, in the same book, argues for the ambiguity of the call for a proper death in the early Rilke and insists that "Rilke's experience . . . enlightens us in spite of him, as if through the mediation of his reassuring intentions it continued to speak to us in the harsh original language."[66] There seems to be something irresistible about dividing Rilke into a good and a bad poet, even for critics such as de Man and Blanchot who show that the division runs within Rilke's poetry at every point and not between his early and later work.

Such separations of Rilke's poetry continue to have effects and sympathetic readers, who repeat the neat separation of Rilke's work into "valid" and "invalid."[67] These critical reactions, as well as those of Spitzer, Benn, Por, Hoffmann, and Huyssen analyzed in the preceding two chapters, can be read as symptoms of something in Rilke's writing that is untimely and thus disturbing for the history and theory of literature.[68] Rilke himself singles out *The Book of Hours* as particularly untimely, describing it as "impossible to date, even if it belongs to the works of my youth" and as "not occupying a place in the series of my productions so much as standing facing them."[69] The *Duino Elegies*, some of which were written twenty years after *The Book of Hours*, are, according to Rilke, "a further elaboration of those essential presuppositions that were already given in *The Book of Hours*."[70]

Rilke poses a challenge to literary history. This challenge, along with the "great luster" and "indifference" of his writing, brings to mind the "haze" and "clear sudden light" *(heller, blitzender Lichtschein)* of the "unhistorical" in Nietzsche's "On the Use and Disadvantage of History for Life."[71] For Nietzsche, the haze of the unhistorical remains within historical consciousness as the possibility of any historical action and the overcoming of a merely historical consciousness. For Rilke, the luster or indifference of poverty appears within literary language as a marker for resistance against every form of propriety and identity—a resistance that is often interpreted as anachronistic instead of untimely.

Exposed Interiors and the Poverty of Experience

Barbarians

In 1933, when Benjamin declares, "We have become poor," he means to give nothing less than a summary account of life in the young twentieth century: trench warfare, the traumatic experience of the metropolis, new forms of mass-produced art, devastating inflation, and the disintegration of traditional concepts of humanity and culture.[1] For Benjamin, the most urgent task for the artist or writer of his day is the recognition of "how poor he is and how poor he has to be in order to begin again from the beginning."[2] Poverty is double here: it is a state that must be recognized and that remains to be realized. It also appears as a means to an end: beginning over.

This call to adopt poverty responds to a historical condition and demands its appropriation, following a Brechtian maxim cited by Benjamin: "Take your cue not from the good old things but from the bad new ones."[3] To come to terms with a bad, new poverty, Benjamin proposes a concept, the "poverty of experience," to differentiate his poverty from other forms of poverty.

Aspects of the poverty of experience can be seen at work in the Benjaminian notions of reproducibility, citation, and the loss of aura. Although not as well known as these other concepts, the concept is central to Benjamin's writings in the 1920s and 1930s. Besides its prominence in the programmatic essay "Experience and Poverty," the poverty of experience assumes various forms and different names in the *Arcades Project*—"Surrealism," "The Storyteller," "The Destructive Character," "The Author as Producer"—as well as in the essays on Brecht and Karl

Kraus. A more general concern with poverty also appears in earlier Benjamin texts, especially in *One-Way Street,* and Benjamin even records that the first text that he wrote "for himself" was about poverty.[4]

"This, of course, is not Maeterlinck's mystical view of poverty," Benjamin states. "Nor is it the Franciscan poverty that Rilke has in mind when he writes, 'For poverty is a great light from within.'"[5] This distancing of Brecht from Rilke and Maeterlinck seems superfluous, because it is hard to imagine that these authors would ever be confused. But Benjamin's intention is not merely to distinguish the poverty of experience from two other writers' notions of poverty. In the essay "Experience and Poverty," he makes clear that he means for the poverty of experience to supplant an entire tradition of thinking about poverty: "our poverty of experience is just a part of that great poverty that has once again acquired a face—a face of the same sharpness and precision as that of a beggar in the Middle Ages."[6] This sentence is crucial for understanding the place of Benjamin's writings on the poverty of experience in the modern canon of texts about poverty. For Benjamin, the poverty of experience replaces the traditional figure of the beggar, and the formulation of this claim implicitly divides poverty into a series of "faces" and a faceless, "great poverty."

The texts examined in the previous chapters reveal a general tendency toward a retreat of the thematic face of poverty: from Baudelaire's beggars to Mallarmé's, from Mallarmé's to Rilke's, and, within the Rilkean corpus, from the urban poor of "The Book of Poverty and Death" to the outcast and the Prodigal Son in *The Notebooks of Malte Laurids Brigge.* In all these cases, thematic poverty serves as a starting point for authors to investigate potential, because, I argued, the nineteenth century understood the poor to be the embodiment of power and powerlessness in the capitalist process of production. The beggar's face never failed to appear, even if it was unrepresentative of poverty in an epoch of industrialization. Benjamin recognizes this untimeliness of the beggar, and his replacement of the beggar's obstinate face seems to require an explicit distancing from it. My task in this chapter will be to examine poverty's new face and to determine its relation to earlier forms of poverty.

Benjamin uses his new concept to discuss such figures as Kraus, Paul Scheerbart, Adolf Loos, and Paul Klee, all of whom appear as escaping survivors of European culture's downfall in the fragment from Benjamin's *Nachlaß* that I briefly discussed in the introduction and that will serve as our entryway into the poverty of experience:

> One must read Paul Scheerbart and, above all, hear his people speaking in order to understand how ornamental our speech is when compared to the stellar Esperanto of his Peka, Labu, and Sofanti; one must imagine along with Bert Brecht the poverty of Herr Keuner—"The thinker does not use one thought too many"—and have glanced with Paul Klee at the clawed feet of Angelus Novus (that angel of prey who prefers to liberate humanity by taking from it rather than to make it happy by giving to it) in order to imagine how the ship carrying them set sail, bringing these emigrants away from the Europe of Humanism into the promised land of cannibalism {In any case we know the ship's name—*Poverty*—and that Karl Kraus is the best hidden stowaway on board}. Scheerbart and Ringelnatz, Loos and Klee, Brecht and S. Friedländer—they all push off from old shores, from the excessively wealthy temples full of images of man solemnly bedecked in sacrificial offerings, so as to turn toward their naked contemporary who lies crying like a newborn in the dirty diapers of this age. What ultimately inspires this crew is the awareness that the establishment of an order *[Einrichtung]* for human existence according to the intensification of production, the improved distribution of consumer goods, and the socialization of the means of production demands more than, and something other than, a cozy doctrine of global delight—that to go along with this intensification of needs there is a corresponding ascetic attitude.[7]

From this presentation of the ship *Poverty* and its exiled passengers, a preliminary sketch of Benjamin's notion of poverty can be made. It includes speech without ornament, minimalist thinking, the abandonment of every inherited conception of humanity, attention to the barrenness of one's contemporaries, and an ascetic attitude that is adopted with a certain telos in mind: a new conception of humanity and culture. In the essay "Experience and Poverty," this destination appears under the term "barbarism," not cannibalism:

> Barbarism? Yes, indeed. We say this in order to introduce a new, positive concept of barbarism. For what does poverty of experience do for the barbarian? It forces him to start from scratch; to make a new start; to make a little go a long way; to begin with a little and build up further. . . . Among the great creative spirits, there have always been the inexorable ones who begin by clearing a tabula rasa.[8]

The new barbarism begins by razing, by creating a tabula rasa, on which not creation but "construction" will take place. In this passage, the new beginning and the tabula rasa are not absolute; this new barbarism begins with "little" but not nothing. Like Nietzsche, he eschews total impoverishment; like the Prodigal Son with his sham sentences, Benjamin's poor start out not with nothing but with a little something.

For Benjamin, clearing the table is the appropriate response to the epoch or, as the preceding passage has it, to one's "naked contemporary." Instead of adopting the consoling or memorializing stances toward World War I common in the postwar years, impoverished artists attempt to take account of (and not recuperate) what was definitively lost.[9] In "Experience and Poverty," the exemplary naked fellow man is the soldier in the trenches of World War I, who stood in the middle of a changed landscape "in which nothing was the same except the clouds and, at its center, in a force field of destructive torrents and explosions, the tiny, fragile human body."[10] Humanity's fragility appears most strikingly on the battlefield and in its experiential and linguistic wake: "Wasn't it noticed at the time how many people returned from the front in silence? Not richer but poorer in communicable experience?"[11] Benjamin insists here on the linguistic nature of the poverty of experience: the soldier returns not with less experience but with less "communicable experience," a fact whose most convincing theorization Benjamin finds in Freud's theory of trauma.[12] This *mal de langage,* as Jean Paulhan calls the muteness of shell-shocked soldiers, appears to Benjamin as a sign of a more general impoverishment.[13] Unable to come to terms with the technological and economic forces that, in the space of a few decades, irrevocably changed human experience, the sole response was a kind of silence, whose explication Benjamin undertakes in his writings from the 1930s.

His texts on the poverty of experience register a retreat from the traditional figures of poverty and, often, from the very term "poverty." The fragment on the ship *Poverty* also reveals a key difference between Benjamin's conception of Baudelaire and his reading of these twentieth-century figures. Chapter 2 showed how, in "The Paris of the Second Empire in Baudelaire," the ship appears as a key metaphor in Baudelaire, and Benjamin compares it to the dandy. But the ship does not leave harbor, just as the modern heroic figure of the dandy is cursed with the nonenactment of his potential, "an out-of-work Hercules."[14] Modernity "moors him fast in the secure harbor forever and abandons him to everlasting idleness."[15] The ship in the fragment is no longer this ship of modernity, because it sets sail for a new world, one that Benjamin initially understands in terms offered by discourses on poverty but that he presents in a different way. In the fragment, Benjamin eventually strikes the sentence in brackets in which he christens the ship *Poverty.* His texts reveal a tendency toward the erasure of the tie to poverty, possibly because even the mention of the word "poverty" recalls the traditional face of the beggar, which can easily distract from the potential inherent in the greater poverty. One can only wonder what other Benjamin texts once included the term "poverty."

This chapter will address those of Benjamin's texts that present two kinds of impoverishment: the exposure of the nineteenth-century bourgeois interior by glass architecture and the reduction of the dramatic and poetic subject in Brecht. Besides presenting the poverty of experience as a conclusion to a certain modern tradition, it will offer a reading of Benjamin's dispersed remarks on poverty with the aim of opening up new perspectives on the authors that Benjamin discusses (especially Scheerbart and Brecht) and on Benjaminian notions that are related to the poverty of experience, such as his conception of the interior and Jugendstil in the *Arcades Project* and that of quotability in his essays on Brecht and Kraus.

Aura's Last Refuge

In Benjamin's writings, glass architecture often serves as an emblem for the "new poverty," because it signals the end of privacy and property, which, he claims, the nineteenth-century interior attempted to defend. Benjamin mentions Le Corbusier, Scheerbart, and Loos as exemplary architects and theorists of a new humanity that would inhabit transparent buildings in a new way: "The twentieth century, with its porosity and transparency, its tendency toward the well-lit and airy, has put an end to dwelling in the old sense."[16] "One must make transparent the interior's social function and expose the illusion of its closure," Adorno writes in a letter to Benjamin, articulating a shared theoretical goal as well as stating the effect of glass architecture.[17] The porosity of twentieth-century architecture exposes the intimacy of interior and exterior, an interdependence that, according to Benjamin, the nineteenth-century interior attempts to conceal.

What, in Benjamin's terms, is the interior? As he presents it in the exposés of the *Arcades Project*, the Parisian bourgeois interior is a symptom of Hausmannization, which made Parisians "no longer feel at home in [the city], and start to become conscious of the inhuman character of the metropolis."[18] As the city began to seem more and more inhuman, the interior takes on an increasingly important role:

> Ever since the time of Louis Philippe, the bourgeois has shown a tendency to compensate for the absence of any trace of private life in the big city. He tries to do this within the four walls of his apartment. It is as if he had made it a point of honor not to allow the traces of his everyday objects and accessories to get lost. . . . He has a marked preference for velour and plush, which preserve the imprint of all contact.[19]

The bourgeois attempts to make up for the loss of a human relation to the city by accumulating signs of humanity in the only place where it was still possible: the home, which gains its definition from its opposition to the street and to the office:

> For the private individual, the place of dwelling is for the first time opposed to the place of work. The former constitutes itself as the interior. Its complement is the office. The private individual, who in the office has to deal with reality, needs the domestic interior to sustain him in his illusions. This necessity is all the more pressing since he has no intention of allowing his commercial considerations to impinge on his social ones. In the formation of his private environment, both are kept out. From this arise the phantasmagorias of the interior—which, for the private man, represents the universe. In the interior, he brings together the far away and the long ago. His living room is a box in the theater of the world.[20]

The private man protects himself in his home and reinforces the difference that Marx analyzes in "On the Jewish Question" between *citoyen* and *homme*. Instead of working toward the emancipatory goal of the unification of the "abstract citizen" and "individual human," the bourgeoisie, in Benjamin's interpretation, reinforces this separation.[21] In its apparent enclosure, the bourgeois interior assumes a metaphorical function, since it aims to stand in for the world and to create the illusion that it contains everything: thus its phantasmagoric character and Benjamin's exposition of how "the nineteenth-century interior is . . . a stimulus to intoxication and dream."[22] The bourgeois dream of completion in its interior parodies the emancipatory image of a complete humanity in Marx.

These characteristics—cloistered, metaphorical, phantasmagoric—make the interior the ideal habitat for the collector, who can "dress up" his rooms to give them the appearance of including the whole world as well as all of history:

> Nineteenth-century interior. Space disguises itself—puts on, like an alluring creature, the costumes of moods. The self-satisfied burgher should know something of the feeling that the next room might have witnessed the coronation of Charlemagne as well as the assassination of Henri IV, the signing of the treaty of Verdun as well as the wedding of Otto and Theophano.[23]

Besides staging this production that brings the outside inside in the form of an illusion and the past into the present as a fantasized masquerade, the collector attempts to transform the objects that share the interior with him:

> He makes his concern the transfiguration of things. To him falls the Sisyphean task of divesting things of their commodity character by taking possession of them. But he bestows on them only connoisseur value, rather than use value. The collector dreams his way not only into a distant or bygone world but also into a better one—one in which, to be sure, human beings are no better provided with what they need than in the everyday world, but in which things are freed from the drudgery of being useful.[24]

The attempt to make every object into a work of art and to free the object from its exchange value only removes its use value. The collector dreams of a utopia for his objects but not for humanity. Just as the "private man" seeks asylum in his home, so too a specific, auratic understanding of art finds in the interior its last "place of refuge."[25]

Glass Architecture

Aura, in Benjamin's classic definition, is the "unique apparition of a distance, however near it may be."[26] Besides being characterized by this juxtaposition of intimacy and distance, Benjamin presents aura as an anthropomorphizing figure:

> Inherent in the gaze . . . is the expectation that it will be returned by that on which it is bestowed. Where this expectation is met . . . , there is an experience of the aura in all its fullness. . . . To experience the aura of an object we look at means to invest it with the ability to look back at us.[27]

Benjamin conceives of the auratic relation as a "transposition" of a "response characteristic of human relationships" to "the relationship between humans and inanimate or natural objects."[28] To have an aura means to return the gaze and thus implies the fantasy of a humanized object. This definition is a variation on the classical definition of prosopopeia, which endows an absent or dead person with the ability to speak. Prosopopeia, as my discussion of Mallarmé in chapter 3 showed, bestows both a face and facelessness, because a face can only be given to that which lacks one.

The loss of aura would mean that the object could no longer be considered invested with human characteristics. The inhabitant of the Benjaminian interior attempts to humanize the art object and emphasizes the anthropomorphic force of prosopopeia while attempting to ignore the inhuman muteness or facelessness that anthropomorphism and thus the aura always also imply. The inhumanity of the aura is projected away from the object upon an exterior that has to be kept at bay so as to maintain, in isolation, the humanized aspect of aura, and this defense of the interior against the intrusion of the inhuman city can be detected in the apparent "fortification" of homes and even individual objects.[29]

Benjamin's analysis of the interior makes explicit the dependence of the human inside and the inhuman outside as well as the strategies that were used to obscure their relation. His theoretical efforts to unveil the social function of the nineteenth-century interior correspond to glass architecture's exposure of that same space, because glass makes explicit and visible the relations between outside and inside that were occulted in the nineteenth century by the interior's fortification.[30] The most concise articulation of Benjamin's understanding of glass architecture occurs in "Experience and Poverty":

> It is no coincidence that glass is such a hard, smooth material to which nothing can be fixed. A cold and sober material into the bargain. Objects made of glass have no "aura." It is the enemy of possession in general. . . . Do people like Scheerbart dream of glass buildings because they are the spokesmen of a new poverty?[31]

Unlike the interior, in which everything is marked as belonging to its owner, glass does not allow for traces to be left on it. It is the opposite of plush. The interior of a glass building cannot serve as a metaphor for the outside, because glass walls do not separate them sufficiently into two distinct spaces, and the constant confrontation with the exterior bans any illusory independence of the interior. Instead of a metaphorical relation to the outside, glass architecture creates a relation of contiguity and similarity, because glass opens up a new space that is both inside and outside instead of attempting to separate the interior from the exterior.

By creating a transparent barrier, glass contests property and the division of interior and exterior in a specific manner that Massimo Cacciari, commenting on Benjamin's praise of "glass culture," describes as follows:

> Only indirectly is glass opposed to possession. The fundamental reason behind its *Kultur* lies in opposing the existence of a place in which the thing (the collected) might be for the individual an inalienable experience. Hence glass does not oppose possession per se, but the idea of an inalienable possession.[32]

The impoverishment brought about by glass architecture remains potential, because it does not actually deliver the interior over to the exterior. The predominance of glass does not lead to complete dispossession but only to the estrangement from the idea of inalienable property. Cacciari's refusal here to bestow a more absolute force on glass architecture must be emphasized so as to dispute the continuation of his own text:

> By showing, producing, manifesting all possession, glass would have it exist only as money, on the market. . . . In spite of its avant-garde pose, which rejects the paternal language and opposes its presumed organicity with the arbitrary and the freely constructive, *Glaskultur* belongs to a perfectly logocentric civilization. Its will to render transparent, to lay bare, to demystify, expresses a utopia that fully and progressively identifies the human with the linguistic:

every secret must be spoken aloud, every interior made manifest, every childhood pro-duced.[33]

In these sentences, Cacciari presents a critique of glass architecture as naively utopian, as the fantasy of pure transparency, but such a complete exposure implies the absence of the glass building itself. Glass buildings are still buildings, and their walls protect at the same time that they expose. Turning away from his position cited earlier, Cacciari's reading here ignores the medial character of glass, because he sees glass architecture as the wish for the destruction of barriers and difference.

Benjamin emphasizes the potential nature of the impoverishment that Cacciari initially points out and that corresponds to what Benjamin calls a "threshold experience" in some of his first notes for the *Arcades Project:*

> The threshold [*Schwelle*] is a *zone.* And indeed a zone of transition. Transformation, passage, flight are in the word "swell" [*schwellen*], and etymology ought not to overlook these senses. On the other hand, it is necessary to keep in mind the immediate tectonic framework that has brought the word to its current meaning. We have grown very poor in threshold experiences.[34]

The exemplary threshold experiences for Benjamin are those of the arcades, the Proustian "falling asleep," boredom,[35] the dream, and Kraus's "night watch."[36] To these experiences, we should add that of "living under glass," in this zone in which the inside is exposed to the outside. Glass architecture reduces the interior but does not eradicate it. The new poor "have to adapt [*einzurichten*]—beginning anew and with few resources," Benjamin writes, and the use of the term *einrichten*—"to furnish" or "to arrange"—to designate impoverished existence here indicates the survival of the interior, even if only as a "few resources."[37]

In "Experience and Poverty," glass does not erase all traces in favor of a pure transparency; it only makes it "hard to leave traces."[38] By stressing the ways in which Benjamin distances his conception of poverty from an absolute position, such as the understanding of glass architecture criticized by Cacciari, it is possible to discern the outlines of an impoverished transition zone, much like the ship *Poverty.* Glass opens up the interior without destroying it.

Habit Production in Scheerbart and Brecht

In "Experience and Poverty," Paul Scheerbart occupies the position of the herald of the new age marked by "glass culture," but his 1914 book *Glasarchitektur* is more than a simple panegyric of the kind of glass architecture that Benjamin proposes in his writings on poverty.[39] The glass walls that Scheerbart proposes would be made of colored glass, which he compares to Tiffany lampshades.[40] This comparison, as well as his praise for the "stylization" of plants and stars, moves Scheerbart closer to Jugendstil or art nouveau, in which Benjamin sees the last attempt to defend aura and the interior and, at the same time, their destruction: "The shattering of the interior occurs in Jugendstil around the turn of the century. Of course, according to its own ideology, the Jugendstil movement seems to bring with it the consummation of the interior."[41]

This doubleness can be seen quite clearly in Scheerbart's *Glass Architecture*. For Scheerbart, glass is far from being the end of ornament, as Benjamin seems to suggest in his bringing together in "Experience and Poverty" of Scheerbart and Loos (whose best-known essay is "Ornament and Crime").[42] But this intimacy with ornament does not keep Scheerbart from proclaiming an end to the closed interior:

> If we want our culture to rise to a higher level, we are obliged, for better or
> for worse, to change our architecture. And this only becomes possible if we take
> away the closed character *[das Geschlossene]* from the rooms in which we live.[43]

This passage contains a phrase that is central to Benjamin's analysis of glass architecture and his interpretation of the nineteenth-century interior: removing the "closed character" or *das Geschlossene,* a phrase almost identical to Adorno's in his letter to Benjamin cited earlier. By showing its dependence on changes in the city and its effect on its inhabitants, the interior loses its isolated character. Glass appears in Scheerbart as both the embellishment and undoing of the interior.[44]

Jugendstil contains opposed forces, and glass architecture develops its destructive tendency. Living under glass opens up the interior to something else and signals a readiness to be liberated or robbed. In "Experience and Poverty," Benjamin cites a Brecht refrain in his discussion of the effects of glass architecture:

A neat phrase by Brecht helps us out here: "Erase the traces!" is the refrain in the first poem of his *Reader for City Dwellers*. . . . This has now been achieved by Scheerbart, with his glass, and by the Bauhaus, with its steel. They have created rooms in which it is hard to leave traces.[45]

For Benjamin, Scheerbart and the Bauhaus carry out a command issued by Brecht; they create spaces in which Brecht's refrain can easily be carried out. "Erase the traces!" is the most frequent Brecht citation in Benjamin's writings on the poverty of experience, and its use of the term "trace" shows how closely Benjamin's theory of glass architecture belongs together with his readings of Brecht. Gershom Scholem recalls a conversation in which Benjamin spoke of Brecht as the writer "who is completing what Scheerbart started so well."[46]

For Benjamin, Brecht's writing shares with architecture a kind of reception different from contemplation: habit, whose architectural variant Benjamin presents in "The Work of Art in the Age of Its Mechanical Reproducibility":

Buildings are received in a twofold manner: by use and by perception. Or, better: tactilely and optically. Such reception cannot be understood in terms of the concentrated attention of a traveler before a famous building. On the tactile side, there is no counterpart to what contemplation is on the optical side. Tactile reception comes about not so much by way of attention as by way of habit. The latter largely determines even the optical reception of architecture, which spontaneously takes the form of casual noticing, rather than attentive observation. . . . *For the tasks which face the human apparatus of perception at historical turning points cannot be performed solely by optical means—that is, by way of contemplation. They are mastered gradually— taking their cue from tactile reception—through habit.*[47]

Benjamin formulates the difference between contemplation and habit as the difference between an "attentive taking notice" *(Aufmerken)* and a "casual notice" *(Bemerken),* and he opposes the specific kind of "living" reception of architecture to the collected contemplation of buildings by tourists. "Dwelling" *(wohnen)* allows for "habituation" *(Gewöhnung),* a kind of relation to art that is not contemplative, and this appropriation of a new habit becomes Benjamin's privileged model for the reception of new kinds of art and the development of new kinds of perception demanded by political and technological transformations.

Benjamin's analysis of habit occurs in the context of his formulation of new categories that would be adequate for discussing the medium of film and its reception, but the "time of historical change" for which Benjamin envisions this new kind of reception is faced with more tasks than the cinema can handle by itself. Brecht's writings, too, require a new kind of reception that is similar to the habituation of architectural reception:

> [Their] principal product . . . is a new attitude. . . . This is something new, and what is new about it is that it can be learned. "The second *Versuch*, the *Stories of Herr Keuner*, represents an attempt to make gestures quotable." . . . [A]nd what is quotable about them is not just their stance, but also the words that accompany them. Yet these words need to be practiced—that is to say, first memorized and then understood. They first have a pedagogical effect, then a political one, and last a poetic one.[48]

Like an actor learning his lines, Brecht's readers should practice his texts before understanding them; they are meant to be assumed as habits. Just as the lived reception of glass architecture succeeds in exposing its inhabitants to the city, the habit of seeing, reading, or performing Brecht leads to the appropriation of new attitudes.[49]

Used and Usable Man

"Anyone who wants to define the crucial features of Brecht in a few words would be smart to confine himself to this sentence: his subject is poverty,"[50] Benjamin writes, and this reduction of Brecht to this "crucial" sentence comes after a reading of Brecht's play *Man Equals Man*, whose plot and central character Benjamin presents in the following way:

> No sooner has [Galy Gay] walked out his own door to buy a fish for his wife, than he meets some soldiers belonging to the Anglo-Indian army who have lost the fourth man in their unit while plundering a pagoda. They all have an interest in finding a substitute as quickly as possible. Galy Gay is a man who is unable to say no. He follows the three of them without knowing what they want with him. Bit by bit, he assumes possessions, thoughts, attitudes, and habits of the kind needed by a soldier in a war. He is completely reassembled.[51]

What interests Brecht and Benjamin in the character of Galy Gay is the process of "reassembly" that he undergoes. As he "assumes" the "attitudes" of the soldiers, he is completely transformed. The extreme, comic facility with which Galy Gay adopts his new assignment reveals that he is nothing but the ability to change, and the play's reduction of his character to this "nothing but . . ." makes visible the ascetic attitude that Benjamin presents, in the fragment on the ship *Poverty,* as the proper response to an impoverished age.

The phrase "man is man" restates the principle of identity, "A = A" or "A is A," which, at least since German Idealism, has been interpreted not as a declaration of abstract identity but as the articulation of a synthetic identity, an identity that includes difference.[52] The first "A" is different from the second "A," and the copula or equal sign is the marker of mediation or synthesis. Benjamin explains "the nature of [Galy's] transformation" by citing an interlude from *Man Equals Man,* which is an extended explication of the play's title. It emphasizes the place of difference in identity by interpreting the statement "man equals man" as a proposition about the possibility of transformation. Change appears as a complement to identity. The play's title may seem to insist on identity, "But Bertolt Brecht also goes on to prove / That you can make as much of a man as you want." Galy Gay's identity includes the openness to transformation and to being "reassembled," and the title's apparent insistence on identity, read through the lens of the interlude, also indicates this openness. It emphasizes that Galy Gay's transformation is not to be understood as a loss: he is "reassembled like a car, / Without his losing anything by it."

As both the interlude and the play's subtitle *(The Transformation of the Porter Galy Gay in the Military Cantonment of Kilkoa during the Year Nineteen Hundred and Twenty-five)* indicate, Galy Gay undergoes a transformation for which he appears to be well suited. We learn from his wife in the play's first scene that he has a "malleable [or weak] mind" *(weiches Gemüt),* which the soldiers of the Anglo-Indian army also sense.[53] One of them says, "His kind change of their own accord, you know. Throw him into a pond, and two days later he'll have webs growing between his fingers. That's because he's got nothing to lose."[54] In this joke, Galy Gay is an amphibian, whose ability to transform would allow him to give up, if necessary, his humanity.[55]

The play focuses on Galy Gay's inhuman ability to be transformed, which is squandered when he is forced into the military. In the first version of the essay "What Is Epic Theater?," Benjamin follows Brecht's lead from the "interlude" and explicates the title *Man Equals Man* as a statement regarding precisely this malleability: "Man equals man: that is not faithfulness to one's own essence, but the readiness to receive something new in oneself" (die Bereitschaft, ein neues in sich selbst zu empfangen).[56] The formulation of this preparedness to receive "something new in oneself" is ambiguous, because, in German, the "in" of "in oneself" could be either "within" or "into." The readiness could allow one to "receive something already there in oneself" or to "receive something from outside into oneself." Galy's transformation can be read both ways; he receives something from the outside—his uniform, his new habits, his new name—and brings to light something inside him, namely, his attitude that enables him to take on the roles given to him.

By the end of the play, nothing is left of Galy Gay but this attitude or *Haltung*. Rainer Nägele's reading of Brecht's *Keuner* stories shows how the Brechtian *Haltung* is "that which subsists and remains under all transformations and . . . is itself a principle of transformation," and the same can be said of Galy Gay's attitude.[57] His transformability exceeds each of the forms that he assumes. According to the 1938 version of the play, he is always "used and accordingly usable" (gebraucht und . . . also brauchbar),[58] and in this phrase Galy Gay's specific way of being used—his conscription—is presented as distinct from his usability, which is not exhausted by any use. *Man Equals Man* does not celebrate Galy Gay's conscription but the ability to be used that exceeds every use and that indicates Galy Gay could have become something completely different.

It would be a grave misreading if only the first aspect of *Man Equals Man*—his conscription—were to be emphasized without a simultaneous insistence on the second, his ability. The play affirms none of the actual transformations that it presents. In 1953, Brecht looks back to *Man Equals Man* and emphasizes exactly this tension between Galy's usability and the ways in which he is used:

> The problem of the play is the false, bad collective (the "gang") and its
> seductive force, that collective that in those years recruited Hitler and his

financial backers, thus exploiting the petit bourgeoisie's indeterminate desire *[Verlangen]* for a historically mature and true social collective of workers.[59]

This late statement by Brecht accentuates the doubleness of Galy Gay's transformation, whose presentation Brecht modified as the meaning of mass movements changed in the 1920s and 1930s.[60] The play aims to show both the "bad collective" and how it exploits the "demand" for another collective. In *Man Equals Man,* this other, "undetermined" demand appears as Galy Gay's transformability, which exceeds every individual role and group. *Man Equals Man* presents the transformation that allows one man to become another; it affirms the "equal" that serves as a marker not for constancy but, instead, for the possibility of change.[61]

My reading of *Man Equals Man* makes clear why Benjamin reduces Brecht's corpus to the treatment of poverty. This is the original context of Benjamin's claim, cited earlier, for a difference between Brecht and Rilke:

> Poverty . . . is a form of mimicry that allows one to come closer to reality *[das Wirkliche]* than any rich man can. This, of course, is not Maeterlinck's mystical view of poverty. Nor is it the Franciscan idea that Rilke has in mind when he writes, "For poverty is a great light from within." This Brechtian poverty is more like a uniform and is calculated to confer a high rank on anyone who wears it. It is, in short, the physiological and economic poverty of humanity in the age of the machine. "The state should be rich, man should be poor; the state should be obliged to be able to do a great deal, and man should be allowed to be able to do very little [der Staat soll verpflichtet sein vieles zu können, dem Menschen soll es erlaubt sein weniges zu können]." This is the universal human right to poverty as Brecht formulates it. He has explored its potential in his writings and has displayed it in public in his own, slight, ragged appearance.[62]

Galy Gay is reduced to a lusterless, malleable attitude that allows him to engage in mimicry and enter into a process of transformation. The poverty that Benjamin sees in him is socioeconomic, but, as the final sentence here shows, it also belongs to a new conception of humanity and a new human right to weakness in the face of the strength of the state and the machine. A right to poverty would allow Galy to be nothing but his reduced, usable attitude and to resist its use by the military or any other entity. The high rank that poverty bestows does not assign its bearer to a specific position; instead, it aims to reduce appearance to the uniformity of an ability that can assume countless other uniforms. It does this by stripping characters and staged events of their definitive nature. This is why Brecht insists, in a text titled "The New Technique of the Actor," that the actor act in such a way "that one sees as clearly as possible the alternative [outcomes] and in a way that his acting allows one to imagine other possibilities."[63]

Even though *Man Equals Man* predates Brecht's conception of the epic theater, it presages his desire, in epic theater, to show a "malleable" and "changeable" world and thus to reduce the staged world to one possibility among many.[64] This impoverishment is the essential gesture of epic theater for Benjamin; the wealth of possibilities it reveals is secondary for Benjamin. The fertility of poverty's uniformity can be seen in the excessive use of Galy's potential—in the way in which the play shows that "you can make as much of a man as you want." Brecht's new humanity is, in itself, nothing but a malleability, and Benjamin reads his texts as the articulation of this new race's right to poverty. He claims a right to weakness and nonenactment that chapter 1 identified in the treatment of the poor by Marx and Foucault and that can also be seen in the beggars and outcasts in Baudelaire, Mallarmé, and Rilke. Brecht's texts play out the tension between an impoverished, potential uniformity and its rich, colorful exploitation. The next section will examine his poetry's variation on this tension.

Quotable Poetry for City Dwellers

At about the same time that Brecht was preparing the first edition of *Man Equals Man* for publication, he wrote a group of poems eventually grouped together under the title *A Reader for Those Who Live in Cities*.[65] This cycle of poems presents a lyrical "I" that shares many characteristics with the protagonist of *Man Equals Man*. Its ten poems offer a set of commands and exemplary depictions suited for a new kind of anonymous city life, and its addressee seems to be a Galy Gay–like figure who can undergo radical change. The first poem's repeated exhortation, "Verwisch die Spuren!" (which can be translated as "Erase the traces!" or "Cover your tracks!") concludes each stanza's call to abandon comrades, parents, and one's own thoughts.[66] The poem's calls for estrangement begin with an evocation of the arrival in the city and the demand to "part company" with one's comrades at the train station. The second stanza calls for its addressee to ignore his parents and to cover his face if he sees them. The call to hide one's face belongs to Brecht's move away from aura; the poem proscribes human relations and thereby a humanized understanding of the artwork. In Benjamin's commentary on this poem, he writes that Brecht presents city life from the perspective of the "fighter for the exploited classes," who is "an emigrant in his own country."[67] "Numb" to the charms, tempo, and entertainment industry of the big city, Brecht is for Benjamin "probably the first major lyric poet to say anything meaningful about city people."[68] The next stanza continues the demands for disavowal by insisting that the addressee never repeat himself and that he "disown" his own statements if he hears them from someone else. One's own words and thoughts, when uttered by someone else, are to be "denied" as part of this strategy of not leaving traces behind.

The imperative "Cover your tracks!" bans continuity and intends to disperse the identity of one's own language and thoughts. The poem's *explicit,* which reads simply "(I was taught that)," continues the earlier stanzas' calls for abandon by abandoning the poem. It is as if the "I" were following its own advice to disown its words. The poem concludes by translating the call for disappropriation into a specifically poetic gesture. The doctrine of disavowal called for by the poetic "I" is not its own but is itself disavowed; "it is not mine," the poem says of its own teaching. Six out of nine poems in the *Reader* conclude similarly with parenthetical remarks that disown the poems they close.[69] Like the anaphoric sentence "Thus spoke Zarathustra" that ends most of the chapters in Nietzsche's eponymous gospel, the Brechtian *explicit* in this cycle points to the constant transformation that takes place within these poems as they switch from one voice to the other. By referring to the preceding lines with the distancing, anaphoric "that" *(das* and *so),* these final lines are estranged from the body of the poem and estrange the poem from itself. Both inside and outside the poem, the final lines' precarious position is emphasized by the parentheses that surround them. In each of the poems of the *Reader,* the self-estrangement of the *explicit* declares that it is distant from the poem and that the poem that precedes it is a citation.

Benjamin writes that Brecht learned from observing "the great canonical literatures, especially Chinese literature" that "the supreme claim which can be made of the written word is that of its quotability."[70] A "quotable" word or phrase indicates, already in its original context, its own being out of place and the possibility of being used elsewhere. In his essay on Karl Kraus, Benjamin explains the full impact of quotability:

> Only when despairing did [Kraus] discover in citation the power not to preserve but to purify, to tear from context, to destroy; the only power in which hope still resides that something might survive this age—because it was wrenched from it.[71]

A quotable phrase bears witness to a future destruction of its context—and its own possible rescue.

The poems in the *Reader* all appear as quotable, estranged from themselves, and addressed to a city dweller with an impoverished attitude like Galy Gay's. Besides the individual voices that are cited in Brecht's poems, the cycle intends to make quotable the gesture of disavowal, the very principle of these poems' composition: the abjuration of every possession, every hold that might bind one to a language or self. What a poem says, in this conception, is not its own, but something from which it distances itself. The lines of the first poem that read "Whatever you say, don't say it twice / If you find your ideas in anyone else, disown them" are intensified in the disavowals repeated throughout the *Reader*. The cycle is run through by the contrast between, on the one hand, a wealth of voices, as each poem seems to cite a different speaker, and, on the other hand, the impoverishing gesture that concludes each poem and distances the speaker from these same voices and these voices' phrases from their contexts.

Brecht and Benveniste

Although Brecht scholarship has chosen to interpret the *Reader* primarily based on this second gesture and to present the cycle in terms of "coldness" or as "inhuman," some Brecht readers have seen a more complex operation at work.[72] In an essay on the putative barrenness *(Kargheit)* of Brecht's poetry, Reinhard Sändig writes:

> Brecht's great ability to use the most diverse linguistic sources worked so strongly to counteract his strived-for barrenness that the question even arises whether the concept of barrenness is appropriate at all.[73]

Walter Delabar observes similarly that the poems' initial "banal and barren" impression eventually changes into a "troubling complexity."[74] This tension is played out within the speaking "I" in the poems. Each poem presents itself as the speech of an "I" before, in the final line, showing that it is the speech of someone else. The fifth poem, for example, begins with the sentence "I'm dirt" and ends with the remark "(That's something I've heard a woman say)." The cycle's complexity consists in its ability to appropriate and present as the words of an "I" the speech of others—from the "most diverse linguistic sources," Sändig writes; and the barrenness of the cycle's language lies in the renunciation of this wealth of voices performed by the "I" of each *explicit*. It is thus in the personal pronoun "I" that wealthy complexity and impoverished barrenness meet and in which we can find the secret of their simultaneity. The "I," along with "you," we learn from Émile Benveniste, belongs to "a set of 'empty' signs, nonreferential in relation to 'reality' and always available, which become 'full' as soon as a speaker assumes them in the instance of discourse."[75] They are "empty" and can become "full" when assumed by a speaker, but, even when they are "full," they retain the characteristic of being "available." Benveniste's use of quotation marks to set off "empty" and "full" indicates the inadequacy of these terms in describing the "I," which is always available, always in excess of the speaker it implies and thus never only full or empty. In Brecht's poems, the fullness of the "I" is undercut by each *explicit* in its insistence on the availability or openness that allowed the position of the "I" to be filled by a different voice each time.

The irreducibility of the availability of the "I" appears in the possibility, noted by Benveniste, that the "I" can always be a cited "I":

> If I perceive two successive instances of discourse containing "I" pronounced by the same voice, nothing guarantees that one of them is not reported speech or a citation in which "I" could be attributed to a different person.[76]

Brecht's *Reader* takes advantage of this aspect of "I" that is not "guaranteed"; it moves back and forth between reported speech (revealed as such only after the fact) and the estrangement of this speech. With this repeated distancing gesture, Brecht's poems insist on the separation of the "I" from what could be misconstrued as its speech and thoughts; and the disavowal of the "I" does not spare the "I" of the Brechtian *explicit*, because there is no guarantee that the parenthetical, distancing "I" that closes most of the poems is the true "I" of the cycle.[77]

There is no way to imprint indelibly the traces of a speaking subject on Brecht's "I," and the *Reader's* insistent foregrounding of the properties of the personal pronoun belongs to its call to "Cover your tracks." The "I" becomes exemplary for the sober, impersonal existence that the cycle advocates; it crystallizes the wealth of the cycle's cited voices and the suspension and estrangement of these same voices. The cycle's calls for a "sober" figure that "creates no stir" and that "speaks quietly" are realized in stenographic form in the poems' impoverished and impoverishing "I."

Hooligans and a New Humanity

The "I" of the *Reader* serves as a marker for what Brecht calls a "new humanity" or a "new man." Brecht removed the poems of the *Reader* from his earlier collection *Manual of Piety (Hauspostille)* because he wanted to write a collection about the "new human being."[78] In the preface to *Man Equals Man*, Brecht insists that the play, too, attempts to present "a new type of man" and goes on to specify what this new man is like: "a great liar . . . an incorrigible opportunist, he can adapt to anything almost without difficulty."[79] It is for this humanity that Benjamin claims the right to poverty.

The juxtaposition of criminal opportunism and adaptability is not unique to *Man Equals Man* and the *Reader*. Many Brecht characters, such as Baal, Fatzer, Edward II, and Kragler, belong to the realm of the outcast and criminal, from which, according to Benjamin's reading, the revolutionary will emerge. Just as Marx would have the revolution emerge from its opposite, capitalism, Benjamin writes that Brecht "wants the revolutionary to emerge from the base and selfish character devoid of any ethos."[80] Benjamin presents the Brechtian hooligan types with these words:

> What they all have in common is the desire to bring about rational political actions that spring not from philanthropy, love of one's neighbor, idealism, nobility of mind, or the like, but only from the relevant attitude. If only the man it belongs to does not delude himself, if only he clings fast to reality, the attitude *[Haltung]* will itself provide its own corrective. Not an ethical corrective: the man does not become any better. But a social one: his behavior *[Verhalten]* makes him useable *[verwendbar]*.[81]

Not motives, but an "attitude" counts for Brecht's protagonists. Their attitude and "behavior" make them "useable," a term that recalls the synonymous "useful" *(brauchbar)* in *Man Equals Man,* in which Galy Gay is reduced to a state of usability.

The emphasis on attitude belongs to a political strategy based on potential and not on positions or motives, and Galy Gay's abandonment of the self is similar to Malte's, even if the political positions and motives of their authors differed radically. The protagonists of the *Notebooks* and *Man Equals Man* are both transformed and impoverished by their surroundings; both figures are forced to renounce their identities and thereby reveal a desire for another kind of collective or community. Rilke's poverty in *The Book of Hours* appears most strikingly in the use of "like," and Brecht's, in the *Reader's* use of "I." In their poetry, both writers emphasize the poverty of those parts of speech that, in themselves, are deprived of meaning and are "always available."[82] Although it could be said that every poet takes advantage of these properties, Rilke and Brecht place them at the center of their texts, and both do so in conjunction with the thematic presentation of poverty. Galy Gay is poor, and the addressees of the *Reader* are poor and are called to become poorer, but, when Benjamin insists that Brecht's "subject is poverty," he means to give a name to Galy's attitude, the *Haltung* that allows him to abandon and assume identities. Benjamin refers to Brecht's interest in socioeconomic poverty, but this seems to be only a remainder of an older tradition of thinking about poverty. It is an insistent one, though, because it still must be mentioned in Benjamin's texts. His desire to separate the potentializing attitude of Brecht's poverty from the tradition of representing socioeconomic or voluntary poverty remains programmatic. The possibility of overcoming humanity and escaping humanism's limitations remains inextricably tied to the socioeconomically poor. Glass architecture alone cannot give a face to potential; Benjamin still seems to need the urban outcasts of Brecht's poems and the poor Galy Gay.

In Transit

The figures of poverty examined in Benjamin's writings are all marked by a kind of doubleness: the culmination and ruin of the interior in Scheerbart's conception of glass architecture; Galy Gay's assumption by a bad collective and his indication of another, possible collective; and the simultaneous barrenness and wealth of poetic language in Brecht's *Reader*.[83] These texts are run through with impoverishing forces that coexist with other, richer textual elements. Such impoverished writings present us with what Benjamin would call "thresholds" and "zones of transition." This is why Benjamin's christening of the ship *Poverty* is not only whimsical, because such a vessel appears as an emblem for transition and for the exposure that these artists and writers search out. His dechristening reveals a desire to create a new face, free of the beggar's traditional aspect. This ship casts off from the "Europe of Humanism," and the ascetic attitude of its passengers anticipates their arrival in "the promised land of cannibalism." The poverty of experience is no telos but a means for achieving a new kind of barbarism. The crew members prepare for this new existence by casting off what might weigh them down: the privacy of their homes, the impressions left on plush upholstery, their voices, and, more than anything else, the notion of a self. But they still need a link to poverty to reach their goal, because the modern experience of potential requires it.

The ship "Poverty" is only one of many images of taking leave in Benjamin's texts on the poverty of experience. Scheerbart's glass buildings and the barren, complex figures of Brecht's *Man Equals Man* and *Reader* are variations on this ship, because they too cast off from the tradition in which they still participate, creating within it an impoverished threshold that leads to something else.

James Ensor, the Destructive Character, and the Obstinate Beggar

The readings of Benjamin in this chapter have shifted attention away from beggars and socioeconomic poverty only to return to them in the image of the impoverished city dweller in Brecht. Benjamin attempts to find a new face for poverty, and in this passage from "Experience and Poverty" that I partially cited earlier, James Ensor's paintings seem to offer a more fitting image of the new poverty:

> We need to remind ourselves of Ensor's magnificent paintings, in which the streets of great cities are filled with ghosts; philistines in carnival disguises roll endlessly down the streets, wearing distorted masks covered in flour and cardboard crowns on their heads. These paintings are perhaps nothing so much as the reflection of the ghastly and chaotic renaissance in which so many people have placed their hopes. But here we can see quite clearly that our poverty of experience is just a part of that great poverty that has once again acquired a face—a face of the same sharpness and precision as that of a beggar in the Middle Ages.[84]

The uncanniness of Baudelaire's beggars reappears in different form in Ensor's paintings. In an article written on the occasion of Ensor's seventieth birthday, Benjamin's concern with the artist's faces takes on another form, and we begin to understand why he finds the new face of poverty outlined "most clearly" in Ensor's paintings of crowds, in which

> [t]he "mass" seems not to be defined or clear-cut. There appears to be a dialectic of the mass and itself, doubled, according to whether it is in the process of being formed or being exposed. The uncovered, the exposed mass is always the throng of tangled snakes that we discover with disgust beneath a rock.[85]

Ensor's paintings reveal within the masses a "dialectic" of formation and exposure, which, in "Experience and Poverty," appears as the relation between the facelessness and face of poverty. As the possibility of bearing ever-new faces, poverty's facelessness is potentially multiple (and disgusting) and never merely one face or figure, just as in Benjamin's translation of Hugo's description of the poor as "a throng." Ensor's masked figures present once again the simultaneously figural and disfiguring force emblematized by the poor in the other chapters of this book. They appear and withdraw from appearance.[86]

Ensor presents the dialectic of the masses by means of a technique of decomposition, whose origin Benjamin finds in the sea air of Ensor's native Ostend:

> Besides breaking down light into an infinite spectrum of colors, sea air dissolves or, rather, erodes rock; it eats away and consumes what is solid. As this image of dissolved, decomposed blocks of stone [in Ensor's painting *Cathedrals*] is brought home to us . . . we come upon a strange aspect of decomposition: the way it brings out the mass character *[das Massenhafte]* and the hidden multiplicity of things. Eroded rock and decomposing flesh reveal the multiplicity of their grainy, cellular composition.[87]

The process of decay reveals the multiplicity that constitutes flesh and stone even when they present the solid appearance of unity. Benjamin breaks down the face of poverty by moving away from the beggar in his attempt to reveal the mass character of the poor. Ensor's singular faces are masks that cover and betray the multiplicity of the classes behind them; this double function of the mask is already visible in the ominous gaze and collective aspect encountered in Baudelaire's beggar as well as in Rilke's insistence on not looking away from the wormy decomposition that Baudelaire makes into a "divine essence" in "Une charogne." Something similar can be sensed in the potentially multiple speakers of Nietzsche's final sentence, "I am your truth." The serpentine mass that emerges in the faces of the poor petrifies its beholder (as in Baudelaire's "The Old Acrobat"), but it also draws its spectators in, forcing them to submit to disturbing, promising transformations. The disgust that Benjamin describes here is only one in a series of affects and effects caused by the encounter with the poor: Baudelaire's paralysis, Mallarmé's hatred, and Rilke's fear.

In *One-Way Street,* Benjamin tells us that this encounter's disaggregating force is the reason behind poverty's millennial prestige:

> All religions have honored the beggar. For he proves that in a matter both as prosaic and holy, banal and life-giving, as the giving of alms, intellect and morality, consistency and principles all fail shamefully.[88]

Here and throughout *One-Way Street,* Benjamin is still interested in the old face of poverty. We see beggars, but their eyes reveal something that we cannot account for, and the texts discussed in the previous chapters emerge from this failure. Narrators like Malte study the poor, but, Benjamin writes, the true readers are the poor themselves:

> We deplore the beggars in the South, forgetting that their persistence in front of our noses is as justified as a scholar's obstinacy before a difficult passage in a text. No shadow of hesitation, no slightest wish or deliberation in our faces escapes their notice.[89]

The understanding of their obstinate reading stance requires that almsgivers and passersby adopt a similar attitude. The poor engage us in a mutual process of "persistent" looking. Earlier in *One-Way Street,* Benjamin presents this reading as a wounding:

> It is impossible to live in a large German city, where hunger forces the most wretched to live on the banknotes with which passersby seek to cover an exposure that wounds them.[90]

> Unmöglich, in einer deutschen Großstadt zu leben, in welcher der Hunger die Elendsten zwingt, von den Scheinen zu leben, mit denen die Vorübergehenden eine Blöße zu decken suchen, die sie verwundet.[91]

It is impossible to live in the midst of poverty because the wounds of poverty cannot be covered up. The exposure of the poor makes them vulnerable and wounds the passerby. Strictly speaking, it is not possible to say whose exposure it is; it is only "*an* exposure," one that could belong to either party. The poor and the passerby are engaged in a relation in which they are both marked by a wounding nakedness that aligns them with Rilke's poor, who are "marked with the mark of final fears / and everywhere disfigured and stripped bare." This nakedness is another form in which multiplicity appears, because, like the mass character of Ensor's paintings, the beggar's barrenness cannot be covered up; it is blank, inexhaustible, obstinate, and contagious.

To understand poverty, we must persistently read this naked surface just as it reads and wounds us. The exposure in Benjamin's text registers the force with which the poor interpellate us as well as the blankness of their impotent withdrawal in the face of every enactment. Paying attention to the difficult passages of the poor and their potential means that we must follow the imperative "to read what was never written," a phrase of Hofmannsthal's that Benjamin suggests as the motto of the "true historian."[92] The texts on poverty examined here contain passages that remain unwritten, virtual figures and insistent absences that mark the place of the poor, the nonwork and impotence that Heidegger identified as crucial to every work and every power. The withdrawal from enactment that characterizes the poor appears in the interruptive force of Rilke's "LIKE," Mallarmé's gold, Nietzsche's virtue, and Brecht's attitude. They register potentials (for another poetic language, for a new understanding of community, for the overman, for the revolutionary subject) and emerge in the encounter with the poor. They often appear, at first, as signs of decomposition, because they break down what exists in order to show that something else could be.

Ensor's decomposing masks ally him with Benjamin's other impoverished artists, who begin not with creation, but with destruction. In each of the authors examined in this study, poverty's destructive force clears the way for something that would not merely replace that which has been destroyed. In Benjamin's portrait of the "destructive character," he writes, "What exists he reduces to rubble—not for the sake of rubble, but for that of the way leading through it."[93] The destructive character destroys without creating more than a "way." Baudelaire's beggar indicates, in the glint of his eye, an uncertain future; Nietzsche's poverty of the richest brings about a poetic language that permits only the possibility of something other than the ascetic ideal; Mallarmé's beggars speak a threatening language whose murmuring runs through his poems and prose without ever emerging as such; the outcasts in Rilke's writings break down every relation of belonging and attribution in favor of a broken poetic language and a new kind of bond with the poor; and, finally, Benjamin's poverty of experience is only a means to an end, to which one adheres in the hope of overcoming traditional notions of humanity and culture. In my final example of impoverished writing, the impersonal, citing "I" of the *Reader* presents as exemplary its abjuration of every possession and every relation that might bind it to its language or identity. For Brecht and Benjamin, the linguistic and conceptual traits that were once associated with the themes of poverty and the beggar attempt to free themselves even of the term "poverty" and to become part of a modern, urban attitude. In the place of the beggar there is glass, "the enemy of possession in general."

The poor, from Baudelaire and Nietzsche to Benjamin and Brecht, appear as messengers of destruction who offer no guarantees and no substitutes for what has been lost. Like Benjamin's preferred messenger, Angelus Novus, the poor come to take away, and, in "Experience and Poverty," the traditional figure of poverty, the beggar, emerges for a moment only to retreat. The other authors examined here already indicate the imminence of this final vanishing in their presentation of the beggar's muteness. Benjamin's attempt to fashion a new face for poverty aims to make the beggar's exit definitive, because he seems to have exhausted his role as a figure for the coincidence of potential and impotence that modern literature finds in poverty. But the figure of the beggar remains in Benjamin's texts, obstinate, even as he seems about to disappear.

Acknowledgments

This book began as a dissertation in comparative literature at the Humanities Center at The Johns Hopkins University. I would like to thank my advisers, Rainer Nägele and Neil Hertz, and my teachers there: Brigid Doherty, Peter Fenves, Wolfram Groddeck, Elizabeth Grosz, and Werner Hamacher. I would also like to express my gratitude to the other faculty members of the Humanities Center and the Department of German, especially Rüdiger Campe, Nahum Chandler, Michael Fried, Susan Hahn, Ruth Leys, Richard Macksey, and Rochelle Tobias.

As I revised the manuscript for publication, many friends, colleagues, and readers offered valuable suggestions and criticism. I thank Anna Brickhouse, Michaele Ferguson, David Ferris, Valerie Forman, Karen Jacobs, Christopher Laferl, Jan Mieszkowski, Michael du Plessis, Darrin Pratt, Sabine Zelger, and my colleagues in the Department of Germanic and Slavic Languages and Literatures at the University of Colorado, Boulder. In particular, I thank Daniel Heller-Roazen for his careful readings of early versions of the manuscript; the two readers for the University of Minnesota Press for their suggestions; and Farideh Koohi-Kamali for her interest in the project.

I especially wish to thank my friends Jeffrey Deshell and Elisabeth Sheffield for their critical responses to the manuscript.

Finally, to Emmanuel David: thank you.

I dedicate this book to my parents.

NOTES

Introduction

1. Charles Baudelaire, *The Parisian Prowler,* trans. Edward K. Kaplan (Athens: University of Georgia Press, 1989), 27–31.

2. Walter Benjamin, *Gesammelte Schriften,* ed. Rolf Tiedemann and Hermann Schweppenhäuser (Frankfurt am Main: Suhrkamp, 1991), 2: 1112 (my translation).

3. Stéphane Mallarmé, *Œuvres complètes,* ed. Bertrand Marchal (Paris: Gallimard, 2003), 2:239 (my translation).

4. Robert Musil, *Der Mann ohne Eigenschaften* (Reinbek bei Hamburg: Rowohlt, 1994), 1191 (my translation).

5. Martin Heidegger, *Basic Writings,* ed. and trans. David Farrell Krell (New York: HarperCollins, 1993), 265. For a discussion of poverty in Heidegger's writings of the 1940s, see Phillipe Lacoue-Labarthe, "Présentation," in Martin Heidegger, *La pauvreté (die Armut),* trans. Philippe Lacoue-Labarthe and Ana Samardzija (Strasbourg: Presses Universitaires de Strasbourg, 2004), 7–65.

6. See Jerzy Grotowski, *Towards a Poor Theatre,* ed. Eugenio Barba (London: Methuen, 1968), and Carolyn Christov-Bakargiev, ed., *Arte povera* (London: Phaidon, 1999).

7. For an introduction to Meister Eckhart, see Reiner Schürmann, *Wandering Joy: Meister Eckhart's Mystical Philosophy* (Great Barrington, Mass.: Lindisfarne, 2001); on Franciscan notions of poverty, see Roberto Lambertini, *Apologia e crescita dell'identità francescana (1255–1279)* (Rome: Istituto Storico Italiano per il Medio Evo, 1990), and Lambertini, *La povertà pensata: Evoluzione storica della definizione dell'identità minoritica da Bonaventura ad Ockham* (Modena: Mucchi, 2000). Modern authors also participate in the long tradition of the transformation of language by the poor and in the face of poverty, which Michael Hardt and Antonio Negri insist on in *Multitude* (New

York: Penguin, 2004), 132. See, for example, the work on thieves' cant by Elisabeth Weber, in "Kassiber, Schibbolim, etc. (von Banditen, Räubern, etc.)," in *Körper/Kultur: Kalifornische Studien zur deutschen Moderne* (Würzburg: Königshausen & Neumann, 1995), ed. Thomas Kniesche, 55–75; and on argot by Alice Becker-Ho, *Les princes du jargon: Un facteur négligé aux origines de l'argot des classes dangereuses* (Paris: Éditions G. Lebovici, 1990).

8. Louis Chevalier, *Laboring Classes and Dangerous Classes in Paris during the First Half of the Nineteenth Century,* trans. Frank Jellinek (New York: Fertig, 1973), 97. Richard Terdiman makes a similar claim in *Discourse/Counter-Discourse: The Theory and Practice of Symbolic Resistance in Nineteenth-Century France* (Ithaca, N.Y.: Cornell University Press, 1985), 315.

9. Chevalier, *Laboring Classes,* 95. On the difficulty of defining poverty, see also Bronisław Geremek, *Poverty: A History,* trans. Agnieszka Kolakowska (Cambridge: Blackwell, 1994), 1–13; on the ambiguity of the term *misère,* see Pierre Macherey, *The Object of Literature,* trans. David Macey (Cambridge: Cambridge University Press, 1995), 94; on the resulting fluctuation of the poor between objects of identification and objects of hostility, see Norbert Preußer, *Not macht erfinderisch: Überlebensstrategien der Armenbevölkerung seit 1807* (Munich: Spack, 1989), 13; see also Raymond Williams's relevant account of the problems of the term "class" in *Keywords: A Vocabulary of Culture and Society* (New York: Oxford University Press, 1983), 60–69.

10. Hannah Arendt, *On Revolution* (New York: Viking, 1963), 54.

11. A concise formulation of this insight can be found in Friedrich Engels and Karl Marx, *Die heilige Familie, oder Kritik der kritischen Kritik* (Berlin: Dietz, 1971), 38. Everything else in Marx, according to Arendt, is "secondary and derivative in comparison" (Arendt, *On Revolution,* 54).

12. Arendt, *On Revolution,* 74.

13. Ibid., 81.

14. Ibid., 81–82.

15. Paul de Man, *The Rhetoric of Romanticism* (New York: Columbia University Press, 1984), 75–76 (my emphasis).

16. Karl Marx, *Capital: A Critique of Political Economy,* trans. Ben Fowkes (New York: Vintage, 1977), 1:272–73.

17. Hardt and Negri, *Multitude,* 134. They argue against the misleading term "industrial reserve army," because "there is no 'reserve' in the sense that no labor power is outside the processes of production" (131). Chapter 1 shows that the text of *Capital* explicitly anticipates their inclusion of the reserve army in the process of production.

18. Marx, *Capital,* 1:798 (translation slightly modified; the emphasis is

Marx's); Marx, *Das Kapital: Kritik der politischen Ökonomie.* Vol. 1, book 1, *Der Produktionsprozeß des Kapitals* (Berlin: Dietz, 1977), 673–74.

19. Marx, *Capital,* 1:799.

20. For a useful discussion of the distinction between questions of identity and ability, see Didier Deleule and François Guéry, *Le corps productif* (Paris: Mame, 1972), 13–14. See also Étienne Balibar, *Masses, Classes, Ideas: Studies on Politics and Philosophy before and after Marx,* trans. James Swenson (New York: Routledge, 1994), 143.

21. On the differences between the beggar and figures of "modern poverty," see Bernhold Dietz, *Soziologie der Armut: Eine Einführung* (Frankfurt am Main: Campus, 1997), 42; and Giovanna Procacci, *Gouverner la misère* (Paris: Seuil, 1993), 11–12. See also Dolf Oehler's remarks on Baudelaire's use of members of the lumpenproletariat to represent the working class in *Pariser Bilder I (1830–1848): Antibourgeoise Ästhetik bei Baudelaire, Daumier und Heine* (Frankfurt am Main: Suhrkamp, 1979), 212.

22. On the temporality of revolt and revolution, see Furio Jesi, *Spartakus: Simbologia della rivolta* (Turin: Bollati Boringhieri, 2000).

23. For a discussion of the specific differences between Hugo's and Mallarmé's relation to the poor, see Anne-Emmanuelle Berger, "Crise d'aumône (Mallarmé reprend Hugo)," *Corps/décors: Femmes, orgie, parodie: Hommage à Lucienne Frappier-Mazur,* ed. Catherine Nesci, Gretchen Van Slyke, and Gerald Prince (Amsterdam: Editions Rodopi, 1999), 237–53. See also Berger's discussion of the change in the representation of poverty that she locates in the 1850s in Berger, *Scènes d'aumône: Misère et poésie au XIXe siècle* (Paris: Champion, 2004), 51.

24. Michel Foucault, *The Order of Things: An Archaeology of the Human Sciences* (New York: Random House, 1970), 251. See also Anson Rabinach's remarks on the nineteenth century's "new image of nature" created by thermodynamics, in which a "stable and homogenous order of natural forms and relations" is replaced by "images of extraordinary power as well as decline, death, . . . entropy, disorder and chaos." Anson Rabinach, *The Human Motor: Energy, Fatigue, and the Origins of Modernity* (New York: Basic Books, 1990), 62–63.

25. Foucault, *The Order of Things,* 300.

26. Berger's *Scènes d'aumône: Misère et poésie au XIXe siècle* interprets poverty in a wide range of nineteenth-century French texts, and her theoretical approach is determined by the discourse of the gift in Marcel Mauss and the related vocabulary of giving and economy in Heidegger, Georges Bataille, and Jacques Derrida. I will refer in my readings of Baudelaire and Mallarmé to

Berger's careful analyses in her book; in addition, I will refer to the interpretations of Mallarmé, Hugo, and almsgiving in the book chapter cited earlier (see note 23). Another study identifies impoverished forms of thought that attempt to do without the subject's imagined mastery over the world and the self, but without focusing on the link between the abandonment of this link and the theme of socioeconomic poverty: Ulrich Fülleborn's ambitious *Besitzen als besässe man nicht: Besitzdenken und seine Alternativen in der Literatur* (Frankfurt am Main: Insel, 1995). Fülleborn covers a time period from the Hebrew Bible to Musil, and his readings of literary and philosophical texts are oriented according to the concept he calls "possessive thinking," which he defines as "a way of thinking for which every relation is important only insofar as it is a kind of possession, a way of dealing with something that only serves utility" (15). But Fülleborn's concepts of possessive and nonpossessive thinking are not tied to socioeconomic conditions, and his readings skirt his authors' encounters with the phenomena of socioeconomic poverty. A similar emphasis on poverty as a notion for explaining new modes of philosophical thinking can be found in Stefano Catucci's rigorous book *Per una filosofia povera: La Grande Guerra, l'esperienza, il senso* (Turin: Bollati Boringhieri, 2003). He situates Georg Lukács's early call for an impoverished philosophy, closer to quotidian life and without transcendent ideals, within a larger philosophical context that includes Benjamin's notion of "the poverty of experience," but his project does not focus on socioeconomic poverty or the nineteenth-century literary genealogy of these modern forms of impoverished thought.

27. Leo Bersani and Ulysse Dutoit, *Arts of Impoverishment: Beckett, Rothko, Resnais* (Cambridge, Mass.: Harvard University Press, 1993), 54, 121, 207–8.

28. Ibid., 5.

29. Ibid., 5, 9.

30. Ibid.

31. The concept of training also appears in Fülleborn, who writes in the first paragraph of *Besitzen als besässe man nicht* of "the acquisition of another possibility for thinking and writing through training *[Einübung]*" (9).

32. Michel Foucault, *The History of Sexuality,* vol. 2, *The Use of Pleasure,* trans. Robert Hurley (New York: Vintage, 1985), 10.

33. Michel Foucault, *The History of Sexuality,* vol. 1, *An Introduction,* trans. Robert Hurley (New York: Vintage, 1978), 145.

34. Ibid., 145; Foucault, *Histoire de la sexualité,* vol. 1, *La volonté de savoir* (Paris: Gallimard, 1976), 190–91.

35. Foucault, *The History of Sexuality,* 1:145 (translation modified); Foucault, *Histoire de la sexualité,* 1:191.

1. Impoverished Power

1. Marx, *Capital*, 1:90.

2. Ibid., 125.

3. Ibid., 940.

4. Étienne Balibar, "Foucault and Marx: Der Einsatz des Nominalismus," trans. Hans-Dieter Gondek, in *Spiele der Wahrheit: Michel Foucaults Denken*, ed. François Ewald and Bernhard Waldenfels (Frankfurt am Main: Suhrkamp, 1991), 39 (my translation).

5. Ibid., 65 (my translation).

6. The English edition of Heidegger's text uses the term "force" to translate the same term that appears in English editions of Marx as "power" *(Kraft)*. Since the Marx translations are more widely used and their terminology widely accepted, I will follow their translation of *Kraft* as "power." See the discussion of the definition of *dunamis* in Charlotte Witt, *Ways of Being: Potentiality and Actuality in Aristotle's "Metaphysics"* (Ithaca, N.Y.: Cornell University Press, 2003), 4. My analysis also draws on Massimo De Carolis, "Il problema della potenza in Nietzsche e in Aristotele," in *Sulla potenza da Aristotele a Nietzsche*, ed. Massimo De Carolis (Naples: Guida, 1989), 7–52.

7. Martin Heidegger, *Aristotle's Metaphysics* Θ *1–3: On the Essence and Actuality of Force*, trans. Walter Brogan and Peter Warnek (Bloomington: Indiana University Press, 1995), 47. I will also refer to the German edition: Martin Heidegger, *Gesamtausgabe*, vol. 33, *Aristoteles, Metaphysik* Θ *1–3: Vom Wesen und Wirklichkeit der Kraft* (Frankfurt am Main: Klostermann, 1981). A more conventional translation of this passage can be found in Aristotle, *Aristotle's Metaphysics*, trans. Hippocrates G. Apostle (Bloomington: Indiana University Press, 1966), 146.

8. "The power to tolerate something from another" and "the behavior of intolerance (insufferability) in reference to a change." Heidegger, *Aristotle's Metaphysics* Θ *1–3*, 73–74.

9. Ibid., 76. Charlotte Witt argues in *Ways of Being* that "the primary meaning of *dunamis* centers on the idea of an agent or an active power," but she also insists that "each agent power or agent requires a corresponding receptivity to change in the object" and acknowledges that "agent powers . . . are not most useful for [Aristotle's] present purposes," which can be found in the attempt to develop an understanding of "two ways of being" ("being X potentially and being X actually") (41–44). Witt's quick dismissal of the question of the priority of activity and passivity bears witness to its relative unimportance in *Aristotle's Metaphysics* Θ. In Heidegger's interpretation, the emphasis on the relation of a tolerating power and an intolerant power instead of on the relation

of an active and passive power belongs to his attempt to orient his analysis of power in way that does not depend on subjectivity, because for Heidegger, power may be what first allows a subject to come to be at all. See the conclusion of Heidegger's reading of Leibniz's interpretation of power. *Aristotle's Metaphysics* Θ *1–3*, 86–87.

10. Heidegger, *Aristotle's Metaphysics* Θ *1–3*, 76–77.

11. Marcel Proust, *Remembrance of Things Past*, trans. C. K. Scott Moncrieff and Terence Kilmartin, revised by D. J. Enright (New York: Vintage, 1996), 1:49. Another modern account of this phenomenon can be found in Freud's notion of resistance, which uses a similar vocabulary to show how the power of the unconscious first appears as resistance. For a summary discussion of resistance in psychoanalysis, see Jean Laplanche and J.-B. Pontalis, *Vocabulaire de la psychanalyse* (Paris: Presses Universitaires de France, 1967), 420–23. The first detailed account of resistance can be found in Josef Breuer and Sigmund Freud, *Studien über Hysterie* (Frankfurt am Main: Fischer, 1991), 285.

12. Proust, *Remembrance of Things Past*, 1:49 (my emphasis).

13. Ibid., 50.

14. Ibid., 51.

15. Heidegger, *Aristotle's Metaphysics* Θ *1–3*, 77.

16. Ibid., 89.

17. Ibid., 91.

18. Ibid.

19. Anson Rabinach locates Marx's notion in a wider context of nineteenth-century discussions of energy *(Kraft)*, and he shows how, in the nineteenth century, the notion of the interdependence of powers relies most explicitly on the theory of the conservation of energy and the concept of labor power discovered and popularized by Hermann von Helmholtz ; see Rabinach, *The Human Motor: Energy, Fatigue, and the Origins of Modernity* (New York: Basic Books, 1990), 45–83.

20. Heidegger, *Aristotle's Metaphysics* Θ*1–3*, 187.

21. My discussion here is indebted to the work of Giorgio Agamben. Agamben draws on Heidegger's analysis, but his concept of potential is different, because, in his discussion of Aristotle and Heidegger, he chooses to omit the concept of enactment. See Agamben, *Potentialities,* ed. and trans. Daniel Heller-Roazen (Stanford, Calif.: Stanford University Press, 1999), especially 182–83 and 187–204; and Agamben, *Homo Sacer: Sovereign Power and Bare Life,* trans. Daniel Heller-Roazen (Stanford, Calif.: Stanford University Press, 1998), 44–47.

22. Heidegger, *Aristotle's Metaphysics* Θ*1–3*, 160.

23. For a discussion of the Megarian position, see Witt, *Ways of Being,* 17–37.

24. Heidegger, *Aristotle's Metaphysics* Θ *1–3*, 145.

25. Ibid., 160 (translation modified); Heidegger, *Aristoteles, Metaphysik* Θ *1–3*, 187.

26. Heidegger, *Aristotle's Metaphysics* Θ *1–3*, 188 (Heidegger's emphasis).

27. Heidegger, *Aristotle's Metaphysics* Θ *1–3*, 180 (Heidegger's ellipsis).

28. Ibid., 109. See also the discussion of Heidegger's notion of *logos* in Reiner Schürmann, *Heidegger on Being and Acting: From Principles to Anarchy*, trans. Christine-Marie Gros and Reiner Schürmann (Bloomington: Indiana University Press, 1987), 175–77; and Françoise Dastur's summary of the evolution of Heidegger's understanding of language in *Heidegger et la question anthropologique* (Leuven: Peeters, 2003), 103–18.

29. Heidegger, *Aristotle's Metaphysics* Θ *1–3*, 115. This revelation of the world occurs in a process of selection that also leaves things hidden, and it is thus tied closely, for Heidegger, to the way in which truth—*alētheia*—reveals and conceals. "In that sense, it can be held that *logos* and *alētheia* 'are the same': *logos* bespeaks the emerging from absence and *alētheia,* the constellation or conflict of presencing-absencing." Schürmann, *Heidegger on Being and Acting*, 175.

30. Heidegger, *Aristotle's Metaphysics* Θ *1–3*, 117.

31. Ibid., 124 (translation modified); Heidegger, *Aristoteles, Metaphysik* Θ *1–3*, 145–46.

32. Heidegger, *Aristotle's Metaphysics* Θ *1–3*, 124; Heidegger, *Aristoteles, Metaphysik* Θ *1–3*, 145–46. See also Heidegger, *Aristotle's Metaphysics* Θ *1–3*, 130–31.

33. Witt, *Ways of Being*, 63.

34. Heidegger, *Aristotle's Metaphysics* Θ *1–3*, 132.

35. See Procacci, *Gouverner la misère*, passim.

36. Marx, *Capital*, 1:799.

37. Ibid., 762–64.

38. Ibid., 776–77.

39. Marx notes that even "the increase of the variable part of the capital and therefore of the number of workers employed by it, is always connected with violent fluctuations and the temporary production of a surplus population, whether this takes the more striking form of the repulsion of workers already employed, or the less evident, but not less real, form of a greater difficulty in absorbing the additional working population through its customary outlets" (Marx, *Capital*, 1:782–83).

40. Ibid., 782.

41. Ibid., 786. "[T]here must be the possibility of suddenly throwing great masses of men into the decisive areas without doing any damage to the scale of production in other spheres" (785).

42. Ibid., 794–96; Marx, *Das Kapital,* 1:670–72.

43. Marx, *Capital,* 1:796.

44. My understanding of pauperism is indebted to Procacci, *Gouverner la misère,* passim, but especially 201–26.

45. Ibid., 249. See Adorno's similar comments on the beggar in Wagner in his *In Search of Wagner,* trans. Rodney Livingstone (London: New Left Books, 1981), 135.

46. Marx, *Capital,* 1:797; Marx, *Das Kapital,* 1:673.

47. Marx, *Capital,* 1:797.

48. Ibid., 272–73.

49. Ibid., 716 (translation modified); Marx, *Das Kapital,* 1:596.

50. Marx, *Capital,* 548.

51. Ibid., 481–82; Marx, *Das Kapital,* 1:381–82. See also Marx's remarks on the crippled worker (*Capital,* 1:486, 568), and on the "destruction" (and not "disturbance," as the translation has it) of the "intensity and flow of [the worker's] vital forces" (*Capital,* 1:460; *Das Kapital,* 1:361).

52. Didier Deleule and François Guéry discuss the worker with similar terms in *Le corps productif,* 44.

53. Marx, *Capital,* 1:797.

54. Nicholas Thoburn, *Deleuze, Marx and Politics* (London: Routledge, 2003), 49 and 63. For a similar account of the proletariat's nonidentity, see Étienne Balibar, *Masses, Classes, Ideas: Studies on Politics and Philosophy Before and After Marx,* trans. James Swenson (New York: Routledge, 1994), 125–49; and Jacques Rancière, *The Philosopher and His Poor,* trans. John Drury, Corinne Oster, and Andrew Parker (Durham, N.C.: Duke University Press, 2004).

55. Thoburn, *Deleuze, Marx, and Politics,* 67.

56. Nicholas Thoburn, "Difference in Marx: The Lumpenproletariat and the Proletarian Unnamable," *Economy and Society* 31, no. 3 (2002): 446. See also Rancière, *The Philosopher and His Poor,* 95–98.

57. Thoburn, *Deleuze, Marx, and Politics,* 63.

58. Ibid., 68.

59. The classificatory disturbances in Marx's text may result from the way in which he conceives of the proletariat as both a class and a nonclass; see Étienne Balibar, "The Vacillation of Ideology," in *Marxism and the Interpretation of Culture,* ed. Cary Nelson and Lawrence Grossberg (Urbana: University of Illinois Press, 1988), 166. For an analogous discussion of the working class as exterior and interior to capital, see Balibar, *Masses, Classes, Ideas,* 143; and Giovanna Procacci, "Social Economy and the Government of Poverty," *The Foucault*

Effect: Studies in Governmentality, ed. Graham Burchell, Colin Gordon, and Peter Miller (Chicago: University of Chicago Press, 1991), 158–59.

60. Gilles Deleuze, "Un manifeste de moins," in Deleuze and Carmelo Bene, *Superpositions* (Paris: Minuit, 1979), 128.

61. Ibid., 129.

62. Ibid., 125.

63. Ibid.

64. Thoburn, "Difference in Marx," 452.

65. Michael Hardt and Antonio Negri, *Empire* (Cambridge, Mass.: Harvard University Press, 2000), 156.

66. Ibid., 157–58; see also Hardt and Negri, *Multitude,* 151–53.

67. Pauperism bears witness to what Balibar calls an "incoercible residue" that registers how the proletariat's power is not absorbed by capitalist production; it shows how "labor-power . . . resists and tends to *elude* the status of pure commodity imposed on it by the logic of capital." Étienne Balibar, *The Philosophy of Marx,* trans. Chris Turner (New York: Verso, 1995), 101–2.

68. Michel Foucault, *Dits et écrits,* ed. Daniel Defert and François Ewald (Paris: Gallimard, 1994), 3:258–59.

69. Ibid., 536. See also Foucault's essay "Nietzsche, Freud, Marx" and the interviews collected in the volumes *Power/Knowledge,* ed. Colin Gordon (New York: Pantheon, 1980), and in Foucault, *Remarks on Marx* (New York: Semiotext[e], 1991).

70. Foucault, *Discipline and Punish,* trans. Alan Sheridan (New York: Random House, 1977), 74, 78–79.

71. Ibid., 138.

72. Ibid., 128, 138.

73. Ibid., 138.

74. On the relation of Foucault to Marx, see Gilles Deleuze, *Foucault* (Paris: Minuit, 1986), 31–38. On the relation of disciplinary power and capital, see also Michèle Barrett, *The Politics of Truth: From Marx to Foucault* (Stanford, Calif.: Stanford University Press, 1991), 123–56; Steven Best, *The Politics of Historical Vision: Marx, Foucault, Habermas* (New York: Guilford, 1995), 110–20; Hardt and Negri, *Empire,* 243 and 453n7; and Barry Smart, *Foucault, Marxism and Critique* (London: Routledge & Kegan Paul, 1983), 113–15.

75. Foucault, *Discipline and Punish,* 221. The problem of discipline is not foreign to Marx, for he, too, insists in *Capital* on the necessity of discipline for the transition from the age of "manufacture" to large-scale industry; see Marx, *Capital,* 489–91, 548–53. For a discussion of the interdependence of discipline, surveillance, and capital, see Deleule and Guéry's *Le corps productif.*

76. This is how Foucault, in an interview from 1977, formulates the relation of his notion of power to economics: "Pour dire les choses très simplement, l'internement psychiatrique, la normalisation mentale des individus, les institutions pénales ont sans doute une importance assez limitée si on en cherche seulement la signification économique. En revanche, dans le fonctionnement général des rouages du pouvoir, ils sont sans doute essentiels. Tant qu'on posait la question du pouvoir en le subordonnant à l'instance économique et au système d'intérêt qu'elle assurait, on était amené à considérer ces problèmes comme de peu d'importance" (Foucault, *Dits et écrits*, 3:146). See also *Dits et écrits*, 3:203: "[I]l s'est trouvé que je me suis occupé de gens qui étaient placés hors des circuits du travail productif: les fous, les malades, les prisonniers, et aujourd'hui les enfants." And this is Foucault in 1978 on *Madness and Civilization* and Marx: "*The History of Madness* caused a lot of trouble, despite everything: this work, which shifted the attention from elevated problems to minimal questions, which instead of discussing Marx proceeded to analyze such trivialities as the internal practices of mental hospitals, etc." (Foucault, *Remarks on Marx*, 96).

77. Foucault, *Discipline and Punish*, 215. Power is not wielded by the state or by the interests of capitalism for the simple reason that for Foucault power cannot be wielded or owned at all; see Deleuze, *Foucault*, 32–33; Foucault, *Dits et écrits*, 3:169; Best, *Politics of Historical Vision*, 140; and Smart, *Foucault, Marxism and Critique*, 114.

78. Foucault, *Dits et écrits*, 3:203–4.

79. Foucault, *Madness and Civilization: A History of Insanity in the Age of Reason*, trans. Richard Howard (New York: Vintage, 1965), 231 (Foucault's emphasis).

80. See the analysis of the relation of this analysis of power to Foucault's later works in Hubert L. Dreyfus and Paul Rabinow, *Michel Foucault: Beyond Structuralism and Hermeneutics* (Chicago: University of Chicago Press, 1983), 7–9.

81. Foucault, *Histoire de la folie à l'age classique* (Paris: Gallimard, 1972), 433 and 435 (my translation). This passage and the following passages are not in the abridged English translation.

82. Ibid., 434 (my translation).

83. Ibid., 439 (my translation).

84. Ibid., 436 (my translation). For Foucault's most extended analysis of the "social space of sickness," see Michel Foucault, *The Birth of the Clinic: An Archaeology of Medical Perception*, trans. A. M. Sheridan Smith (New York: Vintage, 1975).

85. The terminological shift in Foucault's work is worth summarizing:

disciplinary power takes on the new name of "anatomo-politics of the human body" and the new regime of populations and masses is known as "a biopolitics of the population"; together, they make up the "two poles" of biopower and are "linked together by a whole intermediary cluster of relations" (Foucault, *History of Sexuality*, 1:139).

86. Ibid.; Foucault, *Histoire de la sexualité*, 1:183.

87. Michel Foucault, *"Il faut défendre la société": Cours au Collège de France, 1975–1976* (Paris: Seuil/Gallimard, 1997), 218.

88. Ibid., 217–18.

89. Foucault, *History of Sexuality*, 1:140; Foucault, *Histoire de la sexualité*, 1:185.

90. Procacci, *Gouverner la misère*, 39.

91. Foucault, *History of Sexuality*, 1:139; Foucault, *Histoire de la sexualité*, 1:183.

92. Foucault, *Histoire de la folie*, 434 (my translation).

93. Foucault, *The History of Sexuality*, 1:140–41.

94. Ibid., 114.

95. Ibid., 141.

96. It is thus difficult to agree with Dominick LaCapra's reading of Foucault's work as "cut off from traditions of political, social, and cultural analysis—such as those represented by Tocqueville, Marx, and Durkheim—that focused on important institutions—the family, education, the workplace, and the state—and that raised the issue of possible alternative structures for modern societies." Dominick LaCapra, *History and Reading: Tocqueville, Foucault, French Studies* (Toronto: University of Toronto Press, 2000), 121.

2. Let's Get Beat Up by the Poor!

1. Michel Foucault, *Essential Works of Foucault*, vol. 3, *Power*, ed. James D. Faubion (New York: New Press, 2000), 157–58; Foucault, *Dits et écrits*, 3:237–38.

2. See Foucault, *Dits et écrits*, 3:237; and David Macey, *The Lives of Michel Foucault: A Biography* (New York: Pantheon, 1993), 360–62.

3. Foucault, *Essential Works*, 3:161. See Deleuze's remarks on the illuminating effect of power in Deleuze, *Foucault* (Paris: Minuit, 1986), 60.

4. Foucault, *Essential Works*, 3:161.

5. Ibid., 162. Foucault's remark comes as a response to an imagined reproach that his project is "always bound by the same inability to cross the line, to pass to the other side"—in other words, to represent an original existence that escapes power's grasp (ibid., 161).

6. Ibid., 172.

7. Ibid., 174.

8. Ibid., 172. See also Foucault, *Discipline and Punish*, 194. Foucault's analysis of this compulsion to speak dispels any belief in the ability of a text to reflect or represent the infamous or the poor "as they really are" and thus can be read as precisely the "sustained and developing work on the mechanics of constitution of the Other" that Gayatri Chakravorty Spivak has claimed is missing from his writing; see her "Can the Subaltern Speak?" in *Marxism and the Interpretation of Culture* (see chap. 1, note 59), 294.

9. "In *Tableaux parisiens*, the secret presence of the crowd is demonstrable almost everywhere." Walter Benjamin, *Selected Writings*, ed. Michael Jennings (Cambridge, Mass.: Harvard University Press, 2003), 4:323.

10. Ibid.; Benjamin, *Gesammelte Schriften*, 1:622.

11. "Gewimmel," *Deutsches Wörterbuch von Jacob und Wilhelm Grimm*, 6:5831.

12. Marx, *Capital*, 1:940; Marx, *Das Kapital*, 1:802.

13. Here I use the translation in Walter Benjamin, *Illuminations*, ed. Hannah Arendt, trans. Harry Zohn (New York: Schocken, 1968), 169; Charles Baudelaire, *Les fleurs du mal*, trans. Richard Howard (Boston: Godine, 1982), 97. For a recent reading of the place of the crowd in "A une passante," see Dolf Oehler, "Les ressources de l'allégorie: 'A une passante,'" in *Lectures des "Fleurs du Mal,"* ed. Steve Murphy (Rennes: Presses Universitaires de Rennes, 2002), 65–68.

14. Charles Baudelaire, *The Painter of Modern Life and Other Essays*, ed. and trans. Jonathan Mayne (Da Capo: New York, 1964), 9. See the similar formulation in the prose poem "Crowds": "The poet enjoys the incomparable privilege of being able, at will, to be himself and an other" (Baudelaire, *Parisian Prowler*, 21).

15. Benjamin, *Selected Writings*, 4:39; Benjamin, *Gesammelte Schriften*, 1:569.

16. Benjamin, *Selected Writings*, 4:39.

17. Benjamin, *Selected Writings*, 4:60; Benjamin, *Gesammelte Schriften*, 1:600.

18. Baudelaire, *Les fleurs du mal*, 92 (translation modified).

19. Ibid., 93.

20. On this incognito, see Kevin Newmark, "Off the Charts: Walter Benjamin's Depiction of Baudelaire," in *Baudelaire and the Poetics of Modernity*, ed. Patricia A. Ward (Nashville, Tenn.: Vanderbilt University Press, 2001), 72; on its productivity, see Hans-Jost Frey, "On Presentation in Baudelaire," trans. Michael Shae, in *Walter Benjamin: Theoretical Questions*, ed. David Ferris (Stanford, Calif.: Stanford University Press, 1996), 164.

21. Baudelaire, *The Painter of Modern Life*, 28.

22. Ibid.

23. Ibid., 29.

24. Benjamin, *Selected Writings*, 4:60.

25. Ibid.

26. Ibid., 59; Benjamin, *Gesammelte Schriften*, 1:599.

27. Benjamin, *Selected Writings*, 4:9–10.

28. Ibid., 10.

29. Ibid., 9.

30. Baudelaire, *Les fleurs du mal*, 143.

31. Baudelaire, *Œuvres complètes*, ed. Claude Pichois (Paris: Gallimard, 1975), 1:5 (my translation). An English translation of the entire poem can be found in Baudelaire, *Les fleurs du mal*, 5–6.

32. Dolf Oehler, *Ein Höllensturz der alten Welt: Zur Selbstforschung der Moderne nach dem Juni 1848* (Frankfurt am Main: Suhrkamp, 1988), 281. See also the remarks on community in "To the Reader," in Ross Chambers, "Poetry in the Asiatic Mode: Baudelaire's 'Au lecteur,'" *Yale French Studies* 74 (1988): 103–4.

33. Baudelaire, *Les fleurs du mal*, 6.

34. Ross Chambers points out that the political motivation of the possible violence evoked here remains impossible to determine; the poem does not clarify the political intent and context of these hangings (Chambers, "Poetry in the Asiatic Mode," 98). Intensifying Benjamin's remark that Baudelaire denounces his reader as "disinclined," Dolf Oehler writes that the addressee and the poet of "To the Reader" both appear as "completely incompetent and incapable but, precisely because of this incapacity, able to commit the most terrible things" (Oehler, *Ein Höllensturz der alten Welt*, 281). In any case, the poem presents ennui as potential; Leo Bersani has emphasized how ennui in this text must be understood as an "openness to other forms of being" and as an "aptitude." Leo Bersani, *Baudelaire and Freud* (Berkeley and Los Angeles: University of California Press, 1977), 28.

35. Baudelaire, *Les fleurs du mal*, 6.

36. Baudelaire, *The Parisian Prowler*, 69.

37. Ibid., 41.

38. Ibid., 93.

39. Ibid., 23.

40. Jacques Derrida, *Given Time I. Counterfeit Money*, trans. Peggy Kamuf (Chicago: University of Chicago Press, 1992), 137. Derrida focuses on the place of the gift in Baudelaire and explicitly excludes a consideration of poverty: "But this is not the place to go off into an endless discourse, however necessary

it may be, on alms and begging" (ibid.). He chooses to "retain merely a formal trait," this "absolute demand of the other," and the principal link between Derrida's work on Baudelaire and the current study would be the passivity or latency of the poor, which appears in Derrida as the possible openness to the gift.

41. Berger, *Scènes d'aumône*, 197–98. On the experimental disposition, see Avital Ronell, *The Test Drive* (Champaign: University of Illinois Press, 2005), and the discussion of Ronell's reading of Nietzsche in chap. 4.

42. Baudelaire, *The Parisian Prowler*, 13–14.

43. Ibid.

44. All French citations of "Le vieux saltimbanque" are from Charles Baudelaire, *Œuvres complètes*, 1:295–97. I will refer to the English translation in Baudelaire, *The Parisian Prowler*, 27–31.

45. Jean Starobinski emphasizes the opposition between the immobility of the performer and the mobility of his gaze in "Sur quelques répondants allégoriques du poète," *Revue d'histoire littéraire de la France* 67 (April–June 1967): 410. Baudelaire focuses here and throughout *Le spleen de Paris* on the deep, empty "eyes of the poor"; see the prose poems "The Cake," "The Pauper's Toy," "The Eyes of the Poor," "The Counterfeit Coin," and "The Widows." On "The Eyes of the Poor," see Sophie Montreuil, "Pauvreté et modernité dans 'Les yeux des pauvres' de Charles Baudelaire," in *Misères de la littérature*, ed. Geneviève Sicotte and Pierre Popovic (Montreal: Centre universitaire de lecture sociopoétique de l'épistolaire et des correspondances, 1995), 167–85.

46. In his essay on *Madame Bovary*, Baudelaire presents male hysteria as a form of impotence similar to that suffered by the narrator of "Le vieux saltimbanque": hysteria "se traduit chez les hommes nerveux par toutes les impuissances et aussi par l'aptitude à tous les excès" (Baudelaire, *Œuvres complètes*, 2:83). On hysteria and inactivity, see Luce Irigaray, *Speculum of the Other Woman*, trans. Gillian C. Gill (Ithaca, N.Y.: Cornell University Press, 1985), 61 and 71. On the relation of the acrobat to narration, see Bridget Mary Keegan, "Sordid Melpomene: Poetry and Poverty in the Work of Wordsworth, Clare, Hugo and Baudelaire" (PhD diss., State University of New York, Buffalo, 1993), 307. Beryl Schlossman's reading of "A une passante" emphasizes the petrifying effect of that poem's encounter; see her "The Night of the Poet: Baudelaire, Benjamin, and the Woman in the Street," *MLN* 119 (2004): 1017–18.

47. This is a good example of what Leo Bersani identifies as the "pedantic" and "sadistic" attempt to contain the threat of the encounters with difference in Baudelaire's prose poems; see the last chapter ("A Beggarly Ending") of his *Baudelaire and Freud*, 137–51.

48. On the failure to parry shocks in Baudelaire, see Vaheed K. Ramazani, "Writing in Pain: Baudelaire, Benjamin, Haussmann," *boundary 2* 23 (1996): 206.

49. Jean Starobinski, *Portrait de l'artiste en saltimbanque* (Geneva: Skira, 1970), 94.

50. Starobinski, "Sur quelques répondants allégoriques du poète," 410.

51. Cheryl Krueger, "Telling Stories in Baudelaire's *Spleen de Paris*," *Nineteenth-Century French Studies* 30, no. 3–4 (2002), 297.

52. All citations from "Let's Beat Up the Poor!" are from Baudelaire, *Œuvres complètes*, 1:357–59, and Baudelaire, *The Parisian Prowler*, 121–23. The manuscript version of this poem concludes with the apostrophe that may have served to indicate more precisely the kinds of "formulas" that the narrator was acquainted with: "Qu'en dis tu, Citoyen Proudhon?" See Baudelaire, *Œuvres complètes*, 1:1350; and for a recent account of Baudelaire's relation to Proudhon, see Berger, *Scènes d'aumône*, 187–95.

53. Dolf Oehler calls "Let's Beat Up the Poor!" one of the most "compelling" examples of how Baudelaire's poems address themselves to multiple "forces of resistance" (Oehler, *Ein Höllensturz der alten Welt*, 298).

54. Émile Littré, *Dictionnaire de la langue française* (Paris: J. J. Pauvert, 1956–58), 2:1801–2.

55. By adding a determination of the exact kind of action here, my reading offers a variation on Jonathan Monroe's emphasis on how, in this poem, "contemplation gives way to action" and "praxis"; see Monroe, *A Poverty of Objects: The Prose Poem and the Politics of Genre* (Ithaca, N.Y.: Cornell University Press, 1987), 112–24.

56. On this appropriation, see Bersani, *Baudelaire and Freud*, 143. For Bersani, the appropriation is undone by the poem's irony.

57. Émile Benveniste, *Indo-European Language and Society*, trans. Elizabeth Palmer (Coral Gables, Fla.: University of Miami Press, 1973), 422; for the original text, see Émile Benveniste, *Le vocabulaire des institutions indo-européens* (Paris: Minuit, 1969), 2:149.

58. Benveniste, *Indo-European Language and Society*, 422; Benveniste, *Le vocabulaire des institutions indo-européens*, 2:150.

59. Benveniste, *Le vocabulaire des institutions indo-européens*, 2:150. This passage is from a paragraph that is missing from the English translation of Benveniste's text.

60. Benveniste, *Indo-European Language and Society*, 423.

61. See Ernst Kantorowicz's related discussion of late medieval political and artistic theories in "The Sovereignty of the Artist: A Note on Legal Maxims

and Renaissance Theories of Art," in Kantorowicz, *Selected Studies* (Locust Valley, N.Y.: J. J. Augustin, 1965), 365.

62. This equation of equality and violence belongs to a more general phenomenon of Baudelaire's association of the utopian vocabulary of the Revolution with violence; see Debarati Sanyal, "The Tie That Binds: Violent Commerce in Baudelaire's 'La corde,'" *Yale French Studies* 101 (2001): 132–49. For Anne-Emmanuelle Berger, the equality in "Let's Beat Up the Poor!" is based on a specific capacity: the "pure capacité de 'rendre' ou de donner" (Berger, *Scènes d'aumône*, 195).

63. See the discussion of Bouché-Leclercq's definition of divination as the use of "extra-rational means" in François Guillaumont, *Philosophe et augure: Recherches sur la théorie cicéronienne de la divination* (Brussels: Latomus, 1984), 13. On the complex, close relation of divination and reason, see the studies assembled in J. P. Vernant et al., *Divination et rationalité* (Paris: Seuil, 1971).

64. Foucault, *Essential Works*, 3:174.

65. Benveniste treats the enunciations *je jure* and *il jure* as exemplary of this distinction in Émile Benveniste, *Problèmes de linguistique générale* (Paris: Gallimard, 1966), 1:265.

66. Leo Bersani captures this aspect of the poem in his reading, in which he shows how "the sign of the beggar's enslavement is his imitation of the poet"; for Bersani, the poem presents the fulfillment of a fantasy of narcissistic power in which "the poet's influence will spread everywhere; in numerous places and at numerous times, the world will mirror him" (Bersani, *Baudelaire and Freud*, 146). In this reading, the beggar remains completely contained and controlled by the narrator. But Bersani also insists on the reappearance of difference in the form of irony, which can be read most explicitly in the all too perfect conclusion to the narrator's attempt to prove his theory (ibid., 149).

67. Foucault, *Essential Works*, 3:172.

68. Heidegger, *Aristotle's Metaphysics* Θ *1–3*, 157.

69. Deleuze, "Un manifeste de moins," 125.

70. Dolf Oehler, *Pariser Bilder I (1830–1848): Antibourgeoise Ästhetik bei Baudelaire, Daumier und Heine* (Frankfurt am Main: Suhrkamp, 1979), 161.

71. Jeffrey Mehlman emphasizes the passivity and suffering of the encounter with the beggar when he writes that "Let's Beat Up the Poor!" presents "less an exchange of *douleurs* than the *douleur* of a certain kind of exchange." Mehlman, "Baudelaire with Freud: Theory and Pain," *diacritics* 4, no. 1 (1974), 8.

72. Baudelaire, *The Parisian Prowler*, 21.

73. Oehler, *Ein Höllensturz der alten Welt*, 299.

74. Gilles Deleuze, *Negotiations: 1972–1990*, trans. M. Joughin (New York:

Columbia University Press, 1995), 133; cited in Thoburn, *Deleuze, Marx and Politics*, 18.

3. Poetic Rebellion in Mallarmé

1. Paul Valéry, *The Collected Works of Paul Valéry*, ed. Jackson Matthews, trans. Malcolm Cowley and James R. Lawler (Princeton, N.J.: Princeton University Press, 1972), 8:274; Paul Valéry, *Œuvres complètes*, ed. Jean Hytier (Paris: Gallimard, 1957), 1:646.

2. "Un homme qui renonce au monde se met dans la condition de le comprendre. Celui-ci dont je parle et qui tendait vers ses délices absolues par l'exercise d'une sorte d'ascétisme, puisqu'il avait repoussé toutes les facilités de son art et leurs heureux conséquences, il avait bien mérité d'en apercevoir la profondeur" (Valéry, *Œuvres complètes*, 1:621).

3. Valéry, *Collected Works*, 8:293; Valéry, *Œuvres complètes*, 1:659–60.

4. Mallarmé, *Œuvres complètes*, 2:39 (my translation). A summary of this lecture can be found in Michel Gauthier, *Mallarmé en clair ou: L'obscurité poétique "vaincue mot par mot"* (Saint-Genouph: Nizet, 1998), 312–15. For a reading of the lecture in terms of the proper name, see Michael Temple, *The Name of the Poet: Onomastics and Anonymity in the Works of Stéphane Mallarmé* (Exeter: University of Exeter Press, 1995), 40–47.

5. Mallarmé, *Œuvres complètes*, 2:39 (my translation).

6. Ibid., 24 (my translation).

7. Stéphane Mallarmé, *Divagations*, trans. Barbara Johnson (Cambridge, Mass.: Harvard University Press, 2007), 210.

8. Mallarmé, *Œuvres complètes*, 2:212.

9. Maurice Blanchot, *The Work of Fire*, trans. Charlotte Mandell (Stanford, Calif.: Stanford University Press, 1995), 29–30. See also Blanchot, *The Space of Literature*, trans. Ann Smock (Lincoln: University of Nebraska Press, 1982), 48.

10. See Blanchot, *The Work of Fire*, 30.

11. Mallarmé, *Divagations*, 186 (translation modified).

12. Mallarmé, *Œuvres complètes*, 2:66.

13. This passage occupies a privileged position in Pierre Bourdieu's critique of Mallarmé. Bourdieu reproaches Mallarmé for this reverence for the alphabet but does not take into account the transfiguration that emerges from it. Pierre Bourdieu, *The Rules of Art*, trans. Susan Emanuel (Stanford, Calif.: Stanford University Press, 1996), 275–76. See also Pierre Bourdieu, *Méditations pascaliennes* (Paris: Seuil, 1997), 15.

14. Mallarmé, *Divagations*, 211 (translation modified).

15. Roger Pearson, *Mallarmé and Circumstance: The Translation of Silence* (New York: Oxford University Press, 2004), 30. For Mallarmé's critical remarks about journalism, see Mallarmé, *Œuvres complètes*, 2:210, 227, and 698.

16. Jacques Scherer, *Grammaire de Mallarmé* (Paris: Nizet, 1977), 88–93.

17. Ibid., 91 (my translation).

18. Valéry, *Œuvres complètes*, 626. Jean-Pierre Richard discusses Mallarmé's fascination with the newspaper in *L'univers imaginaire de Mallarmé* (Paris: Seuil, 1961), 557–58.

19. Walter Benjamin, "Paul Valéry in der École Normale," in Benjamin, *Gesammelte Schriften*, 4:480 (my translation).

20. See Mallarmé, *Œuvres complètes*, 2:487–654; and Bertrand Marchal's notes on the place of the journal in Mallarmé's œuvre, Mallarmé, *Œuvres complètes*, 2:1712–15. Roger Dragonetti examines Mallarmé's journalism and correspondence in his *Un fantôme dans le kiosque* (Paris: Seuil, 1992). In the letter from 1885 to Verlaine that came to be titled "Autobiography," Mallarmé fondly recalls *La dernière mode:* "dont les huit ou dix numéros parus servent encore quand je les dévêts de leur poussière à me faire longtemps rêver" (Mallarmé, *Œuvres complètes*, 2:789).

21. Gilles Deleuze, *The Fold: Leibniz and the Baroque*, trans. Tom Conley (Minneapolis: University of Minnesota Press, 1993), 31.

22. Mallarmé, *Divagations*, 210 (my emphasis).

23. Mallarmé, ibid.; *Œuvres complètes*, 2:212 (my translation).

24. Scherer, *Grammaire de Mallarmé*, 58.

25. Jacques Rancière, *Mallarmé: La politique de la sirène* (Paris: Hachette, 1996), 40 (my translation). On the word *rien* in Mallarmé, see also Roger Dragonetti, *Études sur Mallarmé*, ed. Wilfried Smekens (Ghent: Romanica Gandensia, 1992), 123.

26. Mallarmé, *Œuvres complètes*, 1:24.

27. Mallarmé, *Divagations*, 210.

28. Mallarmé, *Œuvres complètes*, 2:213. On the value of *aucun* here, see Scherer, *Grammaire de Mallarmé*, 59.

29. Mallarmé, *Divagations*, 207 (translation modified); Mallarmé, *Œuvres complètes*, 2:210. The other aspect of language appears here again as unverifiable, as presented only to divination.

30. Mallarmé, *Divagations*, 208 (translation modified).

31. Mallarmé, *Œuvres complètes*, 2:211.

32. Roger Pearson writes similarly of "Mimique" that "Mallarmé realizes that he is reading the potentially audible, linguistic account of a pattern," and

he concludes that "in 'Mimique' Mallarmé shows us how he means us to read his own poetry. Caught between sound and silence, between text and *'mystère,'* between a poem and what it might mean, we shall be able to delight . . . in the *'attente'* and *'suspens'* that are the *sine qua non* of ecstasy" (Pearson, *Mallarmé and Circumstance,* 66).

33. Mallarmé, *Divagations,* 210–11.

34. Mallarmé, *Œuvres complètes,* 2:213. Mallarmé writes elsewhere about *une vertu* revealed in literature: "une vertu autrement attrayante que ne les voilera une description, évocation dites, *allusion* je sais, *suggestion"* (Mallarmé, *Œuvres complètes,* 2:210). The third aspect—or that which is *autrement attrayant*—that emerges as an accord or relation between two terms is an allusion to another way of writing and thinking about poetry. See Barbara Johnson, *Défigurations du langage poétique: La seconde révolution baudelairienne* (Paris: Seuil, 1979), 211; and Richard, *L'univers imaginaire de Mallarmé,* 527. Vincent Kaufmann writes that the changed relation between genres and between criticism and literature has the effect of "mettre en crise toute spécificité ou toute identité du langage." Vincent Kaufmann, *Le livre et ses adresses* (Paris: Méridiens Klincksieck, 1986), 55.

35. A translation of the poem can be found in Stéphane Mallarmé, *Collected Poems,* trans. Henry Weinfield (Berkeley and Los Angeles: University of California Press, 1994), 23.

36. Mallarmé, *Œuvres complètes,* 1:16. All references to "Aumône" are from this page. Jean-Pierre Richard shows how the movement of torsion, throughout Mallarmé's corpus, appears as the mixture of real and imaginary (which would correspond in "Aumône" to the encounter of the monetary and extramonetary within the coin's torsion) and also can be seen in *le tourbillon, mouvement-clef de la danseuse* (Richard, *L'univers imaginaire de Mallarmé,* 217–18).

37. Earlier versions of "Aumône" included the phrase "I hate useful alms" ("Je hais l'aumône utile"): for these poems, titled "A un mendiant" and "A un pauvre," see Mallarmé, *Œuvres complètes,* 1:122–23 and 108–9.

38. Kevin Newmark discusses a similar Mallarméan "interruption and displacement" that "consists in resisting political and economic conventions precisely by repeating, or translating, their means in quite unexpected and even unpredictable ways" in "Translators, Inc.: Kierkegaard, Benjamin, Mallarmé & Co.," *parallax* 14 (2000), 52.

39. Paul de Man, *The Rhetoric of Romanticism* (New York: Columbia University Press, 1984), 75–76 (my emphasis).

40. Paul de Man, *Resistance to Theory* (Minneapolis: University of Minnesota Press, 1986), 44 (de Man's emphasis). Prosopopeia literally means to create a face, not to give one.

41. De Man, *The Rhetoric of Romanticism*, 81.

42. Ibid., 80.

43. Ibid.

44. All citations from "Pauvre enfant pâle" are from Mallarmé, *Œuvres complètes*, 1:418–19. For an interpretation of the relation of Mallarmé's poems on poverty to his predecessors' poems on the same theme, see Austin Gill, *The Early Mallarmé* (Oxford: Clarendon Press, 1986), 2:214–26; and Berger, "Crise d'aumône (Mallarmé reprend Hugo)," 237–54.

45. "As-tu jamais eu un père? Tu n'as pas même une vieille qui te fasse oublier la faim en te battant, quand tu rentres sans un sou" (Mallarmé, *Œuvres complètes*, 1:418).

46. Berger, *Scènes d'aumône*, 42–43.

47. Ibid., 39.

48. Mallarmé, *Œuvres complètes*, 1:445–46.

49. Mallarmé, *Collected Poems*, 103. On the terza rima in Dante, see Guglielmo Gorni, *Il nodo della lingua e il verbo d'amore: Studi su Dante e altri duecentisti* (Florence: Olschki, 1981), 187–216.

50. Mallarmé, *Collected Poems*, 96.

51. Jean-Claude Milner, *Ordres et raisons de langue* (Paris: Seuil, 1982), 301.

52. Giorgio Agamben, *The End of the Poem*, trans. Daniel Heller-Roazen (Stanford, Calif.: Stanford University Press, 1999), 109–15.

53. An earlier version of the poem, "Monologue d'un faune," ends with the line "Adieu, femmes; duo de vierges quand je vins" (Mallarmé, *Œuvres complètes*, 1:156).

54. All French quotations from "L'Après-midi d'un faune" are from Mallarmé, *Œuvres complètes*, 1:22–25; all English quotations are from Mallarmé, *Collected Poems*, 38–41.

55. Mallarmé, *Collected Poems*, 6; Mallarmé, *Œuvres complètes*, 1:7.

56. Mallarmé's text participates in what Debarati Sanyal calls Baudelaire's "perversion of fraternity" in "The Tie That Binds: Violent Commerce in Baudelaire's 'La corde,'" *Yale French Studies* 101 (2001): 132–49.

57. Mallarmé, *Œuvres complètes*, 1:65 (my translation).

58. On the literary discourse of suicide as a form of opposition and proto-revolution, see Ross Chambers, *Room for Maneuver: Reading (the) Oppositional (in) Narrative* (Chicago: University of Chicago Press, 1991), 102–74.

59. The rhyme that joins the two poems is taken as evidence by Austin Gill that the poems form a series and are not simply a pair of versions of the same poem: "the rhyme they . . . share . . . gives positive testimony that the so-called two versions are in fact separate compositions." He concludes that

"Haine du pauvre" is "an individual poem and not an earlier version of 'A un mendiant' [the first title of 'Aumône']"; see Gill, *The Early Mallarmé*, 2:218–19.

60. Lawrence J. Zillman and Clive Scott, "Terza Rima," *The New Princeton Handbook of Poetic Terms*, ed. T. V. F. Brogan (Princeton, N.J.: Princeton University Press, 1994), 307–8.

61. John Freccero, "The Significance of Terza Rima," in *Dante, Petrarch, Boccaccio: Studies in Honor of Charles S. Singleton* (Binghamton: Center for Medieval and Early Renaissance Studies at the State University of New York at Binghamton, 1987), 6.

62. Leo Bersani discusses a similar tendency in Mallarmé's poetry: his "eerie strategy of celebrating writers and literature as a way of burying them"; see his *The Death of Stéphane Mallarmé* (Cambridge: Cambridge University Press, 1982), 25–47.

63. Mallarmé, *Divagations*, 167 (translation modified). For a commentary on this passage, see Pearson, *Mallarmé and Circumstance*, 123–25.

64. Pearson, *Mallarmé and Circumstance*, 124.

65. On the imprisoning power of a similar *lacet/lacs* in the sonnet "Le vierge, le vivace et le bel aujourd'hui," see Jean-Claude Milner, *Mallarmé au tombeau* (Paris: Verdier, 1999), 21–22.

66. All quotations from "Le démon de l'analogie" are from Mallarmé, *Œuvres complètes*, 1:416–18; the translation is from Mallarmé, *Collected Poems*, 93–94.

67. "Orphelin, j'errais en noir" (Mallarmé, *Œuvres complètes*, 1:423).

68. Mallarmé, *Collected Poems*, 122.

69. Ibid., 121–22.

70. The same emphasis can be seen in his description of the Book in a letter to Verlaine from 1885: "le Livre, persuadé qu'au fond il n'y en a qu'un . . ." (Mallarmé, *Œuvres complètes*, 1:788).

71. See the similar remarks of Leo Bersani on Mallarmé's desire to transform "the signifying process into fixed visual designs" that "produce diagrammatic sense" (Bersani, *The Death of Stéphane Mallarmé*, 76).

72. Valéry writes that Mallarmé read "Un coup de dés" to him in a single, unaccented voice: "Il se mit à lire d'une voix basse, égale. . . . Il a essayé, pensai-je, *d'élever enfin une page à la puissance du ciel étoilé*" (Valéry, "Le coup de dés: Lettre au directeur des *Marges*," *Œuvres complètes*, 1:625). This contradicts the indication in Mallarmé's preface to change intonation according to the typeface (Mallarmé, *Collected Poems*, 122).

73. "Nothing / of the memorable crisis / or might / the event // have been accomplished in view of all results null / human" ("RIEN / de la mémorable

crise / ou se fût / l'événement // accompli en vue de tout résultat nul / humain"). All French citations from "Un coup de dés" are from Mallarmé, *Œuvres complètes*, 1:384–87; all English citations are from Mallarmé, *Collected Poems*, 124–45. One slash will mark a line break; two slashes, a page break.

74. Scherer, *Grammaire de Mallarmé*, 230.

75. Mallarmé, *Divagations*, 133–34.

76. Pearson, *Mallarmé and Circumstance*, 61.

77. Mallarmé, *Divagations*, 130; Mallarmé, *Œuvres complètes*, 2:171.

78. See another Mallarméan formulation of the dancer as an un-individual: "Une armature, qui n'est d'aucune femme en particulier, d'où instable, à travers le voile de généralité, attire sur tel fragment révélé de la forme et y boit l'éclair qui le divinise; ou exhale, de retour, par l'ondulation des tissus, flottante, palpitante, éparse cette extase" (Mallarmé, *Œuvres complètes*, 2:177). A translation of this passage can be found in Mallarmé, *Divagations*, 138.

79. Mallarmé, *Collected Poems*, 69 (translation modified).

80. Ibid., 35.

81. Mallarmé, *Œuvres complètes*, 1:37.

4. The Transvaluation of Poverty

1. Gilles Deleuze, *Pure Immanence: Essays on a Life*, trans. Anne Boyman (New York: Zone, 2001), 78.

2. Ibid., 80.

3. Nietzsche, *On the Genealogy of Morality*, trans. Carol Diethe (Cambridge: Cambridge University Press, 1994), third essay, §27.

4. Ibid., third essay, §24. Nietzsche also describes the ascetic ideal as the separation of a force from what it can do; the invention of an agent separate from activity; and the idea that the strong can hold back and be weak. On the ascetic ideal's separation of humanity from its power, see *On the Genealogy of Morality*, first essay, §13; and Deleuze's presentation of "the becoming-reactive of forces" in *Nietzsche and Philosophy*, trans. Hugh Tomlinson (New York: Columbia University Press, 1983), 64–65.

5. Nietzsche, *On the Genealogy of Morality*, third essay, §27.

6. Friedrich Nietzsche, *Beyond Good and Evil*, trans. Walter Kaufmann (New York: Vintage, 1989), §1. There is a similar passage at the end of *On the Genealogy of Morality:* "what meaning does *our* being have, if it were not that that will to truth has become conscious of itself *as a problem* in us?" (Nietzsche, *On the Genealogy of Morality*, third essay, §27).

7. Nietzsche, *On the Genealogy of Morality*, third essay, §27.

8. Ibid., third essay, §25.

9. Sarah Kofman recognizes that "there is no single essence of the ascetic ideal, but, instead, a plurality of possible meanings," but she unites this plurality under a "typological unity" that precludes the necessary undoing of asceticism from within; see Kofman, "Wagner's Ascetic Ideal According to Nietzsche," trans. David Blake and Jessica George, in *Nietzsche, Genealogy, Morality: Essays on Nietzsche's "On the Genealogy of Morality,"* ed. Richard Schacht (Berkeley and Los Angeles: University of California Press, 1994), 194.

10. Friedrich Nietzsche, *Human, All Too Human,* vol. 2, trans. R. J. Hollingdale (Cambridge: Cambridge University Press, 1996), "The Wanderer and His Shadow," §127 (translation modified); Friedrich Nietzsche, *Daybreak: Thoughts on the Prejudices of Morality,* trans. R. J. Hollingdale (Cambridge: Cambridge University Press, 1997), §195 (translation modified).

11. Nietzsche, *On the Genealogy of Morality,* first essay, §6; second essay, §16.

12. Ibid., third essay, §§7–8.

13. Friedrich Nietzsche, *Kritische Studienausgabe,* ed. Giorgio Colli and Mazzino Montinari (Munich: de Gruyter and Deutscher Taschenbuch Verlag, 1980), 10:233.

14. Nietzsche, *On the Genealogy of Morality,* third essay, §8. On the power of a different kind of chastity, see Nietzsche, ibid., third essay, §§8–9. For a reading of Zarathustrian humility, see Donata Schoeller-Reisch, "Die Demut Zarathustras: Ein Versuch zu Nietzsche mit Meister Eckhart," *Nietzsche-Studien* 27 (1998): 420–39.

15. Pierre Klossowski, *Un si funeste désir* (Paris: Gallimard, 1963), 217 (my translation).

16. My discussion of Nietzsche and Christianity is indebted to Ernst Benz, *Nietzsches Ideen zur Geschichte des Christentums und der Kirche* (Leiden: E. J. Brill, 1956); Didier Franck, *Nietzsche et l'ombre de Dieu* (Paris: Presses Universitaires de France, 1998); Karl Jaspers, *Nietzsche und das Christentum* (Munich: Piper, 1952); Manfred Kaempfert, *Säkularisation und neue Heiligkeit: Religion und religionsbezogene Sprache bei Friedrich Nietzsche* (Berlin: Erich Schmidt Verlag, 1971); and Paul Valadier, *Nietzsche et la critique du christianisme* (Paris: Cerf, 1974).

17. Friedrich Nietzsche, *The Antichrist* in *The Portable Nietzsche,* ed. Walter Kaufmann (New York: Viking, 1968), §32.

18. Ibid., §§29, 33 ("any distance separating man and God—is abolished"), and 34.

19. Nietzsche, *Thus Spoke Zarathustra,* trans. Walter Kaufmann (New York: Penguin, 1966), 28–30 ("On the Teachers of Virtue") (translation modified).

20. Ibid., 30 ("On the Teachers of Virtue").

21. Ibid., 29 ("On the Teachers of Virtue"). In *Beyond Good and Evil,* which a note of Nietzsche's calls the "glossary" for *Thus Spoke Zarathustra,* Nietzsche writes of his task as *"wakefulness itself."* Nietzsche, *Beyond Good and Evil,* trans. Walter Kaufmann (New York: Vintage, 1966), 2 ("Preface"). For the note, see Nietzsche, *Kritische Studienausgabe,* 14:345.

22. Nietzsche, *Thus Spoke Zarathustra,* 101 ("On the Tarantulas").

23. Nietzsche, *The Antichrist,* §32 (translation modified). For the acceptation of *Gleichnis* as "comparison," see "Gleichnis," *Deutsches Wörterbuch von Jacob und Wilhelm Grimm,* 7:8200–8201, especially the quotations from Gottsched and Hegel. Nietzsche repeats this critique of Christ's language three times in *The Antichrist,* twice in §32 and then in §34: "he understood the rest, everything natural, temporal, spatial, historical, only as signs, as occasions for parables" (Nietzsche, *The Antichrist,* §34). I will follow Nietzsche's now antiquated spelling "Gleichnis."

24. On the notion of opposition in Nietzsche, see Heidegger, *Nietzsche* (Pfullingen: Neske, 1961), 1:43. Derrida writes that the relation in Nietzsche's texts between metaphysics and nonmetaphysics must be something other than opposition. Jacques Derrida, *Éperons: Les styles de Nietzsche* (Paris: Flammarion, 1978), 96.

25. Under the third heading for the entry for "Gleichnis," Grimms' *Wörterbuch* lists "similarity," "'ähnlichkeit, gleichartigkeit,' . . . als abstrakter eigenschaftsbegriff auf übereinstimmung des aussehens, der gestalt, des wesens, der gesinnung, u. ä. bezogen" ("Gleichnis," *Deutsches Wörterbuch von Jacob und Wilhelm Grimm,* 7:8191).

26. Nietzsche, *Thus Spoke Zarathustra,* 99 ("On the Tarantulas"). The term "*Gleichnis*" occupies an important position in Nietzsche's conception of language. In *The Birth of Tragedy,* the Apollinian "*Mythus*" of tragedy is described as a "*Gleichnis*" of the Dionysian (see *The Birth of Tragedy,* especially §21). Thomas Böning writes about the importance of the parable for the early Nietzsche in *Metaphysik, Kunst und Sprache beim frühen Nietzsche* (Berlin and New York: De Gruyter, 1988), 458–59.

27. Nietzsche, *Thus Spoke Zarathustra,* 217 ("The Convalescent," part 2). Martin Stingelin equates paronomasia with the relation of the "smallest cleft" in "Nietzsches Wortspiel als Reflexion auf poet(olog)ische Verfahren," *Nietzsche-Studien* 17 (1988), 344.

28. Heidegger insists on Zarathustra's transitional character in "Wer ist Nietzsches Zarathustra?" in *Vorträge und Aufsätze* (Pfullingen: Neske, 1954), 101–26.

29. Nietzsche, *Ecce Homo,* in Friedrich Nietzsche, *On the Genealogy of Morality and Ecce Homo,* trans. Walter Kaufmann (New York: Vintage, 1967), 304 ("Thus Spoke Zarathustra," 6).

30. Friedrich Nietzsche, *The Gay Science,* trans. Walter Kaufmann (New York: Vintage, 1974), §299 (translation modified).

31. Nietzsche, *Kritische Studienausgabe,* 14:267.

32. For an extended reading of Zarathustra, distance, and "dis-dance," see Roger W. Müller Farguell, *Tanz-Figuren: Zur metaphorischen Konstitution von Bewegung in Texten* (Munich: Wilhelm Fink, 1995), 318–47.

33. Nietzsche, *Thus Spoke Zarathustra,* 75 ("On the Gift-Giving Virtue," 1).

34. On giving and taking in Nietzsche, see Derrida, *Éperons,* 89–93.

35. Nietzsche, *Thus Spoke Zarathustra,* 75 ("On the Gift-Giving Virtue," 1).

36. For Nietzsche, the verb "to rob" *(rauben)* must always be understood in relation to the race of *Raubtiere,* the predators at the center of *Beyond Good and Evil, On the Genealogy of Morality,* and the fourth *Dionysus Dithyramb,* "Among Birds of Prey."

37. Joan Stambaugh describes the Nietzschean precedence of "how" over "what" in "Amor dei and amor fati: Spinoza and Nietzsche," in *Studies in Nietzsche and the Judaeo-Christian Tradition,* ed. James O'Flaherty, Timothy F. Sellner, and Robert M. Helm (Chapel Hill: University of North Carolina Press, 1985), 136.

38. Just as the eternal return is a process of differentiation in which only the affirmative returns, the giving virtue takes and gives only what affirms. See the concise presentation of the eternal return as that which "expels all that contradicts affirmation" in Deleuze, *Pure Immanence,* 88; and in Deleuze, *Nietzsche and Philosophy,* 189–94.

39. Nietzsche, *Thus Spoke Zarathustra,* 76 ("On the Gift-Giving Virtue," 2) (translation modified).

40. Ibid., 78 ("On the Gift-Giving Virtue," 3) (translation modified).

41. Nietzsche describes *Thus Spoke Zarathustra* as his "Evangelium" (see Nietzsche, *Kritische Studienausgabe,* 12:234) and himself as the "Evangelist" or bearer of the "Good News" in *Ecce Homo* ("Why I Am a Destiny," 1). He also presents parody as a way of being original: "Perhaps this is where we shall still discover the realm of our *invention,* that realm in which we, too, can still be original, say, as parodists of world history and God's buffoons—perhaps, even if nothing else today has a future, our *laughter* may yet have a future" (Nietzsche, *Beyond Good and Evil,* §223).

42. Nietzsche, *Thus Spoke Zarathustra,* 147 ("The Stillest Hour").

43. Ibid.

44. Ibid., 146.

45. See Klaus Weichelt's remarks on "The Stillest Hour" in his *Zarathustra-Kommentar* (Leipzig: Meiner, 1922), 117–20; and the editors' commentary on a similar instance of Zarathustra's reticence: "Zarathustra pauses here, because he recoils before the pronouncement of his teaching of the eternal return" (Nietzsche, *Kritische Studienausgabe*, 14:307). On the nonrevelation of the eternal return, see Gilles Deleuze, "Conclusions sur la volonté de puissance et l'éternel retour," in Deleuze, *L'île deserte et autres textes: Textes et entretiens 1953–1974* (Paris: Minuit, 2002), 163–77, especially 164; and Michel Haar, *Par-delà le nihilisme: Nouveaux essais sur Nietzsche* (Paris: Presses Universitaires de France, 1998), 176.

46. Avital Ronell, "Street Talk," in *Benjamin's Ground*, ed. Rainer Nägele, (Detroit: Wayne State University Press, 1988), 127.

47. She is testing him, and Avital Ronell shows in *The Test Drive* how, for Nietzsche, "virtue itself, no matter how generous or exemplary, can trip up the one being tested. . . . One can become enslaved to one's virtue . . . and turn oneself into a hospital for the vampirizing other," which is an apt description of the parasitic relation desired by the Stillest Hour. See Ronell's discussion of how, for Nietzsche, "One must desist even from becoming attached to one's own virtues" (*The Test Drive*, 144–45).

48. See the final lines of book 4 of *The Gay Science* that are taken up again in the foreword to *Thus Spoke Zarathustra*: "Behold, this cup wants to become empty again, and Zarathustra wants to become man again"; Nietzsche, *The Gay Science*, §342, and Nietzsche, *Thus Spoke Zarathustra*, 10 ("Prologue, 2").

49. Nietzsche, *Thus Spoke Zarathustra*, 144 ("On Human Prudence"). This recalls Nietzsche's transformed citation from Terence in the preface to *On the Genealogy of Morality*: "everyone is furthest from himself" (Jeder ist sich selbst der Fernste); Nietzsche, *On the Genealogy of Morality*, 3–4 ("Preface," 1).

50. Nietzsche, *Thus Spoke Zarathustra*, 147 ("The Stillest Hour").

51. Nietzsche, *Nietzsche contra Wagner* in *The Portable Nietzsche*, 682–83 ("Epilogue," 2) (translation modified).

52. Nietzsche, *Thus Spoke Zarathustra*, 270 ("The Voluntary Beggar").

53. Ibid. (translation modified).

54. Ibid., 272 ("The Voluntary Beggar").

55. Ibid., 237 ("The Honey Sacrifice").

56. Ibid., 327 ("The Sign").

57. Ibid., 287 ("On the Higher Men," 3).

58. See Deleuze's discussion of "the higher men" in *Pure Immanence*, 96–100; and in *Nietzsche and Philosophy*, 164–66.

59. Nietzsche, *On the Genealogy of Morality,* third essay, §11.

60. See Nietzsche, *Kritische Studienausgabe,* 13:88.

61. Wolfram Groddeck notes the testamentary form of "Last Will" in his *Friedrich Nietzsche "Dionysos-Dithyramben"* (Berlin: de Gruyter, 1991), 2:99. On "Lament of Ariadne," see Bianca Theisen, "Die Gewalt des Notwendigen: Überlegungen zu Nietzsches Dionysos-Dithyrambus 'Klage der Ariadne,'" *Nietzsche-Studien* 20 (1991), 192.

62. Nietzsche, *Kritische Studienausgabe,* 6:388 (my translation). The repetition of this phrase calls into question Philip Grundlehner's interpretation of the poem's final "impression" as "one of continued forward motion"; *The Poetry of Friedrich Nietzsche* (New York: Oxford University Press, 1986), 257.

63. Nietzsche, *Kritische Studienausgabe,* 6:389–92 (my translation).

64. Ibid., 390 (my translation).

65. Ibid., 390 and 392 (my translation).

66. Max Baeumer, "Dialektik und zeitgeschichtliche Funktion des literarischen Topos," in *Toposforschung,* ed. Max L. Baeumer (Darmstadt: Wissenschaftliche Buchgesellschaft, 1973), 310 (my translation); cited in Groddeck, *Friedrich Nietzsche "Dionysos-Dithyramben,"* 2:xviii.

67. Nietzsche, *Kritische Studienausgabe,* 6:401 (my translation, Nietzsche's emphasis).

68. For a theory of anagrams and their possible centrality to (Latin) verse, see Jean Starobinski, *Les mots sous les mots: Les anagrammes de Ferdinand de Saussure* (Paris: Gallimard, 1971), especially 151–54. Starobinski's conclusions are pertinent here in their insistence on the distance between the poet and his or her writing.

69. Nietzsche, *The Gay Science,* §110; quoted in Ronell, *The Test Drive,* 245.

70. Nietzsche, *Nietzsche contra Wagner* in *The Portable Nietzsche,* 682–83 ("Epilogue," 2).

71. See Deleuze, *Nietzsche and Philosophy,* 77 (translation modified). See also Foucault's related discussion of the question "Who is speaking?" in Nietzsche, in *The Order of Things,* 305–7.

72. However, their tentative status in *Nietzsche contra Wagner* should alert us that these last words should be read as a threshold rather than an end point. On the final Nietzsche, see Avital Ronell, *Finitude's Score: Essays for the End of the Millennium* (Lincoln: University of Nebraska Press, 1994), 63–82; and Jean-Luc Nancy, *The Birth to Presence* (Stanford, Calif.: Stanford University Press, 1993), 48–57.

73. Nietzsche, *Kritische Studienausgabe,* 6:407 (my translation).

74. Zarathustra may have even taken over Nietzsche himself, who writes

in *Ecce Homo* of Zarathustra: "he ambushed me" (er überfiel mich); Nietzsche, *Ecce Homo*, 298 ("Thus Spoke Zarathustra," 1). Bianca Theisen insists on the force of "excessive self-citation" and the "multiplicity of fictive voices" in "Lament of Ariadne"; see Theisen, "Die Gewalt des Notwendigen," 195.

75. Gilles Deleuze describes the overman in similar terms—as releasing, estranging—in "The Mystery of Ariadne according to Nietzsche," in Deleuze, *Essays Critical and Clinical*, trans. Daniel W. Smith and Michael A. Greco (Minneapolis: University of Minnesota Press, 1997), 99–106.

76. Nietzsche, *Kritische Studienausgabe*, 6:409 (my translation). Zarathustra condemns this kind of poor wealth and praises poverty in Nietzsche, *Thus Spoke Zarathustra*, 48–51 ("The New Idol").

77. Nietzsche, *Kritische Studienausgabe*, 6:409–10.

78. Nietzsche, *Thus Spoke Zarathustra*, 238 ("The Honey Sacrifice").

79. Nietzsche, *On the Genealogy of Morality*, 7 ("Preface," 5) (translation modified). See also the section on "the morality of sacrificial animals" in Nietzsche, *Daybreak*, §215. Bianca Theisen shows how surrender in "Lament of Ariadne" is not sacrifice in Theisen, "Die Gewalt des Notwendigen," 196.

80. Nietzsche, *Beyond Good and Evil*, §25 (translation modified). Nietzsche also insists in *Beyond Good and Evil* that the "philosophers of the future . . . will not dally with 'Truth'" (Nietzsche, *Beyond Good and Evil*, §210).

81. The conflict between Zarathustra and Truth makes it difficult to agree with Grundlehner's interpretation of these lines as an attempt to make Zarathustra "aware of his foibles by constructive criticism" and that presents Zarathustra's poverty as "paradoxically a prerequisite to genuine wealth" (Grundlehner, *The Poetry of Friedrich Nietzsche*, 286).

82. Nietzsche, *Kritische Studienausgabe*, 6:407 (my translation).

83. Clemens Heselhaus, *Deutsche Lyrik der Moderne von Nietzsche bis Yvan Goll: Die Rückkehr zur Bildlichkeit der Sprache* (Düsseldorf: August Bagel, 1961), 30; Grundlehner, *The Poetry of Friedrich Nietzsche*, 286.

84. Michel Haar, "Présentation," in Friedrich Nietzsche, *Poèmes 1858–1888, Dithyrambes pour Dionysos*, trans. Michel Haar (Paris: Gallimard, 1997), 22 and 20. Nietzsche even writes that "the yearning for a *unio mystica* with God is the Buddhist yearning for nothingness, Nirvâna—und nothing more!" (Nietzsche, *Genealogy of Morality*, first essay, §6) (translation modified). For a presentation of Nietzsche's abandoned project for an Empedocles drama and the relation between Zarathustra and Hölderlin's *Der Tod des Empedokles*, see Marie Louise Haase and Mazzino Montinari, *Nachbericht zum ersten Band der sechsten Abteilung: Also sprach Zarathustra* (Berlin: de Gruyter, 1991), 962.

85. On the use of such "evidence" in literary criticism, see Peter Szondi,

"Über philologische Erkenntnis," in Szondi, *Schriften* (Frankfurt am Main: Suhrkamp, 1978), 1:263–86.

86. Groddeck, *Friedrich Nietzsche "Dionysos-Dithyramben,"* 1:72. The final line of "Lament of Ariane" was also revised many times. See David Farrell Krell, *Woman, Sensuality, and Death in Nietzsche* (Bloomington: Indiana University Press, 1986), 19. Karl Kerényi describes the similar change in attribution in Nietzsche's "Gespräche auf Naxos" and in the seventh dithyramb; Karl Kerényi, "Nietzsche und Ariadne: Gedanken über die Zukunft des Humanismus," *Neue Schweizer Rundschau* 12:7 (1944): 402–12. Nietzsche assigns a high value to renaming and reattribution: "The great epochs of our life come when we gain the courage to rechristen our evil as what is best in us" (Nietzsche, *Beyond Good and Evil,* §116).

87. Nietzsche, *The Gay Science,* §361 (translation modified).

88. Groddeck, *Friedrich Nietzsche "Dionysos-Dithyramben,"* 2:206.

89. Nietzsche, *Beyond Good and Evil,* §1. For this translation, I have also referred to Nietzsche, *Beyond Good and Evil,* trans. Marion Faber (Oxford: Oxford University Press, 1998).

90. Friedrich Nietzsche, *The Birth of Tragedy and The Case of Wagner,* trans. Walter Kaufmann (New York: Vintage, 1967), §21 (translation modified).

91. This indistinction of the Apollinian and Dionsyian appears throughout *The Birth of Tragedy,* but never with this same explicit force; on these "reversals or strategies of detours," see Rainer Nägele, *Reading After Freud: Essays on Goethe, Hölderlin, Habermas, Nietzsche, Brecht, Celan, and Freud* (New York: Columbia University Press, 1987), 93.

92. See Nietzsche, *Thus Spoke Zarathustra,* 159–60 ("On the Vision and the Riddle," 2).

5. Rilke and the Aestheticization of Poverty

1. Erich Heller, *The Disinherited Mind: Essays in Modern German Literature* (Cambridge: Bowes and Bowes, 1952), 101.

2. Furio Jesi, "Rilke, Nietzsche e il nietzscheanismo del primo '900," in *Studi germanici* 14 (1976), 255.

3. Rainer Maria Rilke, *Sämtliche Werke* (Frankfurt am Main: Insel, 1955–66), 6:1020–21. An extreme example of this "nervousness" is Rilke's inability to "resist" Stefan George, discussed by Eudo Mason in his essay "Rilke und Stefan George," in *Rilke in neuer Sicht,* ed. Käte Hamburger (Stuttgart: W. Kohlhammer, 1971).

4. Rilke, *Sämtliche Werke,* 6:1021.

5. On Rilke's relation to Nietzsche, see Heller, *The Disinherited Mind*, 97–140; Jesi, "Rilke, Nietzsche e il nietzscheanismo del primo '900"; and Irina Frowen, "Nietzsches Bedeutung für Rilkes frühe Kunstauffassung," *Blätter der Rilke Gesellschaft* 14 (1987): 21–34.

6. Rilke, *Sämtliche Werke*, 6:1163.

7. Ibid., 6:1170 and 1177.

8. Ibid., 5:417.

9. Ibid., 5:25 and 5:10.

10. Ibid., 5:418–21.

11. Ibid., 5:68–69.

12. Ibid., 5:480.

13. Ibid., 7:299–303. The Mallarmé translations date from 1919.

14. Rilke, *Die Aufzeichnungen Malte Laurids Brigge* (Frankfurt am Main: Insel, 1982), 219.

15. Beda Allemann, "Rilke und Mallarmé: Entwicklung einer Grundfrage der symbolistischen Poetik," in *Rilke in neuer Sicht*, 67–71 (see note 3).

16. Rilke, *Sämtliche Werke*, 2:730.

17. See Blanchot, *The Space of Literature*, 158–59.

18. For a general account of *The Book of Hours*, see Ralph Freedman, "*Das Stundenbuch* and *Das Buch der Bilder*: Harbingers of Rilke's Modernity," *A Companion to the Works of Rainer Maria Rilke*, ed. Erika A. Metzger and Michael M. Metzger (New York: Camden House, 2001), 90–127.

19. My translation. For Rilke's letters, I use the following edition: Rainer Maria Rilke, *Briefe*, ed. Weimar Rilke Archive with Ruth Sieber-Rilke (Frankfurt am Main: Insel, 1987). I will refer to the letters by their date. See also the letter to Heinrich Vogeler from 17 September 1902.

20. Reinhold Grimm, *Von der Armut und vom Regen: Rilkes Antwort auf die soziale Frage* (Königstein: Athenäum, 1981), 28. See also the reading of Rilke's "Konzeption des großen Todes und der absoluten Armut" as "eine Flucht aus der Realität in eine Ontologie" in Walter Seifert, *Das epische Werk Rainer Maria Rilkes* (Bonn: Bouvier, 1962), 140.

21. On Francis/Orpheus in *Das Stunden-buch*, see Walter Rehm, *Orpheus: Der Dichter und die Toten, Selbstdeutung und Totenkult bei Novalis, Hölderlin, Rilke* (Düsseldorf: Schwann, 1950), 421–34.

22. Beda Allemann, *Zeit und Figur beim späten Rilke: Ein Beitrag zur Poetik des modernen Gedichtes* (Pfullingen: Neske, 1965), 283. Allemann gives as examples of these figures the future beloved, angels, and Orpheus.

23. Rilke, *The Book of Hours: Prayers to a Lowly God*, trans. Annemarie S.

Kidder (Evanston, Ill.: Northwestern University Press, 2001), 164–67 (translation modified).

24. Ibid., 206–7. The sixth poem of the first book of *The Book of Hours,* "The Book of the Monkish Life," contains a similar naming within a simile: "And your images stand before you like names" (Und deine Bilder stehen vor dir wie Namen) (Rilke, *The Book of Hours,* 8–9). In *Die Geschichten vom lieben Gott,* Rilke uses the phrase "fast ohne Namen" (Rilke, *Sämtliche Werke,* 4:302).

25. Rilke, *Sämtliche Werke,* 1:356 (my translation). See also the translation in Rilke, *The Book of Hours,* 189.

26. See Martin Luther's translation of the Bible: *Biblia: Das ist die gantze Heilige Schrifft,* ed. Hans Volz (Munich: DTV, 1974), 3:2305.

27. With the interruption of the enumeration of metaphorical attributes and its recommencement as an accumulation of similes, Rilke's poetry here takes on some of the characteristics of what Leo Spitzer calls "chaotic enumeration," even though Spitzer explicitly excludes Rilke from this "modern" phenomenon and claims that Rilke returns to a form of enumeration already surpassed by Whitman. Leo Spitzer, *La enumeración caótica en la poesía moderna,* trans. Raimundo Lida (Buenos Aires: Coni, 1945), 77 and 89–91.

28. Winfried Eckel sees a similar impoverishment at work already in the enumeration of metaphorical attributes in *Das Stundenbuch:* "Man trifft auf Gedichte, die geradezu im Stil unendlicher Litaneien Metapher an Metapher reihen und dabei jedes einzelne Bild durch die anderen ebenso verstärken wie zurücknehmen." Winfried Eckel, *Wendung: Zum Prozeß der poetischen Reflexion im Werk Rilkes* (Würzburg: Königshausen & Neumann, 1994), 40.

29. Metaphor, too, depends on the difference between literary and figural meaning, but simile makes explicit in the "like" that which, according to Hegel, is already present in itself but not fully posited in the metaphor: "in comparison as such both the sense proper and the image are specifically separated from one another, while this cleavage, though present implicitly, is not yet *posited,* in metaphor" (In der Vergleichung als solcher aber ist beides, der eigentliche Sinn und das Bild, bestimmt voneinander geschieden, während diese Trennung, obgleich an sich vorhanden, in der Metapher *noch nicht gesetzt* ist). Georg Wilhelm Friedrich Hegel, *Aesthetics: Lectures on Fine Art,* trans. T. M. Knox (Oxford: Clarendon Press, 1975), 1:407; Hegel, *Vorlesungen über die Ästhetik,* in Hegel, *Werkausgabe* (Frankfurt am Main: Suhrkamp, 1970), 13:516–17.

30. Rilke, *Sämtliche Werke,* 1:355 (my translation). See also the translation in Rilke, *The Book of Hours,* 186–89. This poem echoes 1 Corinthians 4:13.

31. "[V]erlust, verschwendung, überfluß [for Luther, it means all three—

loss, waste, excess], schaden, squalor, hilflosigkeit, mangel, not, verlegenheit" ("Unrat," *Deutsches Wörterbuch von Jacob und Wilhelm Grimm*, 24:1230–34).

32. Anette Schwarz presents Rilke's later project of *sachliches Sagen* as a relation to, and production of, quasi objects that could be considered under the term *Unrat;* for Schwarz, *sachliches Sagen* is an "ascetic non-consumption" and "a process of fermentation that transforms the object into a non-object of desire and thus into a thing that is both undesirable and, above all, inedible— a form of refuse." Anette Schwarz, "The Colors of Prose: Rilke's Program of *Sachliches Sagen*," *Germanic Review* 71, no. 3 (Summer 1996), 196–97. In "Über Kunst," Rilke similarly describes art as waste: "kein Erwerben . . . sondern ein Vergeuden aller wandelbaren Werte" (Rilke, *Sämtliche Werke*, 5:429).

33. Rilke, *The Book of Hours*, 186–87 (translation modified).

34. Ernst Jandl's poem "rilkes widerspruch" foregrounds and replays the impossible juxtapositions often performed by Rilke's "*und*" and "*und dennoch.*" In *Rilke? Kleine Hommage zum 100. Geburtstag*, ed. Heinz Ludwig Arnold (Munich: Edition Text und Kritik, 1975), 24.

35. Rilke, *The Book of Hours*, 192–93 (translation modified).

36. Peter Por, *Die orphische Figur: Zur Poetik von Rilkes "Neue Gedichten"* (Heidelberg: Winter, 1997), 63 (my translation).

37. Bert Herzog, "Der Gott des Jugendstils in Rilkes *Stundenbuch*," in *Jugendstil*, ed. Jost Hermand (Darmstadt: Wissenschaftliche Buchgesellschaft, 1971), 380 (my translation).

38. Hans Bender, ed., *Mein Gedicht ist mein Messer: Lyriker zu ihren Gedichten* (Heidelberg: W. Rothe, 1955), 9; cited in Reinhold Grimm, "Die problematischen 'Probleme der Lyrik,'" in *Gottfried Benn*, ed. Bruno Hillebrand (Darmstadt: Wissenschaftliche Buchgesellschaft, 1979), 206.

39. Grimm, "Die problematischen 'Probleme der Lyrik,'" 206.

40. Gottfried Benn, "Probleme der Lyrik," in Gottfried Benn, *Gesammelte Werke in der Fassung der Erstdrucke* (Frankfurt am Main: Fischer, 1989), 3:513 (my translation).

41. Ibid. (my translation).

42. Ibid. (my translation).

43. Paul Ricouer summarizes these judgments of simile and metaphor in *The Rule of Metaphor: Multi-disciplinary Studies of the Creation of Meaning in Language*, trans. Robert Czerny with Kathleen McLaughlin and John Costello (Toronto: University of Toronto Press, 1977), 24–27. Beda Allemann discusses the relations among simile, metaphor, and symbol in terms that explicitly echo (and modify) Benn's in *Über das Dichterische* (Pfullingen: Neske, 1957), 40–42.

44. Aristotle, *The Art of Rhetoric* III.x.3, trans. J. H. Freese (Cambridge, Mass.: Harvard University Press, 1947), 397. A discussion of the relation between simile, other figures of comparison, and metaphor in ancient rhetoric can be found in Marsh H. McCall Jr., *Ancient Rhetorical Theories of Simile and Comparison* (Cambridge, Mass.: Harvard University Press, 1969). See also Irène Tamba-Mecz and Paul Veyne, "*Metaphora* et comparaison selon Aristote," *Revue des études grecques* 92:3–4 (1979): 77–98.

45. Jacques Derrida, *Margins of Philosophy*, trans. Alan Bass (Chicago: University of Chicago Press, 1982), 239.

46. Grimm cites similar passages on the simile in Claudel and Marinetti in "Die problematischen 'Probleme der Lyrik,'" 214–15. Mallarmé's remark "Je raye le mot comme du dictionnaire" is reported in Édouard Dujardin, *Mallarmé par un des siens* (Paris: Albert Messein, 1936), 50 (my translation).

47. Herzog, "Der Gott des Jugendstils in Rilkes *Stundenbuch*," 378 (my translation).

48. Benn's interpretation of Rilke could be considered as a reading of the hypothetical entrance of St. Francis in "The Book of Poverty and Death," which appears as a "break-in": "But if *you* are there, be heavy and break through" (Bist Du es aber: mach dich schwer, brich ein) (Rilke, *The Book of Hours*, 164–65).

49. Robert Musil, *Precision and Soul: Essays and Addresses*, ed. and trans. Burton Pike and David S. Luft (Chicago: University of Chicago Press, 1990), 247; Robert Musil, "Rede zur Rilke-Feier in Berlin am 16. Januar 1927," in Musil, *Gesammelte Werke* (Reinbek bei Hamburg: Rowohlt, 1978), 8:1240. For Hegel, it is the metaphor that is "always an interruption of the train of thought" (Hegel, *Werkausgabe*, 13:523). For a specific example of an interrupting simile, see Ulrich Fülleborn's discussion of the "shocking power" of a simile in Fülleborn, "Form und Sinn der Aufzeichnungen des Malte Laurids Brigge: Rilkes Prosabuch und der moderne Roman," in *Rilkes 'Aufzeichnungen des Malte Laurids Brigge*," ed. Hartmut Engelhardt (Frankfurt am Main: Suhrkamp, 1974), 193.

50. Musil, *Precision and Soul*, 245; Musil, *Gesammelte Werke*, 8:1237.

51. Musil, *Precision and Soul*, 245; Musil, *Gesammelte Werke*, 8:1237.

52. Beda Allemann describes a similar breakdown of boundaries in Rilke's conception of *Weltinnenraum*: "Die Begriffbildung 'Weltinnenraum' . . . ist ein Versuch, mit Hilfe eines Oxymorons die Aufhebung [der Schranke zwischen Innen und Aussen] zu vollziehen, aber indem in ihm die Begriffe von Aussen (Welt) und Innen doch erhalten sind, bleibt er zwiespältig" (Allemann, *Zeit und Figur beim späten Rilke*, 279). For Winfried Eckel, the relation between God and "I" in *Das Stundenbuch* is characterized by a similar loss of

definition: "Das Buch ist voll von solchen Bildern der Verwebung und wechsel-seitigen Durchdringung" (Eckel, *Wendung,* 40–41). Édouard Dujardin inter-prets Mallarmé's erasure of simile as performing exactly what Musil claims Rilke's emphasis of simile does: "Voilà le secret de Mallarmé. Il ne dit plus: 'Telle chose ressemble à telle autre . . .' Pour lui, cette chose est devenue cette autre" (Dujardin, *Mallarmé par un des siens,* 50).

53. Musil's discussion of the dissolving force of simile in his "Rilke-Rede" contains many elements of Hofmannsthal's presentation of the symbol in "Das Gespräch über Gedichte"; Hugo von Hofmannsthal, *Erzählungen, Erfundene Gespräche, und Briefe; Reisen* (Frankfurt am Main: Fischer, 1979), 502–3.

54. Musil, *Precision and Soul,* 238.

55. Beda Allemann describes a similar transformation of the traditional conception of metaphor in Rilke's poetry (Allemann, *Zeit und Figur beim späten Rilke,* 239).

56. In "White Mythology," Derrida discusses this "economist" theory of metaphor and simile that appears in Aristotle, Cicero, and Quintilian, and he writes, "It seems that what deserves examination here is less the economic consideration in itself than the mechanical character of the explanations to which it gives rise" (Derrida, *Margins of Philosophy,* 222). Derrida's remarks also tie this rhetorical tradition to modern poetry by discussing Breton's dislike for ornament and his insistence on modern poetry's "law of *extreme briefness.*"

57. Rilke, *The Book of Hours,* 196–97 (translation modified).

58. See Ulrich Baer's account and problematization of the notion of per-fection in Rilke's critics in "The Perfection of Poetry: Rainer Maria Rilke and Paul Celan," *New German Critique* 91 (Winter 2004): 171–89.

59. Rilke, *The Book of Hours,* 166–67.

60. In his reading of the poem "Ich liebe dich, du sanftestes Gesetz" from the first book of *The Book of Hours,* de Man presents the dominance of sonor-ity as a sign of mastery: "the mastery of the poem consists in its control over the phonic dimension of language." Paul de Man, *Allegories of Reading: Fig-ural Language in Rousseau, Nietzsche, Rilke, and Proust* (New Haven, Conn.: Yale University Press, 1979), 31.

61. Rilke, *The Book of Hours,* 190–91 (translation modified). August Stahl discusses at length "das Bild des Leisen" in his *"Vokabeln der Not" und "Früchte der Tröstung": Studien zur Bildlichkeit im Werke Rainer Maria Rilkes* (Heidel-berg: Winter, 1967), 62–71.

62. Rilke, *The Book of Hours,* 202–3 (translation modified).

63. Jens Peter Jacobsen, *Niels Lyhne,* trans. Tina Nunnally (Seattle, Wash.: Fjord Press, 1994), 37.

64. Georg Simmel, "Über Geiz, Verschwendung und Armut," *Gesamtausgabe*, ed. Otthein Rammstedt (Frankfurt am Main: Suhrkamp, 1972), 5:542 (my translation). On Rilke's relationship to Simmel, see Hans-Jürgen Schings, "Die Fragen des Malte Laurids Brigge und Georg Simmel," *Deutsche Vierteljahrschrift für Literaturwissenschaft und Geistesgeschichte*, 76 (2002): 642–71; and Neil H. Donahue, "Fear and Fascination in the Big City: Rilke's Use of Georg Simmel in *The Notebooks of Malte Laurids Brigge*," in *Studies in Twentieth Century Literature* 16, no. 2 (Summer 1992): 197–219. Rilke discusses poverty in a letter to Simmel from 18 May 1914.

65. Rilke, *The Book of Hours*, 198–99 (translation modified). In his book on Worpswede, Rilke writes that the life of a monk "does not impoverish" (verarmt nicht) but is instead "the asylum of all the riches" (die Zufluchtsstätte aller Reichtümer) (Rilke, *Sämtliche Werke*, 5:120).

66. See Rilke's letter to Clara Rilke from 16 September 1907. On Rilke's relation to Kierkegaard, see Geoffrey A. Hale, *Kierkegaard and the Ends of Language* (Minneapolis: University of Minnesota Press, 2002), 73–108.

67. Søren Kierkegaard, *Christian Discourses and the Lilies of the Field and the Birds of the Air and Three Discourses at the Communion on Fridays*, trans. Walter Lowrie (New York: Oxford University Press, 1952), 25–26.

68. Rilke, *The Book of Hours*, 190–91.

69. Ibid., 2–3.

70. Ibid., 188–89 (translation modified).

71. Rilke, *Sämtliche Werke*, 5:182.

72. Rilke, *The Book of Hours*, 187 (translation modified).

73. Ibid., 189 (translation modified).

74. Ibid., 188–89.

75. Ibid., 172–73 (translation modified).

76. Ibid., 174–75 (translation modified).

77. Ibid., 206–7.

78. Walter Sokel, "The Devolution of the Self in *Malte Laurids Brigge*," in *Rilke: The Alchemy of Alienation*, ed. Frank Baron, Ernst S. Dick, and Warner R. Maurer (Lawrence: Regents Press of Kansas, 1980), 188. Maurice Blanchot writes similarly of Rilke, "To make death my death is no longer . . . to remain myself even in death" (Blanchot, *The Space of Literature*, 128). For a discussion of the interest in a "proper death" at the beginning of the twentieth century (especially in Jünger, Lukács, and Beer-Hofmann), see Catucci, *Per una filosofia povera*, 156–95.

79. Rilke, *Sämtliche Werke*, 1:356 (my translation). See also the translation in Rilke, *The Book of Hours*, 189.

80. Johann Wolfgang von Goethe, *Maxims and Reflections*, trans. Elisabeth Stopp (New York: Penguin, 1998), 16; Goethe, *Maximen und Reflexionen* (Frankfurt am Main: Insel, 1976), 41.

81. See Rilke, *The Book of Hours*, 8–9; 114–15.

82. "Glanz wird . . . für den widerschein des im blanken, glatten oder kristallinishen körpern zurückgeworfenen lichtes gebraucht [. . .]. diese bedeutung ist die in neuerer umgangssprache zur vorherrschaft drängende" ("Glanz," *Wörterbuch der deutschen Sprache von Jacob und Wilhelm Grimm*, 7:7606). *Glanz* is also an important term in the early poetry that Hofmannsthal chose for his own collected works; see Hugo von Hofmannsthal, *Gesammelte Werke*, ed. Bernd Schoeller and Rudolf Hirsch (Frankfurt am Main: Fischer, 1979), 1:29, 34, 36.

83. In his interpretation of the *Glanz* of the poor, Walter Seifert at first seems to offer a similar interpretation when he writes that the poor have for Rilke "keine positive Innerlichkeit," but then he turns this lack into a sign of the poor being "Chiffren des Absoluten" (Seifert, *Das epische Werk Rainer Maria Rilkes*, 139).

6. An Outcast Community

1. Rilke uses the term "prose book" to describe the *Notebooks* in a letter to Kippenberg from 9 February 1907; he also calls it "mon douleureux livre de prose" in a letter to Pia de Valmarana from 30 December 1913.

2. Rainer Maria Rilke, *Die Aufzeichnungen des Malte Laurids Brigge* (Frankfurt am Main: Insel, 1982), 38 (hereafter *Aufzeichnungen*); Rilke, *The Notebooks of Malte Laurids Brigge*, trans. Stephen Mitchell (New York: Random House, 1982) (hereafter *Notebooks*), 41. I have occasionally modified the translation.

3. Andreas Huyssen, *Modernity and the Text: Revisions of German Modernism* (New York: Columbia University Press, 1989), 123.

4. August Stahl sees such a "flight from the sufferings of quotidian reality into the realm of dreams and fairy tales" as characteristic of the early Rilke. Stahl, *"Vokabeln der Not" und "Früchte der Tröstung": Studien zur Bildlichkeit im Werke Rainer Maria Rilkes* (Heidelberg: Carl Winter, 1967), 27 and 158.

5. Huyssen, *Modernity and the Text*, 137.

6. Ernst Fedor Hoffmann, "Zum dichterischen Verfahren in Rilkes *Aufzeichnungen des Malte Laurids Brigge*," in *Rilkes Aufzeichnungen des Malte Laurids Brigge*, ed. Hartmut Engelhardt (Frankfurt am Main: Suhrkamp, 1974), 235 (my translation). Judith Ryan criticizes Hoffmann's lack of attention to the Paris scenes in "'Hypothetisches Erzählen': Zur Funktion von Phantasie und Einbildung in Rilkes *Malte Laurids Brigge*," in *Rilkes Aufzeichnungen*, 341–74.

7. Hoffmann, "Zum dichterischen Verfahren," 239–40 (my translation).

8. Ibid., 220 (my translation).

9. Ibid., 233–34.

10. Huyssen, *Modernity and the Text,* 137.

11. Hoffmann, "Zum dichterischen Verfahren," 235; Huyssen, *Modernity and the Text,* 118.

12. Rilke describes a similar incident in a letter to Lou Andreas-Salomé from 18 July 1903; see *Briefe.*

13. Martin Heidegger, *The Basic Problems of Phenomenology,* trans. Albert Hofstadter (Bloomington: Indiana University Press, 1982), 173.

14. "The structure of being-in-the-world makes manifest the essential peculiarity of the Dasein, that it projects a world for itself, and it does this not subsequently and occasionally but, rather, the projecting of the world belongs to the Dasein's being. In this projection the Dasein has always already *stepped out beyond itself,* ex-sistere, it *is in* a world" (Heidegger, ibid., 170).

15. Thomas Mann, *Death in Venice and Other Tales,* trans. Joachim Neugroschel (New York: Penguin, 1998), 159.

16. See Rilke's letters to Emanuel von Bodman from 17 August 1901; to Paula Becker-Modersohn from 12 February 1902; to Otto Modersohn from 25 June 1902; to Franz Xaver Kappus from 23 December 1903; and to Friedrich Westhoff from 29 April 1904. See also Rilke, *Sämtliche Werke,* 5:405, 416, 425, 642; 6:1003, 1168.

17. Ellen Key, "Ein Gottsucher," in *Rilkes Aufzeichnungen* (see note 6), 148; Anthony R. Stephens, *Rilkes Malte Laurids Brigge: Strukturanalyse des erzählerischen Bewusstseins* (Bern: Herbert Lang, 1974), 96.

18. Blanchot, *The Space of Literature,* 122–23.

19. See, for instance, Jacques Le Rider's mention of Malte as one of "numerous examples of solitary characters" in Austrian literature around 1900 in his study *Modernity and Crises of Identity: Culture and Society in Fin-de-Siècle Vienna,* trans. Rosemary Morris (New York: Continuum, 1993), 34.

20. Walter Sokel, "The Devolution of the Self in *The Notebooks of Malte Laurids Brigge,*" in *Rilke: The Alchemy of Alienation* (see chap. 5, note 78), 187.

21. Ibid.

22. Käte Hamburger similarly presents Malte as a phenomenological observer of the outcasts. Hamburger, *Rilke: Eine Einführung* (Stuttgart: Klett, 1976), 77.

23. Baudelaire, *Les fleurs du mal,* 276.

24. For Walter Benjamin, the verses of "A une passante" "reveal the stigmata

which life in a metropolis inflicts upon love." His reading of "A une passante" can be found in Walter Benjamin, *Selected Writings*, 4:323–24.

25. Rilke, *Sämtliche Werke*, 5:639. Maurice Blanchot writes in similar terms about sharing separations, because, for him, a shared exposure to one's own death, to that which excludes every relation because of its absolute alterity, is the sole possible basis for community; see Maurice Blanchot, *La communauté inavouable* (Paris: Minuit, 1983), 28, 46, and passim. See also Jean-Luc Nancy's comments on death and community in *The Inoperative Community*, ed. Peter Connor (Minneapolis: University of Minnesota Press, 1991), 15 and passim; and Françoise Dastur, *La mort: Essai sur la finitude* (Paris: Hatier, 1994), 47.

26. Heidegger, *Basic Problems of Phenomenology*, 171–72.

27. *Mitsein* and *Mitdasein* are "structures of Dasein which are equiprimordial with Being-in-the-world." Martin Heidegger, *Being and Time*, trans. John Macquarrie and Edward Robinson (New York: Harper and Row, 1962), 149.

28. Ibid., 156.

29. Ibid., 163.

30. Blanchot, *The Space of Literature*, 130.

31. Ibid., 131.

32. Another formulation of this position can be found in Rilke's letter of 19 October 1907 to Clara Rilke.

33. Huyssen, *Modernity and the Text*, 137.

34. See Baudelaire, *Les fleurs du mal*, 35–36, 212–13.

35. Ibid., 36.

36. Baudelaire, *Œuvres complètes*, 105.

37. See his letters to Emanuel von Bodman from 17 August 1901; to Paula Becker-Modersohn from 12 February 1902; and to Friedrich Westhoff of 29 April 1904. Walter Seifert writes about a postulated "integration of misery and love" in the *Notebooks* (Seifert, *Das epische Werk Rainer Maria Rilkes*, 289).

38. Allemann, *Zeit und Figur beim späten Rilke*, 269.

39. Such a loss of the self should be compared to the moment in Jacobsen's *Niels Lyhne* when the tutor Mr. Bigum insists that he never loses himself: "These chosen points of view and chosen perspectives that he had taken over for his own never, even for a second, took him over" (23).

40. Theodore Ziolkowski, *Dimensions of the Modern Novel: German Texts and European Contexts* (Princeton, N.J.: Princeton University Press, 1969), 31.

41. Giorgio Agamben, *The Coming Community*, trans. Michael Hardt (Minneapolis: University of Minnesota Press, 1992), 1.

42. Ibid., 64.

43. See the discussion of the "empty" faces with neither traits nor memories in the nineteenth entry (*Notebooks*, 59).

44. The lepers, or the *Aussätzigen*, are also a kind of nonappearance or suspension; Anette Schwarz shows how the *Aussätzigen* and *aussetzen* belong together in "The Colors of Prose," 204. See also the remarks on Rilke's use of *aussetzen* in Por, *Die orphische Figur*, 326n235.

45. Walter H. Sokel, "The Blackening of the Breast: The Narrative of Existential Education in Rainer Maria Rilke's *The Notebooks of Malte Laurids Brigge*," in *Reflection and Action: Essays on the Bildungsroman*, ed. James Hardin (Columbia: University of South Carolina Press, 1991), 358.

46. Ibid.

47. See the account of Count Brahe's dictation to Abelone, which relates types of writing that are more authentic (*Notebooks*, 146–54).

48. Judith Ryan presents Malte as suspended between hope and fear in her "*The Notebooks of Malte Laurids Brigge*," in *Deutsche Romane des zwanzigsten Jahrhunderts: Neue Interpretationen*, ed. Paul Michael Lützeler (Königstein: Athenäum, 1983), 75. Elsewhere, Ryan characterizes the "time of the other interpretation" as an "unreachable (though somehow also dreadfully near) future" and the *Notebooks* in general as marked by a "disturbing vacillation between childhood and adulthood, mastery and impotence, reading and experience, the aesthetic and the real." Judith Ryan, *Rilke, Modernism, and Poetic Tradition* (Cambridge: Cambridge University Press, 1999), 197 and 49.

49. See Claire Lucques's devotional works on Rilke for more details on Rilke's relation to St. Francis: "La dette de Rilke à l'égard de saint François d'Assise," *Blätter der Rilke Gesellschaft* 10 (1983): 80–92; *Le poids du monde: Rilke et Sorge* (Paris: Beauchesne, 1962).

50. A historical sketch of German interest in Franciscanism in the nineteenth century can be found in Ambros Styra, *Franziskus von Assisi in der neueren deutschen Literatur* (Breslau: Otto Borgmeyer Buchhandlung, 1927).

51. Ibid., 14 and 38.

52. Jesi, "Rilke, Nietzsche e il nietzscheanismo," 269.

53. Hesse was also interested in the German mystical tradition; see his short writings on Eckhart, Suso, Tauler, Jakob Böhme, and Angelus Silesius in Hermann Hesse, *Gesammelte Werke* (Frankfurt am Main: Suhrkamp, 1970), vol. 11. On Hesse and his relation to mysticism and asceticism, see Sunil Bansal, *Das mönchische Leben im Erzählwerk Hermann Hesses* (Frankfurt am Main: Peter Lang, 1992).

54. On Hofmannsthal, see Susanne Götz, *Bettler des Wortes: Irritationen des Dramatischen bei Sorge, Hofmannsthal und Horváth* (Frankfurt am Main:

Peter Lang, 1998), 23. On Doderer, see Lutz-Werner Wolff, *Heimito von Doderer* (Reinbek: Rowohlt, 1996), 29. Doderer mentions his plans and, later, the completion of a first version in his diary of 1924 and 1925; Heimito von Doderer, *Tagebücher 1920–1939,* ed. Wendelin Schmidt-Dengler, Martin Loew-Cadonna, and Gerald Sommer (Beck: Munich, 1996), 1:180–299 passim. In his notes on Francis, Doderer exclaims, "Rilke *soll da auch nicht vergessen werden!*" (Doderer, *Tagebücher,* 203).

55. From the Franciscan *Regula* cited by Jacques Le Goff, *Saint François d'Assise* (Paris: Gallimard, 1999), 122.

56. Ibid., 126.

57. Judith Ryan presents the hypothetical narration of the Prodigal Son in the context of Malte's remarks throughout the notebooks about narration: "Er entwirft eine Fülle von Möglichkeiten, ohne diese in einem verbindlichen Erzählzusammenhang miteinander verknüpfen zu können" (Ryan, "'Hypothetisches Erzählen,'" 274).

58. Rilke also discusses the gesture of the Prodigal Son (the *Geste der Anrufung ohne Grenzen*) in his Rodin monograph (Rilke, *Sämtliche Werke,* 5:194).

59. "Ungestüm," *Deutsches Wörterbuch von Jacob und Wilhelm Grimm,* 24:882.

60. This distance from the self makes it difficult to agree with Judith Ryan's claim that Rilke's prose book remains "confined in the realm of an experiencing subjectivity" and "confined in his own identity problematics" (Ryan, "'Hypothetisches Erzählen,'" 246 and 271).

61. See the discussion in the introduction of the untimeliness of beggars in the late nineteenth and early twentieth centuries.

62. See Ellen Key's 1911 review of *Aufzeichnungen* (in Engelhardt, *Rilkes Aufzeichnungen,* 148–50; see note 6). See also Eudo Mason on *Stundenbuch* readers' disapproval of later Rilke works in Mason, *Exzentrische Bahnen: Studien zum Dichterbewußtsein der Neuzeit* (Göttingen: Vandenhoeck & Ruprecht, 1963), 185. Ralph Freedman remarks on the "resistance, even derision" that *The Book of Hours* continues to meet (Freedman, "*Das Stundenbuch* and *Das Buch der Bilder,*" 91).

63. This is the conclusion of Reinhold Grimm, *Von der Armut und vom Regen.*

64. Paul de Man, *Allegories of Reading,* 51; Martin Heidegger, *Holzwege* (Frankfurt am Main: Klostermann, 1950), 274. Karl Krolow mentions the shift in appreciation of the early Rilke in his "'Die Zeit der anderen Auslegung wird anbrechen': Rainer Maria Rilkes produktives Zögern," in *Rilke?,* 90–104 (see chap. 5, note 34).

65. Blanchot, *The Space of Literature,* 149, 155.

66. Ibid., 154.

67. Or, in the case of Else Buddeberg, praising Rilke's "invalid" early works only insofar as they prepared for the later "valid" works. Else Buddeberg, *Kunst und Existenz im Spätwerk Rilkes: Eine Darstellung nach seinen Briefen* (Karlsruhe: Stahlberg, 1948).

68. See the discussion of the problem of literary periodization in Paul de Man, *Blindness and Insight* (Minneapolis: University of Minnesota Press, 1983), 166–86.

69. Letter to Rudolf Zimmerman from 3 February 1921.

70. Letter to Witold Hulewicz, stamped 13 November 1925. This undated letter can be found in Rilke, *Briefe,* 3:894–901.

71. Friedrich Nietzsche, *The Use and Abuse of History,* trans. Adrian Collins (New York: Macmillan, 1949), §1.

7. Exposed Interiors and the Poverty of Experience

1. Benjamin, *Selected Writings,* 2:735 (translation modified).

2. Ibid., 2:776.

3. Ibid., 3:340.

4. Ibid., 3:404.

5. Ibid., 2:370 (translation modified). Benjamin misquotes Rilke. Instead of the correct line, "Denn Armut ist ein großer Glanz aus Innen," he writes, "Denn Armut ist ein großer Glanz von Innen." This shows how present this line was in the beginning of the twentieth century but also how it was not read closely.

6. Ibid., 2:732 (translation modified).

7. Benjamin, *Gesammelte Schriften,* 2:1112 (my translation).

8. Benjamin, *Selected Writings,* 2:732.

9. For an account of Benjamin's "resistance to symbolic healing and positive commemoration," see Martin Jay, *Refractions of Violence* (New York: Routledge, 2003), 11–24.

10. Benjamin, *Selected Writings,* 2:732.

11. Ibid., 731.

12. See Benjamin, "On Some Motifs in Baudelaire," in *Selected Writings,* 4:313-55. On Benjamin's relation to psychoanalysis, see also Kevin Newmark, "Traumatic Poetry: Charles Baudelaire and the Shock of Laughter," in *Trauma: Explorations in Memory,* ed. Cathy Caruth (Baltimore: The Johns Hopkins University Press, 1995), 236–55; and Sarah Ley Roff, "Benjamin and Psychoanalysis,"

in *The Cambridge Companion to Walter Benjamin*, ed. David Ferris (Cambridge: Cambridge University Press, 2004), 115–33.

13. Jean Paulhan, *Les fleurs de Tarbes, ou La terreur dans les letters* (Paris: Gallimard, 1973), 23.

14. Baudelaire, *The Painter of Modern Life and Other Essays*, 29.

15. Benjamin, *Selected Writings*, 4:59.

16. Walter Benjamin, *The Arcades Project*, trans. Howard Eiland and Kevin McLaughlin (Cambridge, Mass.: Harvard University Press, 1999), 221.

17. Cited in Benjamin, *Gesammelte Schriften*, 5:1134 (my translation). The analysis of the interior is at the center of Adorno's 1934 book on Kierkegaard, in which it serves as a metaphor for Kierkegaard's philosophy of an *objektloses Innen* and false *Selbstständigkeit*. Theodor Adorno, *Kierkegaard: Konstruktion des Ästhetischen*, in Adorno, *Gesammelte Schriften* (Frankfurt am Main: Suhrkamp, 1979), vol. 2, especially 61–69. See also Benjamin's review of the book: "Kierkegaard: The End of Philosophical Idealism," in Benjamin, *Selected Writings*, 2:703–5.

18. Benjamin, *The Arcades Project*, 12.

19. Ibid., 20.

20. Ibid., 8–9.

21. Karl Marx, "Zur Judenfrage," in Karl Marx and Friedrich Engels, *Studienausgabe* (Frankfurt am Main: Fischer, 1990), 1:55. Benjamin discusses this Marx passage in Benjamin, *Selected Writings*, 2:454–55.

22. Benjamin, *The Arcades Project*, 216.

23. Ibid. (translation modified).

24. Ibid., 9.

25. Ibid. (translation modified). Benjamin characterizes Jugendstil as a phenomenon of flight and insists on the necessity of including a discussion of that which causes the flight (Benjamin, *The Arcades Project*, 550).

26. Benjamin, *Selected Writings*, 4:255.

27. Ibid., 338.

28. Ibid.

29. See Benjamin's citations of Le Corbusier and Adolf Behne on this "character of fortifications" and "on the ideal of 'distinction'" (Benjamin, *The Arcades Project*, 215); see also the discussion in "Central Park" of the "étuis, covers, and cases in which the domestic utensils of the time were sheathed" (Benjamin, *Selected Writings*, 4:173).

30. See Benjamin's equation of transparency proper and metaphorical: "It is the peculiarity of *technological* forms of production (as opposed to art forms) that their progress and their success are proportionate to the *transparency* of

their social content. (Hence glass architecture)" (Benjamin, *The Arcades Project*, 465).

31. Benjamin, *Selected Writings*, 2:733–34.

32. Massimo Cacciari, *Architecture and Nihilism: On the Philosophy of Modern Architecture*, trans. Stephen Sartarelli (New Haven, Conn.: Yale University Press, 1993), 188.

33. Ibid.

34. Benjamin, *The Arcades Project*, 856.

35. "We are bored when we don't know what we are waiting for. That we do know, or think we know, is nearly always the expression of our superficiality or inattention. Boredom is the threshold to great deeds" (Benjamin, *The Arcades Project*, 105).

36. "His night . . . is not a maternal night, or a moonlit, romantic night: it is the hour between sleeping and waking, the night watch" (Benjamin, *Selected Writings*, 2:447).

37. Benjamin, *Selected Writings*, 2:735; Benjamin, *Gesammelte Schriften*, 2:219.

38. Benjamin, *Selected Writings*, 2:734.

39. For a concise presentation of Scheerbart's wide-ranging works, see Peter Halborn, "Paul Scheerbart: Ein komischer Ulkist," in *Über Paul Scheerbart*, ed. Michael M. Schmidt and Hiltrud Steffen (Paderborn: Igel, 1996), 2:364–78; for a contextualization of Scheerbart's theories of architecture, see Udo Kultermann, "Paul Scheerbart und die Architektur im 20. Jahrhundert," in *Über Paul Scheerbart*, 2:188–207. See also Benjamin's surviving essays on Scheerbart: "Paul Scheerbart: Lesabéndio" (Benjamin, *Gesammelte Schriften*, 2:618–20) and "On Scheerbart" (Benjamin, *Selected Writings*, 4:386–88). Benjamin also wrote a longer essay on Scheerbart titled "Der wahre Politiker" that was lost (editorial note, Benjamin, *Gesammelte Schriften*, 2:1423).

40. Paul Scheerbart, "Glass Architecture," trans. James Palmes, in Paul Scheerbart and Bruno Taut, *Glass Architecture and Alpine Architecture* (New York: Praeger, 1972), 47.

41. Benjamin, *The Arcades Project*, 9. "Jugendstil forces the auratic" (Benjamin, *The Arcades Project*, 557). Benjamin cites the following words from Dolf Sternberger, whom Benjamin accuses of having stolen his ideas about the *passages* and the panaroma: "The most characteristic work of Jugendstil is the house. More precisely, the single-family dwelling" (cited in Benjamin, ibid., 550).

42. See Scheerbart, "Glass Architecture," 45, 47, 63.

43. Scheerbart, ibid., 41; Paul Scheerbart, *Glasarchitektur* (Munich: Passagen, Rogner and Bernhard, 1971), 25.

44. This simultaneity of the interior and its destruction corresponds to Manfredo Tafuri's analysis of the historical development of Gropius and the Bauhaus from a "romantic anti-capitalism" and "mythic populism" to a more theoretically and historically adequate theory and practice under the influence of Russian Constructivism. Tafuri, *The Sphere and the Labyrinth: Avant-Gardes and Architecture from Piranesi to the 1970s*, trans. Pellegrino d'Acierno and Robert Connolly (Cambridge, Mass.: MIT Press, 1990), 120–48.

45. Benjamin, *Selected Writings*, 2:734; Benjamin's emphasis.

46. Gershom Scholem, *Walter Benjamin: The Story of a Friendship*, trans. Harry Zohn (New York: Schocken, 1981), 208.

47. Benjamin, *Selected Writings*, 4:268.

48. Ibid., 2:366 (translation modified).

49. On this new mode of reception, see John McCole, *Walter Benjamin and the Antinomies of Tradition* (Ithaca, N.Y.: Cornell University Press, 1993), 190–95.

50. Benjamin, *Selected Writings*, 2:370 (translation modified).

51. Ibid., 2:369.

52. See Hegel, *Enzyklopädie der philosophischen Wissenschaft, Werkausgabe*, 8:237–38; and Hegel, *Wissenschaft der Logik, Werkausgabe*, 6:41–44.

53. Brecht, *Werke*, 2:95 (my translation).

54. Brecht, *Man Equals Man*, 31.

55. Brigid Doherty points to this line as a sign of Galy Gay's malleability in her "Test and Gestus in Brecht and Benjamin," *MLN* 115 (2000), 462.

56. Benjamin, *Gesammelte Schriften*, 2:527 (my translation).

57. Nägele, *Reading After Freud*, 119.

58. Brecht, *Werke*, 2:224 (my translation).

59. Bertolt Brecht, "Bei Durchsicht meiner ersten Stücke," in *Werke*, 23:245 (my translation).

60. See Brecht, *Werke*, 2:406–10, for a reconstruction of the many versions of *Man Equals Man*.

61. In an interpretation of the equal sign in one of the play's earlier titles, *Mann=Mann*, Brigid Doherty writes that it "stands in for operations performed on persons . . . that involve above all the transformation of posture and gesture" (Doherty, "Test and Gestus in Brecht and Benjamin," 451).

62. Benjamin, *Selected Writings*, 2:370 (translation slightly modified); see Benjamin, *Gesammelte Schriften*, 2:667.

63. Brecht, *Schriften zum Theater*, ed. Siegfried Unseld (Frankfurt am Main: Suhrkamp, 1989), 109 (my translation).

64. Ibid., 114 and 9.

65. For the development of this title, and the variations on it, see Brecht, *Werke*, 11:353.

66. Brecht, *Werke*, 11:157; Brecht, *Poems 1913–1956*, ed. John Willett and Ralph Manheim (New York: Methuen, 1976), 131–32. All citations of this poem are from these pages.

67. Benjamin, *Selected Writings*, 4:232–33. Benjamin comments on the first, third, and ninth poems of the *Lesebuch;* Benjamin's self-critique of the commentary on the third poem can be found in ibid., 4:159.

68. Benjamin, *Selected Writings*, 4:233.

69. Brecht, *Poems 1913–1956*, 133–37.

70. Benjamin, *Selected Writings*, 2:370.

71. Ibid., 455.

72. See Helmut Lethen, *Verhaltenslehren der Kälte: Lebensversuche zwischen den Kriegen* (Frankfurt am Main: Suhrkamp, 1994), 170–81; Klaus Schumann, *Der Lyriker Bertolt Brecht 1913–1933* (Berlin: Rütten and Loening, 1964), 153–54; and the summary of interpretations of the *Lesebuch* in Jan Knopf, *Brecht Handbuch: Lyrik, Prosa, Schriften* (Stuttgart: J. B. Metzler, 1984), 56–57.

73. Reinhard Sändig, "Das Prinzip der Kargheit bei Brecht," in *Német filológiai tanulmányok—Arbeiten zur deutschen Philologie* 15 (1981): 99–117 (my translation).

74. Walter Delabar, "Nomaden, Monaden: Versuch über Bertolt Brechts *Aus dem Lesebuch für Städtebewohner*," in *Bertolt Brecht (1898–1956)*, ed. Walter Delabar and Jörg Döring (Berlin: Weidler, 1998), 143 (my translation).

75. Émile Benveniste, "La nature des pronoms," in *Problèmes de linguistique générale* (Gallimard: Paris, 1966), 1:254 (my translation).

76. Ibid., 252 (my translation).

77. Thus Helmut Lethen's conclusion that "Die Souveränität der Grenzziehung zwischen 'Eigentlichkeit' und 'Man' ist dieser Stimme abhanden gekommen," in Lethen, "Brechts Hand-Orakel," *Brecht Yearbook* 17 (1992), 89. Walter Delabar remarks that the notions of "individuality" and "subjectivity" are "unsuitable" for discussing the *Lesebuch* (Delabar, "Nomaden, Monaden," 148).

78. Knopf, *Brecht Handbuch*, 56.

79. Brecht, *Werke*, 24:40–41 (my translation).

80. Benjamin, *Selected Writings*, 2:369.

81. Ibid., 367; Benjamin, *Gesammelte Schriften*, 2:663.

82. Leo Bersani and Ulysse Dutoit discuss a similar syncategorematical poverty in Beckett (Bersani and Dutoit, *Arts of Impoverishment*, 70–71).

83. For Benjamin, the impoverishment of experience and its excess belong together: "With this tremendous development of technology, a completely new

poverty has descended on mankind. And the reverse side of this poverty is the oppressive wealth of ideas that has been spread among people, or rather swamped them entirely—ideas that have come with the revival of astrology and the wisdom of yoga, Christian Science and chiromancy, vegetarianism and gnosis, scholasticism and spiritualism" (Benjamin, *Selected Writings*, 2:732).

84. Ibid., 732 (translation modified).

85. Benjamin, *Gesammelte Schriften*, 4:567 (my translation).

86. Ensor's paintings also recall other Benjaminian faces: the skull whose grin is both expressive and expressionless and which, for Benjamin, is the emblem of the work of art, and the soldier Fewkoombey from the *Threepenny Novel*, about whom Benjamin writes: his "new face" is "barely one" and better understood as "'transparent and faceless' like the millions who live in crowded barracks and basement apartments" (see Benjamin, *Selected Writings*, 3:5).

87. Benjamin, *Gesammelte Schriften*, 4:567 (my translation).

88. Benjamin, *Selected Writings*, 1:486.

89. Ibid.

90. Ibid., 452 (translation modified).

91. Benjamin, *Gesammelte Schriften*, 4:96.

92. Ibid., 1:1238.

93. Benjamin, *Selected Writings*, 2:542.

INDEX

Patrick Greaney is assistant professor of German at the University of Colorado at Boulder.